AMERICAN OVERTURE

Jewish Rights in Colonial Times

MICHAEL GRATZ

portrait by Thomas Sully

AMERICAN OVERTURE

Jewish Rights in Colonial Times

by

ABRAM VOSSEN GOODMAN

PHILADELPHIA
THE JEWISH PUBLICATION SOCIETY OF AMERICA
5707–1947

60

PRINTED IN THE UNITED STATES OF AMERICA
PRESS OF THE JEWISH PUBLICATION SOCIETY
PHILADELPHIA, PENNA.

To

MY WIFE

WHOSE ENCOURAGEMENT
MADE THIS BOOK POSSIBLE

PREFACE

THIS work does not pretend to be a full-dimensioned study of Jewish experience during America's colonial age, although I am glad that a liberal proportion of that story has found its way into my pages. My main consideration has been the interaction of Jewish forces with the early American scene as manifested in the expanding rights of the Jewish minority and in the growing recognition that Jews were men who might aspire to full civic equality. This theme has tremendous meaning in the unfolding of Jewish history and in the upbuilding of the democratic principle as we know it today. It serves fittingly as an American overture.

Now that the typescript has been transformed into a book, I think humbly of the words used by the grandson of Ben Sira when he presented his forebear's work to a Hellenistic public. "Ye are entreated, therefore," he wrote, "to make your perusal with favor and attention, and to be indulgent if in any parts of what we have laboured to interpret we may seem to fail in some of the phrases."

A list of individuals and libraries to whom I owe a debt of gratitude for aid offered and hospitality extended would exhaust the patience of readers. It would be churlish, however, not to thank by name a few of those who showed me great kindness.

Dr. Abram L. Sachar, National Director of the B'nai
B'rith Hillel Foundations, first suggested the subject I
have treated. I have received valued guidance from Dr.
Eugene C. Barker under whom I worked at the University
of Texas. Others who afforded me needed assistance were
Mr. Lee M. Friedman of Boston, Mrs. Caroline Greenfield
of New York, Miss Elena Greenfield of Mobile, Dr.
Marcus Jernegan of the University of Chicago, Dr. Jacob
R. Marcus of the Hebrew Union College, Dr. Rollin G.
Osterweis of Yale University, Dr. Cecil Roth of London,
and Mr. Raphael Semmes of the Maryland Historical
Society.

I have enjoyed special courtesies at the hands of the
librarians of the following institutions: the Harvard
University Library of Cambridge; the Essex Institute of
Salem; the Department of State of the State of Rhode
Island and the John Carter Brown Library of Providence;
the Newport Historical Society; the Connecticut State
Library of Hartford; the New York Public Library and
the American Jewish Historical Society of New York;
the Georgia State Archives, Atlanta; the University of
Texas Library, Austin; the Clements Library of the
University of Michigan, Ann Arbor; the University of
Chicago Library and the Newberry Library, Chicago;
and the Wisconsin Historical Society Library, Madison.

I omit here reference to individuals and institutions
through whose courtesies the illustrations accompanying
my text have been reproduced. Due acknowledgment will
be found elsewhere in the volume.

I am particularly obligated to the congregations at
Austin and Davenport for permitting me to rummage
through library stacks far from home during my summers.
A word of thanks is also due Dr. Henry Hurwitz who
printed the sections dealing with New York and Massachusetts in the *Menorah Journal*. Nor should I overlook
the Colonial Dames of Texas for their encouragement
expressed in a generous grant while I was preparing this
work.

A.V.G.

Davenport,
June 1, 1947.

TABLE OF CONTENTS

LIST OF ILLUSTRATIONS

xiii

AMERICAN OVERTURE

Jewish Rights in Colonial Times

CHAPTER I

HOW A THOUSAND MEN AND WOMEN MADE HISTORY

THE United States has close to five million Jews today. Many of them are newcomers of the first and second generation, refugees from the fires of hate which burn in contemporary Europe. Their hearts thrill with the promise of liberty and hope extended to them by the Mother of Exiles, holding high her lamp beside the golden door.

But the Jew as such is no newcomer in America. He can look backward over a career of three centuries. Musty Dutch manuscripts from the seventeenth century, browned and ancient documents of the Public Record Office in London that have survived the fires of robot and blitz, testify to the early arrival of Jews in this country during the seventeenth century and to their struggle for recognition in those far-off days before religious freedom had become the birthright of every American.

These Jews joined the hosts that crowded ships sailing from Europe in the days when a voyage was adventure. A long procession of vessels ploughed the Atlantic, with their cramped cargoes of suffering humanity ready to endure unimaginable hardships, on the long voyage over, in the hope that the New World would grant them a better life in a better land.

These newcomers from all lands and nations travelled with scanty impedimenta; yet they were carriers of a tangle of beliefs and skills and knowledge that constituted the cultural pattern of Europe. They brought with them a heritage of centuries of civilized living, of art and science and faith. But also in their spiritual luggage they transported a burden of ignorance, superstition, hatred and bigotry.

When they arrived on the American scene they were Europeans — Britons in the main — whose first impulse was to continue with the same institutions they had known in the world they forswore. Oddly enough, the transplanted forms underwent a process of mutation once they had taken root in the new soil. As each passing generation noted, American ways grew more and more distinct from their European archetypes, so that there emerged on the edge of the wilderness a peculiarly American outlook and social philosophy. The catalysts which produced the new system cannot be readily identified, but one may say with assurance that both isolation from the forces at work in Europe and the proximity of the egalitarian frontier played a part.

Nowhere does the difference between the old way and the new appear more clearly than in the changing status of the Jews in the American colonies during the years they were traveling towards their destined independence. The experience of the Jews turned out to be the great confirmation of the American spirit, the testing of its values. Although not numerous even in terms of the sparse population of the eighteenth century, they none the less have significance for us. After all, the minute contents of a test tube may be a clue to the mysterious processes of our universe.

It is salutary to stress the fact that Jews were rare in the thirteen colonies. Otherwise author or reader might overemphasize the weight they carried. Despite the roseate estimates of some Jewish writers on the subject, it is safe to say there were never more than one thousand Jews living among the three million and more inhabitants of the colonies. The Newport community in its heyday totaled at most one hundred and fifty to one hundred and seventy-five Jews.[1] Perhaps New York had as many, or more. Philadelphia, Charleston and Savannah were certainly smaller communities. Even when combining their Jewish populations with the lonely groups in the back country, we still are far from an impressive total.

Yet this handful of Jews were not only the measure of the expanding spirit of a nation, they were also important as the forerunners of modern American Israel, the most fortunate and well placed Jewish group that all the millennia of a people's checkered history have witnessed. Their lot was a portent of the future growth of American Jewry, the promise of equality under the protective banner of the Stars and Stripes.

There was also a third facet in the Jewish experience in colonial times to lend it significance. As part of Israel's ancient story, the thousand Jews in colonial America were witness to the initial steps towards world-wide emancipation. When a Jew voted in New York, when another was elected to office in South Carolina, the original blows were struck in loosing the shackles of a people. It was the first intimation of a chapter of freedom for the Jews of the western world, a chapter so tragically interrupted by the irruption of Nazidom. In terms of Jewry's and mankind's reaching for liberty, the struggle of America's early Jews has global significance.

The story of Jewish rights in the various colonies is a tale in itself. The difficulties they had to surmount, the vestigial bigotry they must overcome in order to live, to worship God, and earn a livelihood there, had dramatic force. Sometimes our tale includes other aspects of their lives; all too briefly does it turn the spotlight on arresting personalities.

The Jews, who were early arrivals in the New World, had long been stock figures in the theater of European life. The conventional portrayal of the day misrepresented the people whose lips had been burned by the coals of prophecy, whose spirit had been tempered in the fires of persecution. Europe looked on the Jew as a mysterious paradox who, in "committing the greatest crime of history," blessed Christianity with the blood of atonement — after which he was fated by God to wander to and fro upon the earth, accursed. The Jews occupied the position of permanent aliens, inhabiting a country but having no part in it. They were thought of as dirty and sly, tricky and dishonest, Satan's apprentices rather than normal human beings.

At the best, Jews were suffered. Nowhere did they

enjoy the full rights of burghers and freemen, although it must be admitted that they were better off than the bulk of the population who belonged to the peasantry. Many occupations were closed to them. They were burdened by taxes levied upon them alone and by onerous restrictions such as those preventing them from owning real property. Frequent insults included special oaths under degrading conditions which were required of Jews, as the usual formula was not considered sufficiently compelling. On occasion they encountered the fury of the mob and the death of martyrs.

For centuries England gave Jews no official recognition. Since the time of their expulsion from the kingdom, during the reign of Edward I, they had been forbidden to set foot in Britain. Even when England was rendered free of Jews, old folk notions clung to the soil. The cult of little St. Hugh of Lincoln, with its ritual murder quality, flourished. The unhappy boy was commemorated in the *Canterbury Tales*, and his relics in the cathedral of Lincoln were credited with miracles.[2] Marlowe's *Jew of Malta*, and the detestable Jew that Shakespeare drew, were intended to satisfy the appetite of the populace for spiced novelties.

At the time when Jews were beating against the gates of England for readmission, they were already making their way into the colonies. Accordingly, two attitudes towards them grew up in Westminster — one concerning their status in Great Britain and the other overseas.

In England, the problem of the Jew's status became a matter of concern during the days of the Commonwealth, when a group of London Marranos reverted to Judaism. Though Jews were expressly forbidden to live in England, Cromwell, as the historian Cecil Roth describes it, followed an oblique policy: he connived at the settlement of the Jews without formally authorizing it.[3] Formal recognition of their right to reside and trade came at the hands of the Restoration monarch, Charles II.[4]

The Jews of England must have considered their lot fortunate when compared with conditions on the Continent. They were not penned in ghettos and, except for a very brief period from 1689 to 1691,[5] they were not made victims of special taxation. The crown was generous in issuing patents of endenization[6] and court procedure did not require the special Jew's oath of witnesses.[7]

Existence in Britain was none the less accompanied by a certain insecurity, as when almost half of the members of the London community were arrested in 1685 for failure to attend church.[8] Another stumbling block to the peace of many of them was the prejudice against their participation in foreign trade. Jews were excluded from mercantile organizations; they suffered disabilities as aliens when they sought a share in overseas commerce. More of the latter shortly.

Probably the most unhappy experience of English Jewry came a century after their return, with the furore over the Naturalization Act of 1753. As we shall presently see, foreign Jews were naturalized without difficulty in the overseas possessions. Now Parliament attempted to do the same thing at home by permitting Jewish aliens to be naturalized without submitting to the sacrament of the Lord's Supper. The bill had passed both the House of Lords and the House of Commons with little or no difficulty, when the tumult was unleashed. Pamphleteers, politicians and rabble, all joined in a storm of defamation and menace against the Jews who were denounced as the future masters of a Britain betrayed. So charged was the atmosphere that the Archbishop of Canterbury anticipated a massacre. Because of the prevailing frenzy, the act was repealed.[9]

Both in Great Britain and its colonies Jewish life was to a large degree shaped by the dominance of the mercantile philosophy of trade. The Navigation Acts of 1660 and subsequent years, sometimes called the Acts of Trade, expressed the spirit of the age. They aimed to advance the welfare of the homeland at the expense of foreign countries and even at the cost of their own colonies. They produced a congeries of regulations which sought to control trade in all its aspects.

As little English money as possible must find its way abroad through the agency of foreign goods or foreign carriers. Ships must be English owned and English manned (no more than one fourth of their crews being aliens). No foreign merchants might trade in the colonies until they had been naturalized or given the rights of free denizens.[10] According to English law, therefore, the Jews were forbidden to engage in commerce because of their foreign origin.

It was through no oversight that Jews suffered from the Acts of Trade. Follow the Navigation Act of 1663 as it passed through the committee sessions and public

readings in the House of Commons, if you will. During
the earlier steps it was described as a proposal "to prevent Encroachments in Trade by the *Jews, French,* and
other Foreigners."[11] Not until the second reading was
the measure called, disingenuously, "a Bill for the Ad-
vancement of Trade."[12]

There was definite hostility to the entry of Jewish
competition in the field of foreign and colonial trade, an
antagonism which was displayed in certain circles both
in England and the American settlements. One of the
arguments marshaled against Jews was the fact that the
international family connections they enjoyed gave them
an undue advantage over run-of-the-mill British traders.
In the West Indies it is striking to note how, when the
merchants protested against the operations of the "subtle"
Jews, the local planters insisted that they required Jewish participation in business to avoid becoming the victims of the extortionate prices which the English dealers
demanded.[13]

Fortunate were the Jews who became denizens through
an inferior form of naturalization; for then they were in
a position to carry on their business in peace. We know
that, as early as 1661, three Jews, with testimonials of
high esteem from the king of Denmark and good reputations in Barbados, received a special license to live in any
colony.[14]

Other Jews also got permission to sojourn and traffic
in the West Indies until they became important elements
in the economics of Jamaica and Barbados. These two
islands boasted the outstanding Jewish communities of

the New World, overshadowing the settlements on the mainland. Today perhaps their annals of two and three centuries ago seem trivial in the light of the subsequent expansion of the Jewish community in the United States, but in colonial times, when the British government considered its Jewish subjects in America, it looked upon them primarily in terms of those in the West Indies.

Any picture of the Jewish communities of Barbados and Jamaica brings out striking contrasts with Jewish experience along the American seaboard. They ordered things differently in New York than in Kingston. Why? Why was the Caribbean story one of persecution, discrimination and bitterness, while on the mainland these heartaches were brushed away with relative ease? As we study the Jewish disabilities which persisted over a long period in Jamaica and Barbados, the story resounds again and again with echoes from the *Judengassen* of Europe.

Barbados until 1786 would not admit Jewish testimony in court when Christians were involved, unless matters of trade were at issue.[15] The very presence of Jews was regarded as "inconsistent with the safety" of the island.[16] Distrust of them and fear of slave insurrection were reflected in the law of 1688 forbidding Jews to keep Negro men and boys as slaves.[17] Another time Jews were not allowed white Christian indentured servants and were forced to rely on their own impoverished coreligionists for whatever labor was required.[18]

Conditions in Jamaica were possibly worse. Jews there were accused of inciting the slaves to rob their masters so that the Jewish merchants could buy stolen goods.[19] Legislation lumped them in the same category as Negroes and Indians.[20] By the law of 1703 they might not own indentured servants or slaves, under a penalty of five hundred pounds, but they might hire white Christians.[21]

In the West Indies there was special taxation levied against Jewish merchants and planters. This was particularly true in Jamaica, where the Jews were saddled with an annual tax of one thousand pounds, which discriminatory impost they bitterly resented. They appealed to the king against this cruel injustice, with the result that Jamaica had to abandon such easy revenue in 1741 despite the vehement protest of its assembly.[22]

As the years passed, Parliament came to recognize that the Jews in the far-off colonies were fulfilling a valuable function in promoting the growth of empire. Accordingly, when a bill to naturalize foreign Protestants in the colonies in America was being prepared in 1740, it also included similar provisions for the naturalization of Jewish aliens. This legislation opened the gates to all foreign Protestants and Jews who had been living seven years in continuous residence overseas.[23]

In order to bar Catholics from the benefits of the act, it obliged applicants to receive the sacrament of the Lord's Supper in a Protestant church less than three months before they took their oath of allegiance.[24] Of course, such a practice would also have excluded Jews, but, since Jews were welcome and Catholics were not, special exemptions were provided for the former. Not only were followers of the Jewish religion excused from

communion, but when taking the oath, they were allowed
to omit the significant words, "upon the true Faith of
a Christian."[25]

By 1753 some two hundred Jews had been naturalized,
the majority in Jamaica. Although similar legislation
for Great Britain was repealed by popular demand, the
attempt to do away with the colonial system of naturalization was defeated in Parliament by a vote of 208 to
88.[26] It worked too well in the colonies. Even the most
parochial-minded, fox-hunting member of the House of
Commons now recognized that England's and America's
interests were different in many spheres. A new society
was growing up beyond the seas.

This period of colonial settlement was an era of gesta-
tion. In preparation for the birth of American freedom,
new forms were being molded and the fate of the handful
of scattered Jews was rich in significance for the morrow.
Their drama was an American overture with a largo
movement at the first, but with a closing section that was
sprightly allegro. It was rich in promise of the America
that was to be.

CHAPTER II

JEWISH RIGHTS IN THE PURITAN CANAAN

THE mind of the New England Puritan was peculiar. It has proved an object of despair to friends and a source of amazement and consternation to enemies. But though it has been analyzed and atomized, it still remains a mystery.

Undoubtedly, one of the chief factors in creating the Puritan type was the effort of the leaders of the Massachusetts Bay theocracy to transpose their image of the Palestine of ancient times to the shores of New England. The Bible was their guide and Moses was their lawgiver. The learning of the seventeenth century and the spirit of classical Israel were accordingly combined in a blend which was both strange and new.

The ancient Hebrew passion for learning was there. It gave rise to a Harvard College only a few short years after the first settlements had been made along the shores of Massachusetts Bay. The respect for God's word demanded the use of the original Hebrew text in order to illumine the finished resonances of the King James version of the Bible. As a result, the vineyard on the banks of the Charles became a proving ground for ministers, where they were required to learn the language which the prophets spake.

In his study on the Harvard of the seventeenth century, Professor Samuel Morison makes the assertion that "the most distinctive feature of the Harvard curriculum was the emphasis on Hebrew and kindred languages."[1] It is significant that such studies were unknown in the British universities of the day;[2] but, as Professor Morison has said, the Puritans, now boasting a state of their own, were in a position to satisfy their "repressed desire for more and better Hebrew."[3]

The ministers of the colony were much concerned with Jewish lore. The disappearance of the ten "lost tribes" of Israel was to them not an event in remote antiquity, but a current issue, and they sought hungrily for evidences that would identify the Indians of their day with the missing Jews. To such a degree was John Eliot stirred by the hope of redeeming the rejected Israelites, that he became the apostle to the Indians and translated the Bible into their tongue.[4]

When the learned Cotton Mather came to describe the witchcraft hysteria that had prevailed in Salem, he introduced his story with a reference to the Talmud. Instead of citing some of the supernatural phenomena reported by authorities of his own day, he dug up the old rabbinical tale of the hanging of the eighty witches of Gaza.[5]

Side by side with the interest in ancient Hebraics went the policy of exclusiveness and repression which characterized the government of Massachusetts Bay. The norm set up by the clergy, who were the true rulers of the province, was one which demanded strict obedience of all and sundry. God's elect were only a small minority, but they had the power and they intended to keep it. For a long time they were able to defeat any attempt of the "ungodly" majority to swamp them by sheer numbers.

Dissent and criticism were curbed by the authorities with an iron hand. The freemen were the privileged members of the community who enjoyed the right to vote, but their ranks were limited to those whose religious doctrines were unimpeachable. Attendance at church was compulsory, and the people were not permitted to criticize the clergy.

In this atmosphere of religious tyranny, there were still some brave souls who would not swallow their protests. Roger Williams, popular and influential minister of Salem, dared to denounce the attempt of the civil authorities to control men's consciences. To escape the wrath of the magistrates, he was forced to flee to the wintry wilderness. The fiery Ann Hutchinson was known for her magnetism and pungent religious opinions, which won for her a group of followers that at one time included the governor himself. But in the end, after a trial that was a mockery, she was banished from the colony as a woman unfit for society.[6]

When one fills out the picture by recalling that the bigotry of the period was so intense against Catholics that no priest could reside in the colony, and that religious frenzy caused the fanatical Quakers to be whipped, exiled and hanged, one might well inquire what chance the Jews had in such an environment. Yet with all the renown the Puritans earned for intolerance, the record of their treatment of the Jews remains without a black mark. On the contrary, the proverbially easygoing Dutch attempted to exclude Jews from New Netherland altogether and, when that failed, they barred them from gainful occupations and imposed a special discriminatory tax upon them. None of these things is to be found in the annals of Puritan Massachusetts.

The Catholics and the Friends belonged to the Christian Church; the Jews did not. But two factors might be noted in order to explain why the latter enjoyed a more hospitable reception. First, the Jews were not regarded as public enemies, plotting against the peace of the state, as Papists were believed to do. Nor did they interrupt religious services with their reprehensible behavior, as was the Quaker custom. Secondly, the Jews did not appear in numbers until the nineteenth century. Had they been a conspicuous minority in Puritan days, they might have suffered from harsher treatment.

The first Jew known in Massachusetts was a man who came before the authorities pleading for aid because of his destitute condition. He was called Solomon Franco — a name that suggested Iberian descent. We hear of him in 1649 when he appealed to the magistrates to assure him the commission which he claimed for supervising a cargo assigned the major general of the colony, Edward Gibbons. The court decided that there was no valid ground for awarding Franco the fees he claimed. But the case was not so easily settled. Franco was penniless, and the authorities accordingly granted him an allowance of sixty shillings, to last him ten weeks, until he could secure his passage to Holland. As a result, this Jew enjoyed Puritan benevolence.[7]

There is no suggestion that Franco sought to establish a residence in Massachusetts. If he had wanted to settle there, he might have run afoul of a law that had been passed in the excitement over the Hutchinson case. This limited the time that a newcomer might stay in a town to three weeks, unless he had the consent of the council or of two of the magistrates to settle. It is obvious that this law could be directed towards the exclusion of undesirables, among whom Jews might have been included.

In the course of time an occasional Jew did settle in Boston and was apparently unmolested. One such resident named Sollomon had the bad judgment to travel towards New Hampshire on a Sunday in 1668. This was no mean offense in a day when men were sentenced to a month in jail if they missed church on Sunday.[8] Sollomon's journey did not pass unnoticed, and he was brought before the court in Ipswich. The outcome of the case may never be known, but one phrase in the brief court record challenges the attention of the passing reader. Sollomon is described as a "Malata Jue."[9] The first Jew living in New England, as far as we know, was of Negro descent! One can only conjecture who this man was. Perhaps he had been born of a slave mother and a Jewish father who had set him free.

The year 1674 was marked by the publication of the earliest tax list of the town of Boston extant, a list that included the name of Rowland Gideon, "ye Jew." He was taxed eighteen shillings for the town and nothing for the county.[10] At this period Gideon was not a person of importance. He was later to remove to England where he became a freeman of the city of London and the sire of a distinguished line.[11]

In 1675, while still in Boston, Gideon and Daniel Baruh, who was probably also a Jew,[12] were awarded £112 in a law suit. The defendant, however, appealed from the judgment, and in his reply Gideon sought to make capital out of his Jewish origin. He reminded the court that God had commanded "owr Father [Moses] that the same Law should bee for the stranger & sojourner as for the Jssraellits," and so he sought the same justice as was accorded the other inhabitants. He therefore committed his case to the judge and jury, "praing for the prosperity of yowr Gouermⁿ and that yow may bee further fathers of this scatered Nation."[13] The Bible precedent was always dear to the Puritan heart, and Gideon cited it with the aim of wringing from the jury of freemen justice for the Jew.[14]

It was politic to make this kind of plea — perhaps one should say it was possible for Jews to live in Massachusetts at all — only because of the revulsion against the tyranny of the theocracy that had swept over the province by this time. The execution of the four Quakers in Boston in 1658 had proved the high watermark of the fanatical rule of the clergy, and an outraged public sentiment, supplemented by a royal command, ended the cruel persecution.[15] Within a short time the Quakers established a meetinghouse in Salem and the unhappy Baptists opened a church in Boston, while even the Episcopal Church was able to take root, thanks to the efforts of Governor Andros.[16]

Aside from the introduction of the Anglican ritual into Massachusetts, the rule of Andros was unpopular, and it came to an abrupt end when the Boston populace imitated their brethren in Great Britain by reproducing the Revolution of 1688 on American shores. The result was that, in New England as well as in old England, the governmental structure was radically altered. Massachusetts was accorded a new charter which increased the powers of the crown, while at the same time it represented a step forward in the field of religious tolerance. No longer could membership in the Congregational Church be insisted on as a prerequisite for the franchise. The new requirements for voting were concerned with the ownership of property, certainly a more equitable and modern basis than had existed theretofore.[17]

At the same time, freedom of worship was extended to all Christians except Papists.[18] This, of course, overlooked the Jews, but there were not enough of them to question the justice of the law. In fact, Boston did not have a Jewish congregation until long after the establishment of the United States, well into the nineteenth century.

One feature of the new charter was the union of Plymouth Colony with Massachusetts. The little Pilgrim community had never had Jews as far as we know, but back in 1645 the staid Edward Winslow wrote his neighbor, John Winthrop, of the outrageous attempt in the general court to pass an act for complete religious toleration. There were to be no exceptions — Turks, Jews and Papists would be permitted to carry on their religious worship without hindrance. The governor, however, intervened and would not allow the ungodly measure to be voted on.

Winslow was so perturbed by this abhorrent effort, which "would make us odious to all christian commonweales," that he prayed: "The Lord in mercy looké upon us, and allay this spirit of division that is creeping in among us."[19]

But with the passing of the old oligarchy in Massachusetts, the age of religious discrimination and injustice towards any denomination was ended. The story of the Jews, who from time to time settled in Boston, was a happy one, untroubled by disabilities and restrictions. There was one curious case, in 1699, when the governor of Massachusetts Bay, the Earl of Bellomont, turned to a local Jew for an expert opinion. James Gillam, a notorious pirate who had been in the habit of attacking ships in the Red Sea, was arrested by the governor's order. Rumor had it that the buccaneer had been converted to Islam during his Oriental sojourn and that he had submitted to circumcision at the time. Bellomont decided to investigate, and he reported: "I had him searched by a surgeon and a Jew in this town: they have both declared on oath that he is circumcised."[20]

In the year 1729 there were probably four Jewish families in Boston, although there may have been even more.[21] While no organized community existed, Michael Asher and Isaac Solomon, two men who engaged in the manufacture and sale of snuff, felt the need for a cemetery. During the early years of the eighteenth century, they set aside a small tract in a parcel of land they bought as a burying ground for "the Jewish Nation."[22] This ended the practice of sending the Jewish dead to Newport for burial.[23] Strangely enough, no mention of the Jewish cemetery is found after 1750.[24]

Jews were not challenged as witnesses in colonial Boston. Michael Asher, the snuff maker, testified in court again and again.[25] A Jew might even serve as constable with the duty of maintaining public order and collecting town taxes for which a commission was paid. Isaac Lopez, a merchant who came to Boston from England in 1716,[26] was elected constable in 1720. The office must have been considered onerous and odious at the time, for, before Lopez was named, a full slate had been selected and every last one of them had declined to serve. Lopez followed the example of the earlier choices by refusing the doubtful honor.[27]

It might be noted in passing that Lopez did not display the highest character in the conduct of his business affairs. Some years later, when he found himself in financial difficulties, he left town, and neither he nor any of his effects was ever found.[28]

Nowhere is it definitely stated that he was a Jew, but his name was borne by prominent Sephardim of both Newport and New York in colonial times, and his business associate was the Jew, Michael Asher. There is little reason to doubt his Jewishness, although absolute proof is lacking.

The most famous of all the Jews in colonial Massachusetts was Judah Monis, the first of his people to become associated with Harvard College. It seems that he was born in Italy in 1683,[29] and that he received some rabbinical training at the academies of Leghorn and Amsterdam.[30] He subsequently immigrated to America, and in 1715/16 was admitted as a freeman in New York. On the court's record he was listed as a merchant.[31] But Monis nursed higher ambitions.

The next time he was heard from, he had removed to Massachusetts where his plans for a new Hebrew grammar which would "facilitate yᵉ Instruction of Youth"[32] could be appreciated. Accordingly, he dispatched a letter to the Harvard corporation on June 29, 1720, with some sort of preliminary draft of the work. The bid for approval apparently met with success, for the intelligentsia of Boston and Cambridge were always anxious to further the instruction of the sacred tongue.[33]

Harvard celebrated its commencement a week after the letter was written, and the college selected this occasion to bestow upon Monis the honorary degree of Master of Arts.[34] Perhaps the expert on Hebrew syntax had long enjoyed the favor of the Harvard corporation; perhaps his letter had been sent at just the right time. At any rate, Monis was the first Jew to be granted a degree by Harvard or any other American college.

But he did not remain a Jew for long. In March, 1722 — less than two years later — Monis was baptized in the college hall before a crowd which jammed the place to enjoy the rare spectacle of a Jew turning Christian.[35] The next month, Harvard appointed Monis instructor of Hebrew.[36] It is open to question whether Monis would have obtained his position (at seventy pounds a year) if he had not joined the Congregational Church.

Cotton Mather was concerned over the thought that ambition might have sharpened the proselyte's zeal. When Monis' conversion *Discourse* was printed, Mather added a preface in which he recalled instances where ex-Jews had become professors of Hebrew and had subsequently reverted to their original Judaism. "There is no cause to fear," wrote the tactful Mather, "that Mr. Monis will renounce his Christianity."[37] But the divine plainly had his doubts.

Such apprehensions were unwarranted. Monis married a lady of Puritan stock and throughout his life was unshaken in his new faith. When he died, he left the bulk of his estate as a permanent fund for the relief of clergymen's widows.[38] The trust is today being administered by the American Unitarian Association.[39]

Many of the details in the career of Monis make interesting reading after the lapse of two centuries. It might be mentioned that he was the author of the first Hebrew grammar published in America and that he described the discouragements which he experienced in teaching the ancient language to a host of unwilling scholars. A full discussion of such matters, however, would carry us too far afield.

From our point of view, the most significant fact in

A Prospect of the Colledges in Cambridge in New England

HARVARD COLLEGE IN 1726

engraved by William Burgis

EZRA STILES

portrait by Nathaniel Smibert

the career of Monis is that, while still an unconverted Jew, he was entered on the rolls of Harvard College as the recipient of a degree. Puritan exclusiveness notwithstanding, the Massachusetts institution affords a wholesome contrast to Oxford University which did not permit a Jew to obtain his degree until 1870.

One more example of the generous policy that prevailed in Massachusetts towards the Jew and we are through with that phase of our story. The incident concerns the application of the Naturalization Act of 1740 with its regulations regarding foreign Protestants and Jews. In Massachusetts apparently the Act of 1740 was almost superfluous, for only four men were naturalized in the province between 1740 and 1780.[40] This was an indication of the relative homogeneity of the population which included few foreign Protestants and Jews who might desire the privilege of naturalization.

One of these men who transferred his allegiance was Aaron Lopez, the merchant prince of Newport. Brought up a Marrano in Lisbon, he had crossed the ocean to the thriving seaport of Rhode Island, and there he had doffed the mask of Catholicism behind which he had hidden his Jewish sentiments all his life. He reverted to his ancestral faith; he changed his Spanish name to the Hebrew Aaron; and presently he sought to alter his political allegiance by becoming a British subject.

Unfortunately for Lopez, the Rhode Island court blocked his efforts on the ground that he was not a Christian.[41] He therefore transferred his residence to Swansea, over the line in Massachusetts. Accordingly, in the year

1762, after an interval of only five weeks, the court at
Taunton made Lopez a subject of King George III.[42]
Once more Massachusetts displayed its liberalism.

There was a strong bond which united the colonists of
the Connecticut Valley with the settlements of Massachusetts Bay. Hartford, let us remember, was settled by
Thomas Hooker and his congregation from Newtowne,
as Cambridge was called. A separate colony, however,
was that organized at New Haven by Puritans who came
directly from England. It was not until 1665 that the
two areas were united to form the single province of
Connecticut.

The colony was not the habitat of ferocious bigots,
as legend has suggested. The worst of the Blue Laws
were the spiteful invention of the Reverend Samuel
Peters, an embittered Tory who used them as the instrument of his vengeance. Truth has never caught up with
his code, which is still widely accepted.[43] Not that Connecticut was liberal in the modern sense, for a close bond
between church and state existed there similar to that
which prevailed in Massachusetts Bay.

Still the occasional Jews who ventured into the region
faced no special disabilities because of their religion.
Probably the spirit of the time excluded them from the
freemanship, although there was no formal religious requirement for admission. It was a difficult position to
attain, none the less, as the records reveal that in the
period between 1639 and 1662 only one person out of
thirteen was admitted as a freeman.[44]

We have every reason to believe that the earliest Jews

to appear in the Connecticut and New Haven colonies came out of New Netherland. Their place of origin was unfortunate, for a bitter rivalry flourished between Dutch and Britons for the domination of the Connecticut Valley to which both laid claim. It was only natural that the English settlers of Hartford resented the presence of any merchants from the Dutch colony, and the latter were accused of selling the Indians firearms which might be turned against the settlers.[45] In 1650, the sale of goods by foreigners at wholesale or retail was prohibited for the space of a year.[46] It was not until 1654 that "the order for the restraint of trade with the Dutch & other foreigne natyons" was repealed.[47]

We may be sure that the anti-Dutch and anti-foreign atmosphere continued even after the repeal of this legislation. The Jews who entered the Connecticut scene at this period certainly ran afoul of considerable anti-alien sentiment, and the first one mentioned, David the Jew, met with trouble. The general court at Hartford objected to his business methods and fined him twenty shillings in 1659 for such misdemeanors as "going into houses when the heads of ye families wr absent, and tradeing prvision from children."[48]

Even after the law against foreign traders had been repealed, it was not easy for one to settle in Connecticut. Connecticut, says the authority on the subject, was the strictest of all New England colonies in excluding outsiders who sought admission as inhabitants.[49] In 1660 the law was made to read that anyone accepted as an inhabitant of a town had "to be of an honest conversation" and must be "accepted by a maior part of the Towne."[50] Far from being a dead letter, this law was invoked from time to time in order to exclude men and women of "dishonest conversation" who sought residence in Connecticut communities.[51]

Jews who came to Hartford had to get past this hurdle. In 1661, several appeared in the town and took lodging in the house of a prominent citizen, John Marsh.[52] The question of their status was brought up at the town meeting, and it was voted that they might "have liberty to soiorne in ye Towne for seaven months."[53] We have no means of knowing whether the Jews had sought to remain for a longer period.

Jews were not deprived of the privilege of becoming inhabitants, even though it was necessary to secure the approval of a majority of the townspeople. No less a person than David the Jew, who had been heavily fined for trading with children, was permitted to establish himself permanently in Hartford. His name and that of "Jacob Jew" were included among the list of inhabitants in 1670.[54]

It is not to be doubted that Jacob Jew was the Jacob Lucena who was caught in the toils of the law that same year, providing one of the most amazing episodes in the annals of colonial Jewry. The affair, it may be said, reflected scant credit upon him, but it did honor to the courts of the colony.

Lucena was charged with immoral behavior and tried before the court of assistants at Hartford on October 11. Several witnesses appeared against him, and the court found "that the sayd Jacob Lucina hath been frequent & notorious in his lascivious daliance & wanton carriage & profers to severall women." He was fined twenty pounds, which he was to pay the public treasury within a month or else furnish satisfactory security for future payment. Should he fail to meet the penalty, he was to be whipped severely. Meanwhile the court ordered Lucena to remain in prison until the money was received or the stripes laid on. After his release he was to be banished from the colony and not to return "with out Lycinse from the court upon payne of severe corporall punishment."[55]

The fine was heavy, and Lucena immediately petitioned the general court, which was the equivalent of a colonial assembly, that it be reduced. The response of this body to his appeal was remarkable. "The court," says the record of the session held at Hartford on October 13, "see cause, considering he is a Jew, to shew him what fauore they may, abate him tenn pownds of his fine."[56] Why should his Jewish religion have provided extenuating circumstances for the guilty Lucena?

The case did not end here, however, for Lucena objected to paying ten pounds too. He must have enlisted the aid of Asser Levy, the well-known Jewish leader of New York,[57] for we find the latter petitioning the court to grant his friend further clemency. Accordingly, the judges saw fit, on May 11, 1671, to reduce the penalty to five pounds, "as a token of their respect to the sayd Mr. Assur Levy."[58]

This little incident refutes the reputation of seventeenth century Connecticut for bigotry and intolerance. First, we have Lucena, a Jew, accepted as a resident by a majority of the inhabitants. Next, various witnesses report on his licentious conduct, and the court fines him twenty pounds. Yet, because of his Jewish faith and his Jewish friend, he ultimately pays only a quarter of the sum. Perhaps the spirit of colonial Connecticut is not thoroughly understood by our generation.

A word of comment on the prevalence of adultery and fornication, according to the court records of the period, may be in order. Students of the seventeenth century note that infractions of the moral code were so commonplace that they perhaps outnumbered all other types of cases tried. Jacob Lucena and Jacob Lumbrozo, whom we meet in Maryland,[59] were implicated in such matters. It is notable that so few Jews were caught up in the licentiousness of the age.

Occasional Jews settled in Connecticut during the balance of the seventeenth century and a few more entered the colony as the eighteenth century unfolded. For instance, we know of an Abram Pinto, who was located in Stratford by 1725.[60] In all probability his son was the Jacob Pinto who was living in New Haven in 1755 and joined the Congregational Church. Three of Jacob's sons went to Yale and two of them, Solomon and William, were graduated in the class of 1777.[61] Ezra Stiles, the Newport minister who was later to become president of the college,[62] spoke of the "two Jew Brothers Pintos who renounced Judaism & all Religion."[63] Evidently they were no better as Christians than as Jews.

Whatever the defections of the Pintos, there were

already traces of Jewish life in New Haven, as Stiles discovered on a visit there in 1772. He reported that a family of Venetian Jews, who numbered eight or ten souls, had recently arrived. On Sabbath they conducted their worship in a room that had been equipped with special fittings. "If there shd. hereafter be a Synagogue in N. H. it must not be dated from this," wrote Stiles.[64]

Probably nothing would have pleased the Judeaophile Stiles more than to have seen a Jewish congregation organized on the spot. Technically, the religious picture in Connecticut was such that there might have been some complications, but the casual way in which Stiles referred to the establishment of a synagogue suggests that the legal difficulties would not have been insuperable.

In Connecticut the church was under the patronage of the state, and the established religion, that is Congregationalism, was supported by taxes. In fact, by the law of 1735, if the minister did not get his salary, the tax collector had to pay the amount due from his own estate.[65] Attendance at church services continued to be compulsory even as late as the eve of the Revolution. Protestant dissenters, who participated in the worship of their own sects, were excused from going to the Congregational Church.[66] (Probably Jews were not expected to visit any Christian service.)

Episcopalians, Quakers and Baptists, who protested against support of the established church, were exempt from such contributions if they were members of their own societies.[67] If Jews had been in sufficient numbers to organize a congregation, perhaps they too would have secured the same exemption.

Connecticut did not disestablish the state church until 1818, when all Christian denominations were placed upon an equal footing. Jewish congregations had to wait until 1843 for recognition,[68] when one synagogue was already several years old.

If 1843 seems a late date for Jewish religious forms to be acknowledged as within the law, what can one say of New Hampshire whose constitution does not yet give official sanction to Judaism? That document states that "Every denomination of Christians . . . shall be equally under the protection of the law."[69] By inference that same security is denied non-Christians. The neglect of a state of the American union to guarantee the protection of the law to the faith of Israel is an anachronism in the twentieth century scene.

Little need be said about Jews in colonial New Hampshire. The few who penetrated into its northern woods soon lost themselves amid the general population. Their legal position was much as it was in Massachusetts. The Congregational Church was established by law, and the provisions for voting and the freemanship were also similar. It is only today, with state recognition limited to Christianity, and the emphasis on the hiring of Protestant schoolteachers, that New Hampshire seems backward.

New England now counts its Jews by the hundreds of thousands. Some few of them have their roots deep in America's soil. Their ancestors lived in this country when the inhabitants were subjects of the English king. But most of the Jews are themselves immigrants or the children of newcomers. Their saga has been told by Mary Antin in *The Promised Land*.

Seated on the steps of the Boston Public Library, she might well ponder over her two existences — the childhood in mediaeval Polotsk and the new life in twentieth-century Boston. But the miracle of rebirth, the privilege of sharing in the riches of contemporary America, could be hers only because of the ideals and traditions that were born in the colonial towns which emerged from the forests that once covered New England.

CHAPTER III

RETREAT FROM ROGER WILLIAMS

THE gods, wrote Vernon Parrington, "were pleased to have their jest with Roger Williams by sending him to earth before his time." Then the gifted critic continued: "Democrat and Christian, the generation to which he belongs is not yet born, and all his life he remained a stranger among men."[1]

Does the reader require proof that Williams was foreign to his age? Merely turn to his career, observe the ideals voiced in his writings, the projects launched by his boundless energy and the compromises his successors made with his principles. Jews settling on the shores of Narragansett Bay met with experiences which point the tale of the little men who followed in the train of the giant.

Williams was the sort of nonconforming spirit who led a revolt against the religio-political order of the day. His efforts sired a system based on the doctrine of absolute separation of church and state and the inviolability of the individual conscience. What is more, he went beyond the field of philosophical speculation to attack the unholy alliance of clergy and civil government which seventeenth-century New England knew only too well.

The character of such an insurgent exacted a life of protest and personal sacrifice. Williams crossed the ocean

32

and assumed the leadership of one of Salem's churches. But not for long. His nonconformity drove him into the snow-swept forest where he found shelter among the savages. Eventually, as we know, he established Providence at the head of Narragansett Bay as an asylum for outlaw spirits like himself.

Williams' works, published in the main during two extended visits to England, voiced his philosophy. *The Bloudy Tenent of Persecution* denounced not only the wars over religion which took their toll of lives in the name of the Prince of Peace, but also the spirit of intolerance which made martyrs out of victims for conscience's sake. It was God's will, he pleaded, that freedom of worship be granted men of all nations, whether pagans, Jews or Turks. Religious uniformity in the civil state was not the will of God, for true Christianity would flourish only where diverse and contrary consciences were recognized.

Williams' writings were studded with declarations such as these: "A national church was not instituted by Christ Jesus. That cannot be a true religion which needs carnal weapons to uphold it."[2] ... "Forcing of conscience is soul rape."[3] ... "No civil state or country can be truly called Christian, although true Christians be in it."[4]

When Williams was in England in 1652, he entered with gusto into a movement that involved one of the burning issues of the time. Since Edward I had driven them out in 1290, Jews had been unwelcome in Britain, but now many an ardent Puritan urged that they officially return. The restoration of Israel to Britain under the protecting aegis of the Commonwealth had both a mystical significance and a special appeal. Of course, there was an opposition who thought it best for England to remain *judenrein*. In order to show this faction the true light, Williams wrote a pamphlet on Major Butler's *Fourth Paper* which was unknown to later generations until 1874.[5]

He blamed the execution of Charles I and the fall of the house of Stuart on "the *unchristian oppressions, incivilities* and *inhumanities*" of England against the Jews.[6] Only by making decent amends to them would the state pacify the wrath of the Most High.[7]

Williams advocated reconciliation between Jew and Gentile and believed that Christians should take the initiative. It was, he said, "the *Duty* of the *Civil Magistrate* to break down that superstitious *wall* between us Gentiles and the Jews, and freely (without their asking) to make way for their free and peaceable Habitation amongst us."[8] This policy did not find formal acceptance in England at the moment, although the government closed its eyes to the handful of Jews who took up residence. It was in America that the full sweep of Roger Williams' thesis found play.

A motley populace settled in the Narragansett country. At Providence, Portsmouth, Newport and Warwick lived wild Ishmaels whose nonconformity made them unwelcome elsewhere. They included Baptists, Quakers, Antinomians and Seekers, the latter being Williams' own faith.

Rhode Island's open-door policy towards Quakers

served more than any other factor to make this colony a
thorn in the flesh of neighbors who banned the pesti-
lential sect. They sought to change the welcome to exclusion, but their efforts were in vain,[9] and the result was
that the "libertines" of Rhode Island were "generally
hated by the other colonies."[10] Such sentiments prevailed not only among the English but even among the
Dutch. The Rev. Joannes Megapolensis, the spiritual
leader of New Amsterdam,[11] called William's colony "the
receptacle of all sorts of riff-raff people, and . . . nothing
else than the sewer (latrina) of New England. All the
cranks of New England retire thither."[12]

The free atmosphere of Rhode Island (marked to be
sure by disputatious wrangles) can readily be traced to
the untrammeled spirit of Roger Williams.

> I desire not that liberty for myself [he cried] which
> I would not freely and impartially weigh out to all
> the consciences of the world besides; therefore, I
> humbly conceive that it is the express and absolute
> duty of the civil powers to proclaim an absolute free-
> dom of conscience in all the world.[13]

How was this program of religious freedom carried out?
It was achieved in the charter of 1637 by a decision to
keep a rigorous silence on matters of religion. The document spoke of "civil government" and "civil laws," and
declared that the will of the majority was to prevail for
the public good, but "only in civil things."[14] It is evident
that the realm of theology was beyond the province of
government.

Years later, in 1663, the colony secured another charter

from the Crown. The people on their part were eager to preserve their "full libertie in religious concernments," and Charles II complied with their wishes by declaring that it was his royal pleasure for no one to be molested because of religious opinion, provided he did not disturb the civil peace.[15] What a contrast to the intolerant policy of Parliament at home!

The law of 1665, enacted in response to five proposals of a royal commission, was another step in the direction of religious equality. Its definition of the qualifications for the ranks of freemen was sweeping. "All men of competante estates, and of civill conversation" who submitted "to the civill magistrate, though of differing judgments," were eligible to vote or hold office.[16] With one magnificent stroke, seventeenth-century Rhode Island removed all disabilities from Jews, Catholics and Turks.

The famous parable of the ship of state, so close to the heart of the founder of Rhode Island, was fulfilled. The state, he wrote in a letter, was comparable to a ship going to sea with many hundred souls. None of the Papists, Protestants, Jews or Turks on board are forced to attend the ship's worship, nor must they abandon their own forms. At the same time, the captain maintains order and discipline among crew and passengers alike.[17] Religious freedom was more readily realized than the civil control which Williams advocated. The Rhode Island ship of state carried its complement of assorted Protestants. At length, came the Jews.

It was natural for them to go to Rhode Island. Not only did it present the unique phenomenon of a state without an established church, but also Roger Williams actually voiced the hope that he and the Jews might have contacts together. This was little short of an invitation for them to establish homes in the new community.

In addition, there were definite geographical reasons to draw the Jews thither. Newport and Venice have been compared to each other. Both are islands whose merchant fleets formerly ploughed the seas.[18] The goal of much of the maritime commerce of Newport was far-off Barbados, and the recently published letters of Peleg Sanford have brought home to us the long voyages of the Newport ships which set out with cargoes of horses and provisions and returned with Barbados molasses and rum.[19] Now Barbados boasted not only molasses and rum, but also a considerable Jewish community.[20] Nothing was more natural than for the ship captains to have dealings with Jewish merchants there and occasionally to carry one as passenger on the home voyage.

The earliest Jewish names in the town records of Newport were those of men who had removed to Rhode Island from the West Indian center. The date of the first arrivals, however, cannot be determined.

There is, to be sure, a fantastic tale about Jews introducing the Masonic ritual in the year 1658. Mr. N. H. Gould of Newport claimed to own a seventeenth-century manuscript which furnished the proof that Abraham Moses was given his Masonic degree on the second day of Rosh Hashanah — of all times![21] The document was in such a bad state of preservation, said Gould, that he could not permit it even to be photographed.[22] Scholars have come to the conclusion that if such a paper does exist, it is a hoax.[23]

There may very well have been Jews in Newport in 1658, despite our lack of conclusive evidence. The earliest local reference to them which is probably authentic dates from 1677. Almost always the acquisition of a graveyard has been the first step in the founding of a new Jewish community, and in the case of Newport the cemetery deed furnishes significant telltale evidence — the names of the two Jews who acquired a tract of land for burial purposes. They were Moses Pachecho and Mordecai Campernell,[24] and we know something of their careers, thanks to the researches of Wilfred S. Samuel.

Pachecho came originally from Hamburg. He emigrated to Barbados, and in 1662 we find him petitioning the king for denization. Later, as we know, he was at Newport, where he and Campernell secured the land for the cemetery. (The cemetery, by the way, has become a famous landmark of Newport, and its dead have been immortalized in a poem by Longfellow.)

Shortly after the acquisition of the burial ground, Campernell sailed to Barbados and undertook to persuade his relatives and friends to settle in Rhode Island. A contingent of Barbados Jews removed to Newport in 1679, apparently as a result of his arguments.[25]

The newcomers, with their Spanish and Portuguese names, were merchants in many, if not all, cases. The logical calling was intercolonial trade for which their family connections in the West Indies especially qualified them. There was one fly in their ointment, however —

the Navigation Acts of 1660 and subsequent years. There
was good reason for their concern. As we have seen,[26] no
foreign merchants might enter the colonial trade unless
naturalized or granted the rights of free denizens. In
New York, the Jews were fortunate under English rule.
They enjoyed the rights of free denizens after the transfer
of the province; foreign trade was open to them. But in
Rhode Island it was different.

Fortunately for the Jews of Newport and many other
communities, the Acts of Trade were only fitfully enforced and it was a rare event to find violators punished.
The Rhode Island Jews, however, were apprehensive
about their uncertain status, and a group of them petitioned the Assembly in 1684 for an official declaration
concerning their rights and privileges. At least that must
be inferred from the Assembly's response which is buried
in the official minutes of that body; the original petition
has been lost.

The answer declared that the Jews might "expect as
good protection as any stranger, being not of our nation
residing amongst us in this his Majesty's Colony, ought
to have, being obedient to his Majesty's laws."[27] The
response was proper, for the provincial lawmakers could
hardly have been expected to repudiate the acts of the
realm. A strict enforcement, however, would have driven
the Jews out of business.

The Assembly's declaration recalled a similar statement made by the Assembly of Barbados guaranteeing
their rights as foreigners almost thirty years before.[28]
The situation had changed somewhat, however, thanks

to the restrictive Navigation Laws which had been enacted in the interval. Despite provincial reassurances,
the Jews of Newport had reason to be uneasy in view of
the threat embedded in the king's statutes.

Less than a year later, the remote fear became a present menace due to the intervention of Major William
Dyer. Dyer has been an enigmatic figure consistently
neglected by historians. Before considering his role in
Rhode Island Jewish history, we might dip briefly into
his earlier career.

His mother was Mary Dyer, the unfortunate Quaker
woman, who defied the Boston magistrates and got her-
self hanged.[29] This did not prevent William from joining
the retinue of James, Duke of York,[30] which won him the
collectorship of the port of New York.[31]

Dyer seemed to antagonize the citizens wherever he
worked, although it is hard to say whether the conflicts
were due to sterling integrity or consummate venality.
The New York merchants were furious over his tax collecting, and in 1682 they charged him with forcing the
payment of illegal customs duties, but on second thought
they changed the accusation to one of treason.[32] Transported to England for trial,[33] Dyer must have been over-
joyed when none of his accusers appeared and he received
his vindication and freedom.[34]

Meanwhile, the harassed official lost none of the favor
he had enjoyed with members of the British government.
On the other hand, with enhanced prestige, he was able
to cross the ocean and take office as surveyor-general of
the customs of all the American colonies, with head-

quarters in Boston.[35] It was his duty to administer the
Navigation Laws, and he seized ships and imposed fines
with a heavy hand. The men of Boston made violent
threats against him — because of his faithful conduct,
he claimed;[36] because of his malice and dishonesty, said
the others.[37]

Rhode Island was part of Dyer's domain where his
highhanded methods won the same hostility as in Massachusetts. There was a clash with Governor William
Coddington over the case of Captain Thomas Paine, the
"arch-pirate," when Coddington refused to have the sea
captain arrested.[38] A few months later, Dyer faced the
governor once more in seeking to press another important prosecution. This involved nothing less than the
right of the Jews of Rhode Island to conduct their
business.

Only a single documentary source exists for one of the
most dramatic episodes in American Jewish history.[39]
The record is inadequate and incomplete; it is only a
brief transcript of the suit, but it serves to suggest something of the suspense and excitement which must have
stirred the little Jewish community of two and a half
centuries ago to its very foundations.

It is clear that the Barbados Jews newly established
at Newport, and the intercolonial trade they conducted,
caught Dyer's watchful eye. These Jews — these foreigners — were patently violating the Navigation Laws
by trafficking in sugar and molasses from overseas. Dyer
proceeded by presenting his charges against seven men
and one woman to the governor. Four of the men belonged

to the Campernell family. There were also Saul Brown, Abraham Burgos and Aaron Verse. The woman was the widow of Simon Mendez, who apparently took over his business.

With what were these people charged? Our source says they were to be tried "as Aliens &c." This must mean that the Jews were conducting export and import trade closed to them as foreigners. Dyer must have had a good case against them, for the governor directed the general sergeant to seize the property of the accused pending trial.

On March 31, 1685, the case was called. At the session of the general court which met at Newport, Governor Coddington presided, and other important officials of the province were present. The defendants, of course, appeared. The grand jury was sworn and the trial was set to open. But Dyer, who had initiated the proceedings, was nowhere to be found. He was represented by a proxy — such men were called attorneys in those days — but he had failed to give bond for the property he had distrained.

Because of Dyer's default the defendants entered a nonsuit. The governor was of the opinion, however, that there were weighty reasons to proceed to trial. The consent of the defendants was required and, once they agreed, Major Dyer suffered a resounding defeat. He was obliged to pay costs to the amount of fifteen shillings, eight pence. As for the Jews, their property was returned and their right to trade went unchallenged.

The brief statement of facts leaves a number of questions unanswered. Why did the governor of Rhode Island proceed against the Jews at Dyer's insistence? There was no love lost between the two men and Coddington would have hesitated to oblige his enemy by seizing the property of the seven defendants unless pretty weighty arguments existed. Only a few months before he had refused to turn Captain Paine over to Dyer.

If Dyer had such a good case, why then did he default when the trial opened? His non-appearance and the costs which were levied upon him suggest defeat and humiliation that must have stung. A historian has no right to speculate, but it is only human to ask what manner of intrigue behind the scenes was responsible for the dénouement of a courtroom drama which died aborning.

A sequel to this incident has no little significance. On the first Tuesday of September, 1688, Abraham Campanell, one of the defendants in the case, was licensed as a freeman by the court which held its sitting at Rochester.[40] So far as we know, he was the only Jew admitted to this privilege in all the history of colonial Rhode Island.

The fact is that the law of 1665, which threw open the ranks of freemen to men of all religions, was cruelly amended at some unknown time. Just how this happened it is hard to say, but when the laws of Rhode Island were codified and published in 1719, a new statute as of March 1, 1662, was printed in its stead. The revised version read "that all Men Professing Christianity and of Competent Estates, and of Civil Conversation ... (Roman

Catholicks only excepted)" were to be admitted as freemen.[41] Under the new dispensation, Jews, Catholics and
unbelievers no longer enjoyed civil equality.

The Rhode Island somersault involves several mys-
teries. Why, for instance, was the law of 1662 imbedded
in the colonial records while the law of 1665 was never
cited? Certain authorities would dismiss the first version
as a piece of fiction derived from the careless copying of
some clerk. They maintain that the disabilities imposed
on Catholics and non-Christians go back to the original
law.

In substantiation of this hypothesis it has been argued
that Roger Williams as a pamphleteer was one thing and
Roger Williams in action was something radically different. For example, Williams could write Endicott in
1664: "I am far from glancing the least countenance on
the consciences of Papists."[42] This suggests that even he
might have sanctioned Catholic disabilities.

Another school of historians advances the claim that
both of the conflicting acts governing freemen were
genuine. They say, however, that the change may have
come early, and they find very useful for their thesis the
fact that on October 31, 1666, the General Assembly
commissioned John Clarke "to compose all the lawes of
the Collony into a good method and forms, leaveing out
what may be superfluous and adding what may apeere
unto him necessary."[43] Though any changes were subject
to the approval of the next Assembly,[44] the procedure
seems haphazard and irregular.

Clarke may have felt a personal dislike for non-Pro-

testants and transferred his prejudice to the statute books
without meeting with any objections from the leaders of
the colony. Strangely enough, however, the records say
not a word on any revisions by Clarke. If the liberal
form of the freemen's law was abolished early (or never
existed), we find some inconsistency in the fact that
Campanell was granted his license in 1688. It is worth
pointing out, however, that during the colonial period
there were some instances where laws were liberally
interpreted when they seemed to discriminate against
Jews while remaining inflexible barriers to Catholics.

There is still another theory, shared by men like Charles
Andrews. They say that nothing was done on the issue
till long after the passing of Roger Williams.[45] Let us
suppose that the records were silent because no steps
were taken to limit the qualifications for freemen. In
that case, it was not until 1728 that the General Assembly
approved the provincial code *in toto* (with the religious
test for freemen intact). That act left little doubt
of the Assembly's intention to disqualify Jews and
Catholics.

From that date, if not earlier, Catholics, Jews and non-
believers suffered from civil disabilities in colonial Rhode
Island. In justice to the colony, however, it must be said
that it remained a secular state. As Sidney Rider put it,
the religious tests did "not entrench upon the principle
of Religious Liberty. Every individual could enjoy his
religion untaxed for any other man's religion; but he
could not vote or hold office, and it was these two conditions only which constituted a freeman."[46]

Rhode Island as conceived by its founder was to occupy a peak position far above the surging currents of the seventeenth century. As fulfilled by the passing years, it reverted to standards more in accord with the time. This we may regret, but the community on the shores of Narragansett Bay was made up of men, not gods, and as men they erred.

CHAPTER IV

CHIAROSCURO IN EIGHTEENTH-CENTURY
RHODE ISLAND

FEW towns in America are lovelier than Newport. Tree-lined streets with old houses dating back to days of colonial elegance, Cliff Walk and its many pretentious displays of *fin de siècle* splendor, and everywhere vistas of the blue Atlantic and quieter waters of Narragansett Bay, combine to make the bustling town one of the places that no well traveled American should miss.

There is a special Newport legend centering about the early Jewish community whose descendants have vanished from the scene, leaving behind a colonial synagogue to Jews of more recent vintage. That synagogue, the oldest Jewish edifice in the United States, has made Newport a patriotic shrine where latter-day Jews steep themselves in memories of courtly gentlemen in white perukes who conducted great mercantile enterprises and prayed in the accents of medieval Spain.

Like so many other traditions, the Jewish legend of Newport has grown with the passing years until we are asked to believe that Newport was a garden spot in the Isles of the Blessed. We have had conjured for us the picture of a tremendous Jewish community, living under ideal conditions, untroubled by any of the annoyances to which Jews elsewhere are heir. The fact is that the actual community did not attain great size, nor did it enjoy a truly golden age. There was much that was fine in the Newport setting, but there was also much to depress the Jewish residents there. Life was not bathed in endless golden sunshine; but there was rather an atmosphere of chiaroscuro made up of contrasting light and darkness.

One is able to reconstruct the seventeenth-century Jewish Newport only through shards and shreds, so little of its record[1] has survived. For a time there was little or no Jewish life in Newport, but after it revived we are much more fortunate as regards source material. A wealth of letters and accounts in the vaults of the Newport Historical Society throb with the personality of eighteenth-century Jews and fairly clamor for publication. Other manuscripts of interest are found in the archives of the State Capitol in Providence and elsewhere. When the published and unpublished annals of pre-Revolutionary Newport are finally combined, we shall at last enjoy the type of historical study which that venerable Jewish community deserves.

Perhaps the warmest of all our contemporary sources is the already published diary of Ezra Stiles. Stiles was the most colorful figure associated with Jewish life in Newport, although he served as observer rather than as participant. He may be described as a provincial New England scholar with the inclinations of an encyclopedist. For a long time he was minister of the Congregational church in Newport, and later distinguished himself as president of Yale College.[1a]

His insatiable desire for knowledge drew him to the study of the Bible in the original and to the mystical depths of the *Zohar*. He was excited by travelers' tales of enclaves of Jews in remote parts of Asia, but he also embraced the opportunity to study Jewish lore and life in his own Newport.[2]

He frequented the synagogue, which was consecrated in 1763, and made the *hazzan* of the community, Isaac Touro, his companion and teacher. He watched the Jews in their homes and made careful notes on their customs. Whenever a rabbi visited Newport (six came to town between 1759 and 1775),[3] the Congregational divine sought him out to discuss perplexing problems in Jewish theology or biblical exegesis. A remarkable friendship grew up between him and Rabbi Hayim Carrigal of Hebron, Palestine.[4] So attached did the two become that Stiles sought the portrait of "the Venerable Hocham"[5] for the Yale College library.[6]

Full details about every aspect of Jewish life he could discover found their way into his writings, particularly the inexhaustible pages of the *Diary* which was kept from 1769 until long after Stiles had left Rhode Island. In 1760, he catalogued the Jewish families of Newport and counted fifteen households consisting of fifty-eight souls.[7] Nine years later he declared there were twenty-five families in the town.[8] In 1774, a provincial census showed Newport to have 9,209 inhabitants,[9] but a search among the census sheets reveals only one hundred and twenty-one Jewish men, women and children at Newport.[10] Certain Jewish residents seemed to have been omitted from the list, but it is safe to say that the Jews did not number more than two per cent of the population.

This is quite different from the fantastic figures later assigned to the Jews of Newport. Governor William C. Cozzens declared in an address in 1863 that "some hundreds of wealthy Israelites" had moved to Newport between 1750 and 1760.[11] H. T. Tuckerman could write in *Harper's New Monthly* of 1869 that the synagogue had "boasted eleven hundred and seventy-five worshipers."[12] (The tiny building could have accommodated this throng only in relays.) Even a recent writer has stated that "there were about two hundred Jewish families in Newport" on the eve of the Revolution.[13]

The economic life of the Jews centered in ships, shops and warehouses, and the leading citizens of the community were merchants. Jewish vessels hailing from Newport visited harbors the length of the Atlantic coast and frequented the West Indian islands in great numbers, exchanging New England products for sugar and molasses. Some of the ships pursued the infamous triangular route, sailing to Africa to buy kidnaped slaves with Newport rum, exchanging the human cargoes for molasses in Jamaica, and returning home with the ingredients for more rum.[14] That was before the sufferings of the unhappy blacks had excited compassion.

Whaling was another of the shipowners' interests, and Jacob Rodriguez Riveira is said to have introduced the manufacture of candles from spermaceti brought into Newport.[15] Out of this new industry came in 1761 the

INTERIOR OF THE SYNAGOGUE, NEWPORT, R. I.

JACOB RODRIGUEZ RIVERA
portrait by Gilbert Stuart

organization of the United Company of Spermaceti Candlers, an early form of the American trust. The members divided the spermaceti among themselves and controlled prices. Both in the original agreement and later cartel of 1763 Jewish names were prominent. Four of the eight participating in the second instrument were Jews.[16]

The outstanding Jewish merchants belonged to the Lopez family, which had originated in Portugal where its members had formerly lived as Marranos. The first of the family to come to Newport was Moses Lopez, who had been naturalized in New York in 1740.[17] For some years he translated Spanish letters and papers for the government without accepting fees, and in 1750 he petitioned the Assembly to exempt him from all other personal duties in the colony because of this special form of service. The favor was granted.[18] In 1753 he petitioned the Assembly again, this time for the right to manufacture potash by a secret process, and he was given a ten-year monopoly in the field.[19]

Far more important than Moses was his young half-brother, Aaron, who came to Newport in 1752.[20] Through his papers in the Newport Historical Society, we may trace his career from its modest beginnings up to the time when he owned more than thirty vessels, in whole or in part, just before the Revolution.[21] Lopez was one of those entering the spermaceti combine,[22] and later he undertook to ship goods to Bristol, England. This project proved very unwise and resulted in his owing Henry Cruger, his agent there, almost eleven thousand pounds in 1767.[23]

Lopez did not repudiate the obligation. Instead he pursued an aggressive policy of opening up new trade contacts in Jamaica and elsewhere. By diversifying his interests, he added to the success which now rewarded his efforts. In time he not only paid his debt to Bristol, but he became the leading shipowner in Newport.

Ezra Stiles was of the opinion that there was no merchant in America whose trade was more extensive.[24] But he respected Lopez more for character than for gold. After the Revolution had destroyed his commerce and his wealth,[25] Lopez met his death in a carriage accident in 1782. Stiles, who was now president of Yale, wrote a eulogy that approached almost the limit of hyperbole. He called him:

> that amiable, benevolent, most hospitable & very respectable gentleman . . . Without a single Enemy & the most universally beloved by an extensive Acquaintance of any man I ever knew. His Beneficence to his Fami & Connexions, to his Nation, & to all the World is at most without a Parallel.[26]

It is worth while citing this fulsome eulogy of Stiles even though we get somewhat ahead of our story, for it augments the character and reputation of a man who was made the victim of an outrageous piece of discrimination when he sought to become naturalized. The procedure should have been an easy one. In compliance with an act of Parliament of 1740, to benefit Protestants and Jews who lived in an English colony for seven years, it should have been possible to become a British subject by appearing in court with the proper proofs. Jews were exempt from communion and were not required to swear upon the "true faith of a Christian."

James Lucena of Newport, formerly of Portugal, secured his naturalization at the hands of the Rhode Island General Assembly in December, 1760, apparently without difficulty.[27] When Aaron Lopez and Isaac Elizer sought to do the same the following year, conditions had radically changed. Lopez was not yet the great merchant prince of later years, but his integrity was surely well known. This humiliating experience was a black mark on the government of the province which has never been satisfactorily explained.

The affair began in 1761 when the two men applied to the Superior Court for naturalization.[28] They were given no satisfaction. Then they turned to the General Assembly for aid. The lower house voted on October 30 that their petition would be granted if they appeared before the Superior Court and took the oath of allegiance. The legislators, however, wanted Lopez to understand clearly that he was not to enjoy the privileges of a freeman:

> Inasmuch as the said Aaron Lopez hath declared himself by religion a Jew [they stated], this Assembly doth not admit himself nor any other of that religion to the full freedom of this Colony. So that the said Aaron Lopez nor any other of said religion is not liable to be chosen into any office in this Colony nor allowed to give vote as a free man in choosing others.[29]

Even this grudging and limited recognition of the petitioner's rights did not receive the concurrence of the upper house. That body considered the matters of naturalization beyond the Assembly's province (Lucena's case the year before nothwithstanding). The act of Parliament had stipulated that the courts were to be the instruments of naturalization, and so Lopez and Elizer were shunted back to the Superior Court for satisfaction.[30]

The court now considered the applications and rendered its amazing decision on March 11, 1762. Ezra Stiles, the ubiquitous, was present on this momentous occasion, and he was so impressed that he gave a description of the proceedings in his *Itineraries*. Posterity can enjoy a dramatic courtroom scene by reading his account. He wrote:

> And on the Eleventh Day of March 1762 Sentence was pronounced upon the Criminals successively brot to the Bar; first upon Jno. Sherman a noted Thief & Burglar for Burglary, sentenced to be hanged; secondly upon Fortune an abandoned Negro who set Fire to the Warehouses at End Long Wharf 19th. Feb^r. which did Damage £5,000. ster. & endangered the Conflagration of the Town, sentenced to be hanged; Thirdly upon — Lawton for Perjury in swearing to an acco^t. which he had falsely forged against another, sentenced to the Pillory &c . . . And then the Jews were called to hear their almost equally mortifying sentence and Judg^t: which dismissed their Petition for Naturalization. Whether this was designedly, or accidental in proceeding upon the Business of Court I dont learn.[31]

Stiles took the trouble of copying down the verdict of the court. It declared that the Act of 1740 had been designed to increase the population of the colonies.

Inasmuch as Rhode Island had become so crowded that some of its residents had settled in Nova Scotia, the act did not apply there.

> Further [said the court] by the charter granted to this colony, it appears that the free and quiet enjoyment of the Christain religion and a desire of propagating the same were the the principal views with which this colony was settled, and by a law made and passed in the year 1663, no person who does not profess the Christian religion can be admitted free in this colony. This court, therefore, unanimously dismiss this petition as wholly inconsistent with the first principles upon which the colony was founded and a law of the same now in force.[32]

Stiles felt the action of the court warranted some philosophical observations on the Jewish question. He wrote:

> I remark that Providence seems to make every Thing to work for Mortification to the Jews, & to prevent their incorporating into any Nation; that thus they may continue a distinct people.[33]

It seemed to him that popular resentment had brought about the revocation of the rights of naturalization briefly enjoyed by the Jews of England, and the tumult over the same question in New York.[34] This situation, he said, "forebodes that the Jews will never become incorporated with the people of America, any more than in Europe, Asia, and Africa."[35]

Samuel Arnold, the author of the nineteenth-century *History of Rhode Island*, which is still the standard work on the subject, was unsparing in his judgment of the court's opinion.

> The decision in the case of Lopez [he wrote] appears irregular in every respect. It subverts an act of Parliament, violates the spirit of the charter, enunciates principles never acted upon in the colony, and finally dismisses the case on a false issue.[36]

He could find only one ground to explain it all—party spirit resulting from the feud between Chief Justice Ward and Governor Hopkins. "Some of the details of that contest, herein recorded, exhibit as gross violations of right and of usage as does this decision, but none so utterly absurd," wrote Arnold.[37] Today one is not quite as certain as he was just what interpretation of the court's arbitrary verdict would be correct.

Lopez was no doubt outraged by the cavalier treatment administered by the judges, but he was not dismayed; for he immediately instituted action to secure in Massachusetts the naturalization denied in Rhode Island. On March 29—just eighteen days after the defeat in Rhode Island—Lopez's Boston agent, Henry Lloyd, was already writing about some special inquiries he had made. His relative, it appears, was surveyor-general, and the latter had learned from the governor and chief justice of Massachusetts Bay that all that Lopez needed was a certificate, with a Rhode Island seal, attesting to his seven-years' residence there. With such credentials Massachusetts would allow him to take the oath of allegiance.

Mr. Lloyd also turned to Sam Fitch, a local attorney at

law, for advice. The lawyer stated that it was necessary for Lopez to establish residence in Massachusetts before he could appear at the session of the Superior Court where the oath would be administered. Lloyd's own advice was for Lopez to consult with the chief justice himself on his next visit to Boston.[38]

Lopez retained Fitch to advise him on arrangements to be made before his coveted naturalization could be attained. He had to transport his family to Swansea, across the Massachusetts line, to comply with the residential requirements, and a troublesome job it must have been both for him and Mrs. Lopez.

Fitch directed Lopez and Elizer to bring to the court session at Taunton sworn proofs that they had lived at least seven years in Rhode Island and also witnesses whose depositions might be taken in open court. He also reminded them in his letter that they should "remember without fail" to take along the text of the Naturalization Law of 1740 and the wording of the oath prescribed for Jews, "as there will be no books at Taunton."[39]

On October 12, Lopez appeared before the Superior Court in Taunton. Elizer, perhaps discouraged by the annoying requirements of a Massachusetts residence, did not accompany him. Lopez produced a certificate from "the Honble John Gardner Esq. Deputy Governor of the English Colony of Rhode Island & Providence Plantations in New England in America," declaring "that Aaron Lopez and Isaac Elizer two gentlemen professing the Jewish Religion," had lived for seven years in the colony and had "ever deported themselves as good and loyal subjects of his Britannic Majesty."⁴⁰ (Apparently Gardner overlooked the fact that they were as yet unnaturalized.)

Following his naturalization at Taunton, Lopez resumed his residence at Newport and did not return to Massachusetts to live until the British captured Newport during the Revolution, and he, a staunch patriot, fled to Leicester. It was while returning to Newport after the war was over that Lopez met his death.

As for Elizer, he secured his naturalization in a different fashion. After failure in Rhode Island and discouragement in Massachusetts, he turned to New York for satisfaction and finally took the oath of allegiance, July 23, 1763.⁴¹

The Lopez naturalization case highlights the inferior status of the Jews of Rhode Island at this time. They might enjoy equal economic opportunity and freedom of worship without the necessity of supporting a state church by their taxes; but they were second class citizens who could not vote or hold office, whose rights might be further abridged at the whim of Court or Assembly. To say that their pride was hurt is not mere surmise, as is proved by the case of Moses M. Hays of Newport who was unjustly accused of being a loyalist in 1776. When asked to subscribe to the Test, he refused, although he favored the patriot cause, he stated. But, he went on to declare, "I am an Israelite and I am not allowed the liberty of a vote, or voice in common with the rest of the voters, though consistent with the Constitution."⁴²

It would be unfair to suggest that the Jews were regarded as outcasts because of their political disabilities.

Nor were they treated in society as though they belonged
to lesser breeds without the law, for much good will existed
between Jew and Christian. We note, for example, that
when Rabbi Hayim Carrigal preached in the synagogue
on Shabu'ot, 1773, Governor Wanton and other high
officials of the colony looked on.[43] Of course, Ezra Stiles
was present too, and by way of reciprocity the Palestine
leader occupied a pew in the Congregational church while
Dr. Stiles delivered one of his long New England ser-
mons.[44]

Newport Jews also participated in the cultural life of the
community. Two of them, Moses Lopez and Abraham
Hart, joined the company when the historic Redwood
Library was incorporated in 1747.

From the viewpoint of culture, the greatest achievement
in eighteenth-century Rhode Island was the founding of
Brown University. The Newport community did not
appear to play a role in the furthering of this institution,
but other Jews did. The story of the early link between
American Jews and the fledgling college is refreshing, not
only as a contrast to the shabby treatment of Lopez,
but also because it dramatizes some of the differences
between American and English universities during the
period.

Like the other eight colleges on American soil before the
Revolution, Brown welcomed students of all religious
predilections.[45] One must not imagine that a sectarian
spirit was lacking in the higher education of the eighteenth
century. Just as Harvard and Yale were under Congrega-

tional control, and King's College (Columbia) was
Episcopalian, and the College of New Jersey (Princeton)
was Presbyterian, so Brown was the answer to a Baptist
yearning for self-expression in the field of higher education.

The charter which the fledgling institution, later to
become Brown University, secured from the General
Assembly was a broad document. It declared that the new
academy was to be a "Liberal & Catholic Institution,"
without religious tests, where "full free Absolute and
uninterrupted Liberty of Conscience" might be enjoyed.[46]
The program of the College of Rhode Island was in no
sense revolutionary or unique, but nowhere else was a
more enlightened conception of the roles of religion and
education embodied.

It goes without saying that the charter welcomed
youths of every faith and assured them equally generous
treatment during residence, whatever their beliefs. It
was only slightly less liberal regarding the religious background of professors and other college officers, who might
be drawn from all denominations of Protestants. This
was not generally considered as a form of sectarian bias,
for the exclusion of Catholics was axiomatic at the time.
What was perhaps more out of the ordinary in the case
of the College of Rhode Island was the fact that the
charter prohibited religious instruction of a sectarian
nature. This seems surprising in view of the fact that
the institution was under Baptist direction.[47]

Rhode Island College was handicapped at the start
by the fact that it was without the prestige which the

older colleges had won through the years. When it opened its doors at Warren, Rhode Island, in 1765, it began its career with one student.[48] Up to 1769 only twenty-nine students had been matriculated.[49] The new school was not only short of pupils, it was also short of funds. Fortunately, it possessed an able and youthful president in the person of James Manning, who set about to create an adequate endowment. Canvassers were authorized to collect funds, among them the Rev. Morgan Edwards who spent a year in Great Britain and Ireland.[50] In 1769 the Rev. Hezekiah Smith sailed to Charleston to obtain contributions from merchants and planters in South Carolina and Georgia.[51] One of those approached was Moses Lindo.

Lindo came to Charleston from England in 1756,[52] turned planter and also acted as a merchant specializing in indigo for export. His superiority in his chosen field won him the office of "Surveyor and Inspector-General of Indigo, Drugs, and Dyes."[53] Lindo was greatly impressed by Hezekiah Smith's account of the school at Warren with its atmosphere of tolerance and enlightenment. He gladly joined the local patrons by pledging twenty pounds South Carolina curency. This was the equivalent of less than three pounds sterling.[54]

The enthusiasm inspired by Smith is echoed in the letter Lindo wrote his New York agents, Messrs. Sampson and Solomon Simson. (The name of this firm was worthy of a place in a novel by Dickens.) Under the date of April 17, 1770, he asked them to send five pounds York currency, which was the value of the twenty pounds

South Carolina, that he had pledged to the trustees of the "New College." He wrote:

> The Reason y^t [55] Induces me to be a Benefactor to this College is y^{ir}[56] having no objection of Admitting y^e[57] Youth of our Nation without Interference in Principals of Religion. If so my donation shall exceed beyond ye bounds of y^{ir} Imagination —

(Lindo was familiar with the practice of English universities in excluding Jews, but he did not seem to realize that American colleges had no such barriers.)

The letter continued in a mellow vein as the writer recalled his salad days at school in England.

> I presume this College is like Merchant Taylor's School in London where I went every day for three Years as well as two of my Brothers from nine to one O'Clock. There was at ye time above 800 boys, Sons of ye principal Merchants & trading people in ye City. I have lived to see two Lord Mayors & seven aldermen, & many toping merchants my School-Fellows. — Which I assure you was no small service to me when I was a Broker on ye Royal Exchange —.[58]

Lindo displayed an understandable pride in his contacts with the great at the Merchant Taylors' School. One is a little surprised therefore to find none of the three Lindo brothers listed in the register of that ancient seminary.[59] Mr. Girlen, headmaster of the school, writes that Jews were excluded from the student body from 1731 to 1761 by order of the court. However, he states that he feels sure, "That if Lindo and his brothers had been pupils here before 1731, or after the rescinding of the order, they would not have been missing from the Register, which, as far as the eighteenth century goes, is, I believe, very complete."[60]

A copy of Lindo's letter was received by the Rev. Hezekiah Smith, and we can imagine with what excitement the message was heard by the trustees and fellows of Rhode Island College. When the annual meeting was held at Providence (for the first time) on September 6, 1770, they voted:

> That the children of JEWS may be admitted into this Institution and intirely enjoy the freedom of their own Religion, without any Constraint or Imposition whatever.[61]

The trustees were undoubtedly anxious to get a share of the Lindo largess, but for some reason they delayed almost four months before writing him of their vote. Then they sent a lengthy letter, dated January 1, 1771, which began as follows:

> Sir
>
> The College, now building at Providence in the Colony of Rhode Island, is instituted upon the most catholic, and benevolent Principles that could be devised, being designed, solely, for training up Youth in the Practice of Virtue and the Knowledge of the useful Arts and Sciences: and not to initiate them in wrangling, polemical Questions, and useless Disputes; accordingly it is provided in the Charter, by which this Institution is incorporated, that the Scholars shall be put under no religious Tests, or Restraints whatsoever; but shall be absolutely free, and have full Liberty, to attend their own Forms of public and

private Devotion; and without Hindrance, or Interruption, worship God in the Way they, or their Parents may think best.

With this introductory statement out of the way, the trustees went on to consider Mr. Lindo's offer. The institution was free and open, they declared, and at their business meeting "they had particularly noted" the statement that, if the youth of the Jewish nation were freely admitted, Lindo's donation would "exceed beyond the Bounds of their imagination."

The letter proceeded:

Upon Consideration of your Letter and what Mr Smith added upon the same Subject, the Corporation came to a Resolution, which they entered on their Journals, that all such Youths of the Jewish Nation and Religion, as shall offer themselves for that Purpose, shall be received, and admitted into College Standing, on the same Terms as Christian Youth are there received: that they shall during their Continuance there, enjoy equal Priviledges & Advantages in all Respects with others, and shall be permitted freely to enjoy their own Sabbaths, Feasts and Fasts, without Hindrance, or Molestation; and shall not be compelled, or called upon, to attend any Christian Worship or Service whatever. And the same exact Care shall be taken of their Morals as of other Youth in this Seminary; and also, that all the Honors, Advantages, and literary Degrees shall at all times be conferred upon them, as are upon other Students in College, according to their Standing & Proficiency in Learning.

Further, it hath been thought fit to inform you, that,

at any Time hereafter, when there is a sufficient Number of Jewish Scholars in this College to defray the Expense, they may, if they choose it, have a Tutor of their own Religion, who may have the immediate Care of their Education, subject to the Direction and Revision of the President. Unless they should prefer raising a Fund, and establishing a Professor of the Hebrew, & Oriental Languages, either of which, or both, to us, will be equally agreeable.

This was a noteworthy statement of broadmindedness. It is especially significant in view of the fact that the college charter had limited the faculty to Protestants, and is one more indication that, with all the fury directed at the Catholics at the time, Jews might even be considered part of the Protestant camp. At any rate, the welcome extended Jewish students was worthy of the founder of Providence, Roger Williams.

The concluding paragraph of the letter reads as follows:

This College has as delightful a Situation, and as healthful an Air as any in America: the Morals of the Youth will be as safe, and their living as good and as cheap, as in any Part of the Continent. We wish you therefore to become a further Friend to this infant Institution; which can chiefly be done by supplying it with many Scholars; and in the next Place by generous Donations towards endowing it; for which last Purpose we have inclosed a Subscription Book, which together with this Letter, we hope you will recommend to your Friends, in the way you may think best on the whole matter.[62]

The college needed further endowment badly, but

much as Lindo's money might be welcome, it would be cruelly unjust for us to accuse the trustees of carrying out a policy of expediency. A historian of Brown has remarked: "The Corporation must have known, however, that catholicity might repel as well as attract gifts."[63] As for Lindo's philanthropy, he never made good on his pledge to provide generously for Rhode Island College.[64]

Under these circumstances, it is surprising to learn that the school proceeded to formulate an even more advanced policy to protect the rights of any Jewish students enrolled. This was made clear in the college laws of 1774 which provided:

> That every Student attend publick Worship every first Day of the Week steadily at such Places as he, his Parents or Guardians shall think proper; provided that any who do not attend with any Officers of Instruction, produce Vouchers when Demanded of his steady & orderly Attendance.
>
> N. B. — Such as regularly & statedly keep the Seventh Day, as a Sabbath, are excepted from this Law; & are only required to abstain from Secular Concerns which would interrupt their fellow Students.[65]

One might argue that such regulations did not have Jews alone in mind. Seventh-Day Baptists were also Sabbath observers. There is, however, no mistake about the intent of a later section which reads as follows:

> That if any Student of this College shall deny the being of a God, the Existence of Virtue and Vice; or that the Books of the old and new Testament are of

divine Authority, or Suggest any Scruples of that Nature or circulate Books of such pernicious Tendency, or frequent the Company of those who are known to favour such fatal Errors, He shall for the second Offence be absolutely and forever expelld from this College. Young gentlemen of the Hebrew nation are to be excepted from this Law.[66]

Even a hasty reading of this paragraph makes it clear that Jews might be atheists and destroyers of morality with impunity, while all others showing such tendencies would be expelled from college for the second offense. This was liberalism carried *ad absurdum*.

The authorities came to realize the flaw in their discipline. Following a long recess which the Revolution brought about, the school resumed and in 1783 set up a new code of student laws. Again there was a rule providing for the expulsion of students guilty or irreligion. It was followed by this statement:

Young gentlemen of the Hebrew Nation are to be exempted from this Law, so far as it relates to the New Testament and its authenticity.[67]

There is an ironical aspect about all the precautions which Rhode Island College took to protect and safeguard Jewish students in the exercise of their religion. No Jewish lad ever matriculated until long after the institution had changed its name to Brown. This paradox may be readily explained.

Merchants' sons who might follow in their fathers' footsteps did not receive an academic education in those days. Colleges catered primarily to prospective clergymen and attorneys, and Jews at that time were business-men, not ministers or lawyers. Moreover, outside of the community of Newport, which rapidly languished and died after the Revolution, there was no appreciable community within an easy radius of Providence.

Whether or not a Jewish student ever sat at the feet of James Manning does not really matter. In the twentieth-century quest of freedom and democracy, Brown's early record should constitute a blueprint for our times. That venerable institution on the hill overlooking Providence pursued a religious philosophy so broad, so enlightened, so universal, that its campus might well be described as holy ground.

Aaron Lopez

t' Fort nieuw Amsterdam op de Manhatans

A VIEW OF NEW AMSTERDAM IN 1626–8

CHAPTER V

TEN YEARS UNDER PETER STUYVESANT

WHEN the first Jews arrived in the New Amsterdam which Peter Stuyvesant ruled, the view from the ship could hardly have been impressive. In the year 1654, the town was a Dutch village clustering at the tip of Manhattan Island, with a population of less than a thousand.[1] There was a fort, to be sure, and also a diminutive church, and a tavern recently converted into the *stadt huis*.[2] Among the straggling rows of buildings, one out of every four was a taphouse, according to the count of the director-general himself.[3]

The elaborate provisions for toping were suggestive of the frontier; and the frontier, as everyone knows, was a place where life was dynamic and feuds and rancors burned fiercely. There was no Arcadian calm in New Netherland to prove an exception to the tradition. Under "the misrule of Peter Stuyvesant," as Channing called it,[4] constant strife flared between the governor and the Nine Men, who were named to be his advisers as representatives of the people. They knew that Stuyvesant cared little or nothing for the interests of the citizenry who had crossed the ocean to settle the province. His efforts were all expended for the benefit of his masters, the directors of the West India Company, who sat in their commodious offices in Amsterdam. In the white heat of their resentment, the Nine Men finally appealed for redress to the States-General of the Netherlands because of the tyranny, the ruinous taxes, and the neglect of religion and education to which they had to submit.[5] Some small concessions were the result.

The tumult that existed in the fields of politics and commerce also extended to matters of religion. No one could complain, however, that the provisions for ecclesiastical affairs were not explicit. There was a perfect understanding between the governor and the church — in this case the Dutch Reformed. No other religion was to be publicly admitted, according to the Charter of Freedoms and Exemptions granted by the West India Company in 1640.[6] In addition, the authorities were expected to promote the interests of the dominant sect. The Nine Men were not only appointed to represent the people; they were also required to promote "the preservation of the pure Reformed Religion." Members of the municipal court of New Amsterdam likewise swore "to help maintain the true Reformed Religion and to suffer no other." As matters stood, a dissenter could not even be clerk of the court without doing violence to his conscience.[7]

Church and state were thus yoked together. Dissenting religions could hold no worship outside of the family circle. A man who was a heretic in the eyes of the Reformed Church might not serve in office. Meanwhile, the population of the colony was growing more and more cosmopolitan. As the membership of divergent faiths increased, friction with the clerical and lay authorities was bound to occur.

Stuyvesant matched the local clergy in a zeal for the one faith that merited the applause of the classis in Amsterdam. The directors of the Company also were in sympathy with the religious program, although they were obliged to warn the governor that he should moderate his crusading ardor for the sake of expediency.[8]

It was the Dutch Lutherans who first made an issue of the right to public worship. For some time many of their number had joined in the devotions of the Reformed Church,[9] and the directors of the Company even dared cherish the hope that they would be completely won over to the dominant faith.[10] But the Lutherans were not satisfied. Time and again they petitioned for the right to bring over a minister of their own denomination from Holland.[11] Stuyvesant is said to have declared he would rather resign than make such a concession,[12] and our scanty records suggest that he clapped some of the Lutherans into prison, for which he was roundly criticized by his superiors.[13] The directors were emphatic in their answer to the pleas of the Lutherans, however; they declared in March, 1654, that the members of the church were to have neither public worship nor a minister of their own.[14]

But the Lutherans did not flag in their efforts. If they were entitled to their own clergy at home, they argued, they should be afforded the same privilege in the New World.[15] Their perseverance was all but crowned with success. The directors of Amsterdam weakened, and agreed to close their eyes to a violation of the rules.[16] A minister accordingly sailed for New Netherland,[17] and the Lutherans were happy; but they had bargained without the thought of the classis of Amsterdam, ardent defender of the True Faith. This body exerted such pressure upon the directors of the Company that they had reason to repent of their generosity,[18] and the hapless clergyman was forced to sail home again.[19] This was as far as the Lutherans got under Dutch rule.

If such treatment was accorded Dutch dissenters, what success could the various English groups in the province hope for? As a matter of fact, the Dutch divided these newcomers into three groups for each of which there was a different policy.

Most of the settlers were Presbyterians and Congregationalists who were permitted to build their own churches with the support and sympathy of the authorities.[20] In the sight of Reformed, both of these organizations were orthodox, particularly the Presbyterians, who enjoyed the same ecclesiastical government as the Dutch Church.[21] The settlers belonging to these two sects were accordingly treated as coreligionists and granted full religious rights. As Zwierlein put it: "They were not granted . . . freedom of religion, but freedom of their religion."[22]

The second group was the bulk of English dissenters, unorthodox in doctrine and polity, who were suffered rather than welcomed. These men might carry out their religion as conscience dictated within the privacy of their homes, but they were courting disaster if they attempted public worship. When the Reformed divines denounced the services conducted by unauthorized persons on Long Island,[23] a proclamation was issued by the governor and council threatening dire punishment for such religious meetings. Those who officiated were to be fined one hundred pounds Flemish, while those in attendance were to pay a fourth of that amount.[24] Before many months had passed, a poor cobbler of Flushing, claiming a commission from Christ to go out and baptize people, was driven from the province for his pains.[25]

The Quakers, those "instruments of Satan," formed the third division of English settlers and courted martyrdom when they entered New Netherland to defy the authorities with their aggressive propaganda. Many of them were arrested and expelled. Ships that landed Quakers were subject to confiscation, and the penalty for harboring one for a single night was fifty pounds.[26] But their cause flourished under persecution.

Stuyvesant tried severe measures. A Quaker preacher named Hodgson was sentenced to two years' hard labor at a wheelbarrow. He refused to work, and in consequence was so horribly tortured that citizens, hardened though they were to the brutalities of the seventeenth century, cried out in protest.[27] Although the policy of arrests, fines and expulsions continued, we find the magistrates of Rustdorp (Jamaica) complaining, in 1662, that the majority of the inhabitants of their village were "followers of the abominable sect."[28]

Even harsher punishments were contemplated. But the directors of the Company, who themselves had scant use for Quakers, finally stayed the hand of the governor. They ordered him to follow the more expedient and tolerant ways of the city of Amsterdam as good policy in building up a weak and underpopulated province. With this, in 1663, the Quaker persecution came to an end.[29]

So much for general religious conditions in the colony. What was to be the fate of the Jews in New Netherland?

The Jews were not welcomed. They were no more wanted in the province than in various cities of the mother country which closed their gates to them during the period. However, as we shall presently see, the New World Dutch were not to succeed in their policy of exclusion as the cities at home had done. Strangly enough, the handful of Jews who approached New Amsterdam had weapons and resources that exacted a grudging surrender from the numerous foes who opposed their settlement and for a long time denied them even the bare right to earn a living.

As one studies the records of the period, it seems as though there were not a single friend of the Jews among all the people in the colony. Not once is anyone mentioned as rising to plead the cause of these strangers; but we note how burgomasters and train-bands, how clergy and governor, were all against the Jews.

In the case of Stuyvesant, it is interesting to speculate to what degree he had been soured as a result of a recent experience with Jews on the island of Curaçao. Among Stuyvesant's duties was the government of that distant possession by remote control from New Amsterdam. Curaçao was not prospering, and the Company had even considered abandoning it as a liability. At this time, a Jew, Jan de Illan, approached the directors with an offer to settle in Curaçao colonists who would cultivate tobacco, indigo and other crops. In return, he should be granted the rights of patroon. Stuyvesant gave his approval to the project,[30] and the directors consented, but not without a measure of skepticism concerning the outcome.[31]

Before long, reports were received that the Jewish settlers had abandoned agriculture. Instead, they were exporting horses and lumber from the Company's preserves[32] and were importing goods which they sold to the inhabitants at extortionate prices, it was said.[33] Stuyvesant had welcomed these Jews to Curaçao, no doubt, because they represented a much needed farming element. His disappointment over their commercial propensities was not calculated to make the reception of their fellow Jews on Manhattan Island any easier. At any rate, these reached New Amsterdam in the midst of the resentment that must have filled Stuyvesant's heart with pious indignation.

The newcomers came during 1654 in two groups. During the summer, some Jews, anxious to trade, appeared in the colony.[34] That is practically all we know about them, but it is very likely that they belonged to the class of itinerants who came to New Netherland to barter for furs and then returned home again with rich profits in peltries. This class of merchant was regarded with strong dislike by the permanent inhabitants of the province, who resented the way the transients sailed off with the cream of the profits, while the burghers stayed home to endure the perils and hardships of colonial life.[35] Jacob Barsimson, who arrived in August, was the only one of the first group of Jews who is known by name,[36] and he seems likewise to have been the only one to establish a permanent home in New Amsterdam.

The second group, arriving at the beginning of September, provoked a storm. First, there were twenty-three of them, and, secondly, they were frightfully poor.[37] They arrived on board the *Saint Charles*, also referred as the *Saint Catrina* in court records.[38] Their port of origin was Cape Saint Anthony, which cannot be satisfactorily identified today.[39]

It is believed, however, that these immigrants were refugees from Recife, in Brazil, which had just been captured by the Portuguese. The Jews who had dwelt there under Dutch rule were now compelled to go into exile. To be sure, the terms of surrender had stipulated that Jews and non-Catholics enjoyed the same right to remain in Recife as in Portugal. But this was an Irish bull. In Portugal they were regarded as heretics and surrendered to the Holy Inquisition for trial.[40] Threatened with the flames of the auto-da-fé, the Jews scattered, and we may believe that one shipload of fugitives made its way to New Amsterdam.

The Jewish passengers on the *Saint Charles* were described by the Reverend Megapolensis as "healthy, but poor."[41] Poor they were — so poor, in fact, that the ship's captain, Jacques de la Motthe, had them haled into court for failure to pay their passage money in full. When arranging for the voyage, they had made themselves jointly responsible for all fares. It was a matter of twenty-five hundred guilders, but so far only 933 had been paid. The court ordered that the goods of the Jews should be seized and publicly sold to pay the debt.[42] When this decree was carried out, it developed that all their belongings were not sufficient to satisfy the judgment. The plaintiff now demanded that two of the Jews be held in jail until the entire account was settled, and David Israel and Moses Ambrosius were chosen as sureties.[43] They were probably released when funds arrived from Holland.[44]

Meanwhile the Jews of New Amsterdam were in desperate straits. All their goods had been sold to satisfy their creditor, and they were penniless in a strange land. With a show of resentment, the church authorities had to feed them at a cost of several hundred guilders. Pastor Megapolensis wrote Amsterdam that the Jews came to his house several times "weeping and bemoaning their misery." He suggested that they go for aid "to the Jewish merchant" (probably Barsimson who was shown by the tax records to have been a very poor man himself),[45] but "they said he would not lend them a single stiver."[46] One can well imagine the anger of the deaconry as they disbursed the money of the church for these alien, unbelieving Jews.

As Stuyvesant saw the problem, there was only one solution: The Jews must go! Accordingly, six days after the two hostages had been imprisoned for the unpaid debt, we find the governor writing the Amsterdam Chamber of the West India Company that the deaconry had "in a nice way" ordered the Jews to depart, even though most of the penniless wretches preferred to remain. (As if they could go anywhere else!) These Jews, he pointed out, were poor and might become a charge on the community. Indeed, this came true when the deaconry assumed their care. Moreover, Stuyvesant argued, the Jews were notorious for "their usury and deceitful trading with the Christians," and they were repugnant both to the inferior magistrates and to the people. By way of conclusion, he requested "that the deceitful race — such hateful enemies and blasphemers of the name of Christ —" should in the future not be allowed to "infect and trouble this new colony."[47]

Stuyvesant informed his superiors back home that the Jews had been ordered to go, but he apparently hesitated about carrying out the command. We hear of nothing being done to force them to leave New Amsterdam for some time; apparently it was thought wiser to await the approval of the home authorities. But events dependent on decisions in the motherland were slow in unfolding, what with the long time necessary for letters to cross the Atlantic and the slowness with which the directors arrived at their own conclusions. And so both Governor Stuyvesant and the Jews accommodated themselves to a long wait.

Months passed and, early in the new year, the situation was further complicated by the arrival of more Jews in the province. The new immigrants had come directly

from Holland. They reported, according to Pastor
Megapolensis, that they were the vanguard of a great
movement of Dutch Jews who were even planning to
build a synagogue in New Amsterdam. This caused,
"a great deal of complaint and murmuring" among the
people.[48] They not only had a Jewish problem on their
hands, but one of growing proportions.

This aggravation of the Jewish issue seems to have
aroused the authorities from their lethargy. In March,
1655, not very long after the new influx had appeared,
the question of the expulsion of the Jews was laid before
the municipal court. The *Schout-Fiscal*[49] — Cornelis Van
Tienhoven, who was dismissed in disgrace a year later —
appeared before the burgomasters and *schepens*, or aldermen, who formed the court, and told them of the decision
just made by the director-general and the supreme
council. They were commanding the Jews to depart from
the province forthwith. Then Van Tienhoven inquired
if the members of the court had any objections. The
burgomasters and the *schepens* replied that they had
none, and that the resolution should be carried out.[50]
Still, nothing further appears to have been done regarding the expulsion of the Jews.

At this time, too, the leading clergyman of New Amsterdam, John Megapolensis, also decided to exercise
what pressure he could on the directors in Amsterdam
to render a decision on the Jewish question. His best
approach was through his own superiors, the classis of
Amsterdam; and so he wrote them, on March 18, asking
them to use their influence in counteracting the Jewish

peril. He was troubled about the Jews for two reasons: their greed, which would injure the community economically, and their religion, which would do spiritual damage by increasing the variety of creeds which he saw bedeviling New Netherland.

As he wrote his letter, he was inspired to eloquence:

> These people [he declared] have no other God than the Mammon of unrighteousness and no other aim than to get possession of Christian property, and to overcome all other merchants by drawing all trade towards themselves. Therefore we request your Reverences to obtain from the Messrs. Directors, that these godless rascals, who are of no benefit to the country, but look at everything for their own profit, may be sent away from here. For as we have here Papists, Mennonites and Lutherans among the Dutch; also many Puritans or Independents, and many Atheists and various other servants of Baal among the English under this Government, who conceal themselves under the name of Christians; it would create a still greater confusion, if the obstinate and immovable Jews came to settle here.[51]

Such words are typical of Megapolensis, the Catholic-born zealot of the Reformed Church. Just as he had opposed the Lutheran effort for separate worship and reported Quaker activities to the authorities, so now he attempted to prevent the Jews from getting a foothold in the colony.

Meanwhile, the interested parties were awaiting some word from the Dutch West India Company. No one could be sure what the outcome would be, but there was reason to expect that the company officials would uphold Stuyvesant and confirm the exile of the Jews. Only three years before, they had written him a letter condemning the Jewish people. The Jews, they had said, "are a crafty and generally treacherous people in whom therefore not too much confidence must be placed."[52] Was that still their opinion and would it determine their policy?

Fortunately for the Jews whose fate wavered in the balance, they also had powerful advocates abroad — the rich and influential Sephardic community of Amsterdam. It was located in the main center of the West India Company, and seven of its number were among the Company's one hundred and sixty-seven stockholders in 1656.[53] As a factor in the commercial life of the city, the Jews were too important to go unheeded. When a "Petition of the Jewish Nation" expressing concern over the refugees in New Netherland was received by the Amsterdam directors in January, 1655, the counterattack against Stuyvesant, Megapolensis and their allies began.

The petitioners described themselves as "merchants of the Portugal nation residing in this city."[54] They argued that it would do great harm to the "Jewish nation" for the directors to put obstacles in the way of Portuguese Jews who desired passports that they might travel or live in New Netherland. What was more, such a policy would be "of no advantage to the general company, but rather damaging."

The petitioners pointed out that many Jews had lost their wealth in the overthrow of the Dutch power in Brazil, where they had loyally defended the government with blood and treasure. Now they were penniless refugees whom the petitioners had to support at great expense.

New Netherland, they continued, was a spacious land that stood in need of more loyal settlers who would increase tax receipts and promote trade. When the authorities of Amsterdam accorded the Jews the same rights as the other inhabitants, and the French and English permitted the Jews to live and trade in their West Indian islands, how could the Company follow a less liberal course? This was all the more unjust, as many of the stockholders were Jews who had lost heavily in their investment.

Therefore the remonstrants requested that the "Jewish nation" be granted the right to live in the country. In addition, they desired the same liberties as the other inhabitants, the same right to travel and trade, on condition that they assumed similar obligations.[55]

In the face of this array of logic, sharpened by the allusion to the strength of the Jewish stockholders, the directors gave way. Preserved with the petition is a marginal note in another hand which has been identified as that of Hans Bontemantel, a director of the Amsterdam Chamber.[56] It reads as follows: "Granted that they may reside and traffic, provided that they shall not become a charge upon the deaconry or the Company."[57]

This decision was conveyed to Stuyvesant in the form of a letter sent on April 25, 1655, in reply to his communication of seven months before. The directors employed with the governor a tact which may have been thoroughly sincere. They agreed "that the new territories should no more be allowed to be infected by people of the Jewish nation, for we foresee therefrom the same difficulties which you fear." Nevertheless, after due consideration, they had decided that such a policy would have been unfair in view of Jewish sacrifices in Brazil and Jewish investments in the Company. Therefore, Jews were to be admitted to New Netherland for residence and trade, "provided the poor among them shall not become a burden to the company or to the community, but be supported by their own nation. You will now govern yourself accordingly."[58]

This result was not at all to the governor's liking, and so he wrote another letter on October 30, pointing out the folly of according Jews rights. The letter itself has been lost, but we have an abstract of it which reads as follows: "To give liberty to the Jews will be very detrimental there, because the Christians there will not be able at the same time to do business. Giving them liberty, we cannot refuse the Lutherans and Papists."[59]

This letter, written in the midst of the Lutheran agitation for their own worship, was an artful blend of economic jealousy and religious hatred. If the Jews conduct business, the Christians cannot; if they have liberty to trade, the Lutherans will demand liberty to worship. But, as was obvious to the directors, there could be no possible connection between giving the Jews certain economic and civil rights, which the Lutherans already enjoyed to a greater degree, and the public proclamation of the Augsburg Confession.

Accordingly, they undertook to clarify this muddled

interpretation of Jewish privileges. In a letter dated March 13, 1656, they pointed out that the Jews of New Netherland were being granted the same civil and political liberties as in Holland. This did not mean, however, that they were entitled "to carry on their religion in synagogues or gatherings." As long as there was no request for such a concession, there need be no concern; but should the Jews begin to press for the privilege, Stuyvesant was to refer the matter to the authorities in Amsterdam.[60]

Of course, it was useless for the Jews to hope for the right to conduct public worship. By the law of February 1, 1656, there was to be no type of religious assembly, except family prayers, outside the confines of the established Church.[61] Even the Dutch Lutherans had been unable to break through the vested privilege of the Dutch Reformed Church in religious matters. Least of all could a denomination as hated as Judaism be expected to storm the barriers successfully.

But the Jews tried. Stuyvesant wrote that they had many times requested the "public exercise of their abominable religion," and had been refused.[62] At about the same time, the directors on their side were advising the governor that the Jews "may exercise in all quietness their religion within their houses," and proposing that they build their homes close together in some quarter of the town, as had been done in Amsterdam, so as to facilitate their meeting together for prayer.[63] This seems to have been a concession going beyond the provisions of the law limiting the dissenters to family worship.

The Jews of New Amsterdam did not set up for themselves a "ghetto of convenience" under Dutch rule. At the same time, they were never permitted to establish a synagogue. In one way, however, they were accorded quasi-recognition; a special burial-ground was set aside for their dead.[64]

Whether or not they were permitted to establish a synagogue, the Jews of New Netherland had won a great victory in acquiring the rights conceded them by the directors of the West India Company. The local authorities had attempted to keep the unwelcome settlers from the province altogether; their superiors in Amsterdam not only vetoed this exclusion, but accorded the Jews the same rights as at home. Nevertheless, it remained to be seen how effective a command from Europe would be on the banks of the Hudson. A governor implacable and bitter, a clergy fiercely opposing every faith but its own, and a population bigoted and suspicious of Jews would not be eager to carry out the dictates from abroad. Attempts were made to circumscribe the opportunities of Jews to an extreme not justified by the provisions of the Company. Negroes and Indians were of course denied many rights, but Jews were the only European settlers who suffered from economic disabilities as well as religious handicaps.[65]

In all fairness to the local authorities, it must be conceded that many of the Jewish disabilities were based upon precedents in Amsterdam which the directors themselves invoked. In the Dutch metropolis, Jews might not perform military service, nor conduct retail business, nor work at handicrafts. It is significant that in the campaign for emancipation which was now opening on American soil, the energetic attacks of the Jews on their handicaps won victories over several of the disabilities patterned on the traditions of Amsterdam as well as over those imposed in the province without authority.

One of the first battles to enlarge their rights was provoked by an attempt to keep them out of the guard and to impose a special poll tax in lieu of the service exacted from other citizens. This took place when elaborate preparations were being made for the *opera bouffe* war against New Sweden in August, 1655. While volunteers were enlisted for the expedition with the promise of bonuses in case of injury,[66] others were required for guard duty at home in case the impatient Indians were tempted to attack New Amsterdam in the absence of the force. Should Jews also be allowed to mount guard?

That question perplexed the officers of the trainbands of the town. Certainly all hands were needed; but it could not be denied that citizens experienced a certain disgust at the thought of serving with Jews or sharing the same guardhouse with them. Moreover, nowhere in the Netherlands, as far as known, could Jews join the town guard. The officers wondered whether the community's need or its prejudice should gain the upper hand, and so they decided to refer the matter to the governor and the council.

The authorities decreed that Jews were not to serve. Exemption from military duty was something to be

coveted, however; and lest the Jews congratulate themselves overmuch on their good fortune, every male of
them between sixteen and sixty was to pay a special tax
of sixty-five stivers a month.[67] Such a tax was indeed
discriminatory, but it was the type of humiliation that
the Jews had known in many countries in Europe.

That the levy was oppressive is indicated by the com-
parison of its rate with some of the expenses of the Swedish expedition. On the same day that the Jews' tax was
put into effect, two pilots familiar with the Delaware
River were engaged at the rate of three guilders per day.[68]
A week's wages for both of them was more than realized
by what one Jew paid in six months. Or let us take
another instance. Two days after the Jews' levy was
decreed, the government chartered three sloops with
nine hands at a cost of eighteen guilders a day.[69] Ten
Jews paid for a day's expense for men and ships alike in
less than six months.

The poor among the Jews could not afford to pay the
tax. In November, two of the less affluent members of
the community, Jacob Barsimson and Asser Levy,[70]
petitioned the governor and council for either the right
to bear arms or else exemption from the Jews' tax, "as
they must earn their living by manual labor." The
authorities rejected their request with a sneer. If the
petitioners were insistent that they were injured by the
regulation, they were free to leave the province and go
anywhere anytime.[71]

The tax resolution was never repealed, but it became
a dead letter. By the spring of 1657, Asser Levy was

serving in the guard, like any ordinary citizen.[72] No doubt, others of his people did likewise.

The Jews were barred from the retail trade, but they were in no way reconciled to the situation. The first trouble developed even before it was certain that they were to remain in New Netherland. On March 1, 1655, Abraham de Lucena was summoned to court on two charges: keeping his store open during the sermon and selling at retail. Under the tradition of strict Sunday observance, it was a violation of the law for any citizen to do business during church hours; but to sell at retail was normally a perfectly legal transaction. It was a crime only for Jews.

At the hearing, the *schout* demanded that de Lucena be deprived of his business and fined six hundred guilders to boot. The defendant knew so little Dutch, however, that he was unable to follow the proceedings, and the court decided to defer a verdict until the next session.[73] The records have nothing to say of further action, but one may assume that the heavy fine proposed was never inflicted.

Fine or no fine, retail trade was closed to the Jews. Word came from the directors in Amsterdam to strengthen the position of the local authorities: Jews were not to have retail shops.[74] Little good did this message accomplish. Even before it was sent, the Jews had entered the retail trade. We find in the records of the court a pointed observation that Jews and foreigners were as much encouraged to sell at retail as were the citizens themselves.

This was in March, 1656, only twelve months after the de Lucena case.[75]

The Jews had less success in trying to rid themselves of the disabilities which closed the field of handicrafts. In Amsterdam the guilds would not admit them, thus effectively keeping them out of the various trades.[76] This same policy for New Netherland was sustained by the directors in a letter to Stuyvesant.[77]

We know, however, of the attempt which a Jewish baker made to break through the barriers and set himself up in business. In April, 1657, Jacob Cohen Henriques asked for permission to bake and sell bread as the other bakers did, "but with closed door." Apparently he was reconciled to conduct his business as a wholesale venture and not maintain the customary open door of the retail trade. With all the precedents that the mother country afforded, it was a simple matter for the court to reject this petition.[78]

One trade only was open to the Jews, that of slaughtering, which merited special consideration, as in Amsterdam, because of the observance of *kashruth*.[79] In October, 1660, the authorities decided that the time had come to control and regulate the butchering in the community by placing it in the hands of sworn slaughterers who submitted to special regulations. Two of the thirteen butchers initiated at the time were Jews: Asser Levy and Moses Lucena. Because of their religious beliefs, they were exempted from the killing of hogs.[80]

When the oath was imposed, the Christian butchers swore "in the presence of the Most High," and asked for

the help of God Almighty. Even though there was nothing Christological in the oath, it seems that the Jews were
not permitted to use it. They were apparently compelled
to employ another formula — "the oath which the Jews
are accustomed to take."[81] This, without doubt, was an
allusion to the humiliating oath *More Judaico* which was
forced upon the Jews in the Middle Ages and became
a fixture throughout Europe for centuries.[82]

Judging from the evidence of the court records, the
Jews were active in commerce. Their interests included
domestic trade and the traffic in exported and imported
goods. They handled such wares as brandy, butter,
tobacco and shoes.[83] The traffic closest to the merchant's
heart, however, was the fur trade.[84] Beaver pelts figured
so prominently in the economy of the province that they
actually became a legal medium of exchange,[85] and were
honored also with a place on the seals of New Netherland
and New Amsterdam alike.[86]

The burghers of the province resented the intrusion
of outsiders into this lucrative field. In order to keep the
foreign merchants from taking a rich share of the trapper's
spoils, a law had been passed in 1648 limiting the fur
trade to those who actually owned real estate in the
province.[87] The statute was later disallowed by the
Amsterdam directors because they considered it impracti-
cable.[88] Jewish competition was just as unwelcome as
any from abroad, and an attempt was made to bar Jews
from the commerce which formed the province's main
support.

The ban, however, was a direct violation of the right to trade granted by the Company. In the fall of 1655, a group undertook to test the disability in two ways: by the dispatch of goods to be exchanged for furs in the South River (Delaware River) region, and by a protest to the governor and council. Accordingly, three men, Abraham de Lucena, Salvador d'Andrade and Jacob Cohen Henriques, submitted a petition on November 29. Inasmuch as the directors had given them the same right to travel and trade as the other inhabitants enjoyed, they respectfully requested that privilege on the South River and at Fort Orange.

The Jews had the law on their side. Stuyvesant, nevertheless, voted "that the petition be denied for weighty reasons." Van Tienhoven argued that "it would be injurious to the community and the population of the said places to grant the petition of the Jews." The council finally decided to deny their suit, but since the Jews had already shipped goods to the South River, they might send one or two of their number to dispose of them and then immediately return to New Amsterdam.[89]

Within a month after this setback, the Jews suffered another blow when their right to own property was brought into question. Salvador d'Andrade, who had joined in the petition for fur-trading privileges, bought his dwelling when it was put up at public auction. Claiming that he expected a favorable reply, he now approached Stuyvesant and the council to confirm his right to the purchase. They decided that the Jew should not be allowed to acquire the property "for pregnant reasons."[90]

The original owner of the house, Teunis Cray, seems to have been as angry and as disappointed as d'Andrade himself over the arbitrary decision. We find him petitioning a few weeks later for the right to transfer the property to d'Andrade. Otherwise, he requested that the governor and council take possession at the original price of 1,860 guilders. The authorities, however, declined to follow either course,[91] and the house was subsequently sold to someone else.

By now, the leaders of the Jewish community were up in arms. A second petition of grievances was presented with five signers, the three who had signed the first protest and Joseph d'Acosta and David Frera. They made clear their resentment at being excluded from the fur trade and prevented from buying houses. They reminded the governor that each of the five signers had recently been taxed one hundred guilders for strengthening the defenses of the city.[92] If they must contribute like other citizens, the petitioners asked for the opportunity to enjoy the same liberties, including the rights which had just been denied them.

This time Stuyvesant and his colleagues did not brush aside the plea in haste. They replied, however, that the Jewish payment of the tax for defense brought them the same security as everyone else. The question of owning property was being referred to the directors in Amsterdam and, pending their decision, was being refused.

What of the Jewish right to trade in furs? There was no specific answer to that claim, but the response of governor and council did state that the Jews enjoyed

the same liberty as the order of the Amsterdam directors
had implied.[93] There is every reason to believe that this
was a grudging acknowledgment of the Jews' right to
enter the fur trade, for only three months later Stuyvesant
was telling Amsterdam that Jewish rights were in no way
restricted. They traded, he said, "with the same privilege
and freedom as other inhabitants." This letter ended on
an ironic and crestfallen note: "What they [the Jews]
may obtain from your Honors time will tell."[94]

It did not take long for Stuyvesant to learn what Jewish representations to the directors of the Company had
won from "their Honors," for a letter was at that moment
en route to him. Its contents must have made the old
martinet of Manhattan turn livid. His superiors informed
him that they had learned with displeasure that the New
Netherland authorities had disregarded the rights of the
Jews, who were permitted to trade and own real estate
as in Amsterdam. "We wish that this had not occurred,
but that your Honors had obeyed our orders which you
must hereafter execute punctually and with more respect,"
read the stern note.[95] Another battle for Jewish rights
had seemingly been won.

As it turned out, however, the struggle for trading
rights under Dutch rule had one more chapter. The
establishment of a new institution in the life of the
colony — the burgher right — contained a threat seemingly directed against Jewish participation in retail business. The circumstances under which the matter was
first broached, on January 8, 1657, looked ominous. The
council minutes reveal that the burgher right and retail

selling, "practiced to the present time both by Jews and all foreigners," were up for discussion simultaneously.[96]

As finally passed, the burgher right law contained no reference to the Jews. Its intent, as expressed in the preamble, was to obtain protection against outsiders who took the bread out of the mouths of citizens by trading in the best places, and then deserted the country in time of war.[97] Two classes of citizenry were established. The exclusive great burgher right, with its high fee, suggested an attempt to found a provincial aristocracy. We are, however, more concerned with the small burgher right, which became a requirement for anyone running a business, keeping a store, or following a trade. The cost of this privilege was twenty guilders.[98]

The Jews had reason to be apprehensive. Their right to the retail trade had never been confirmed by the directors of the Company and was questioned at the time that the law was first suggested. Accordingly, when applications for either burgher right were invited in April, only one Jew appeared before the court. The candidate was Asser Levy, who had led the attack on the special Jewish poll tax almost two years before. His claim to the small burgher right was to prove a test case.

Levy requested that he be admitted as a burgher, and gave as grounds for his petition that he was a member of the guard, and that he had formerly been a burgher in the city of Amsterdam, as was proved by the certificates he produced. The court, however, was against giving him the burgher right. After deliberation, it voted that Levy could not be admitted to citizenship — by them. He

PETER STUYVESANT

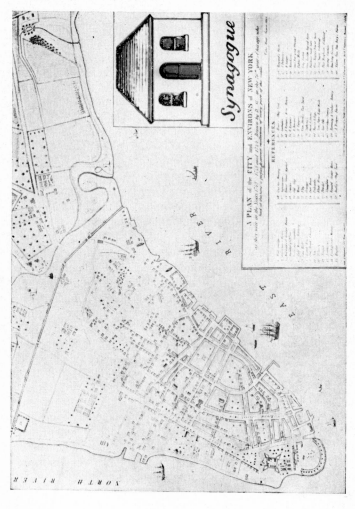

The insert of the synagogue appears at the top of the original of this map among representations of other church buildings.

should therefore apply to the director-general and the council for the privilege.[99]

Levy now retired from the picture and the campaign was taken over by four of the wealthy Jews of the community — d'Andrade, Cohen, de Lucena and d'Acosta. A few days after the verdict of the court, they submitted a petition to the governor and council on behalf of their people. They expressed surprise at the denial of citizenship by the burgomasters; they cited the rights the directors of the Company had granted; they argued that the Jews had assumed the obligations of citizens; and they therefore requested the director and the council to instruct the burgomasters to admit them to the burgher right.

This is exactly what was done, for Stuyvesant's heart was no longer in the fight against the Jews. He and his two colleagues notified the burgomasters that they were "charged to admit the petitioners . . . and their nation to the Burghership."[100] From then on, the burgher right was within the reach of a Jew.

The Jews had fought round after round with Peter Stuyvesant and had emerged victorious. The governor, however, while defeated, was not convinced. In 1660, when he ordered some young Negro slaves from Curaçao for his bowery, he declared that he thought the blacks "preferred before Spaniards and unbelieving Jews."[101] But his hands were tied. The Jews remained and, what is more, they prospered.

CHAPTER VI

PROGRESS UNDER BRITISH RULE

TEN years to the day after the Jews were first mentioned in the records of New Netherland—on September 7, 1664 — the English under Nicolls clamored for the surrender of the province. And so New Amsterdam became New York, and the proprietorship of His Royal Highness, James, Duke of York, replaced the regime of the Dutch West India Company. There was a new flag, a new name, a new law.

Much had happened to the Jews during the ten years they had lived and struggled under Stuyvesant. At first the right to live in the province had been refused them, and was secured only on appeal to Amsterdam. Even with this privilege won, there were many more hurdles to be surmounted before life became endurable. Jews were excluded from guard duty against their will, and had to pay a special tax. They could not open retail stores, nor traffic in furs, nor own property. Even the burgher right was at first denied them. But each of these disabilities was at length removed within three years of the arrival of Jews in New Amsterdam. Long before Stuyvesant's rule had drawn to a close, the Jews of the province could claim fuller rights than their coreligionists in many a Dutch city, and their status compared favorably with conditions in Amsterdam itself.

But all their disabilities had by no means vanished. They could not build a synagogue or hold public worship. They were barred from all handicrafts, and every office was closed to them. Moreover, even though they paid their taxes in full, they could expect no aid from the government in providing for their poor, their orphans and their aged. Much still remained to be done in the years that lay ahead. What would be their lot under English rule?

On the surrender of the city, the conquerors agreed to terms that were indeed generous. The concessions even permitted magistrates then in office to continue, provided that they took the oath of allegiance to the English king. Regarding the common people, it was stipulated that all the inhabitants were to continue as "free denizens."[1] Under articles such as these, even Jews might live in New York in the future as in the past. This was reassuring, for at the time that New Amsterdam fell into the hands of the English, it was impossible to tell just what their fate might be. In London itself, the Jews had dared to live openly for less than a decade, and so those in New York could point to no precedent to guarantee them security under the new regime.

The specifically religious section of the Articles of Capitulation furnished some cause for disquiet. To be sure, it was stated that: "The Dutch here shall enjoy the liberty of their consciences in Divine Worship and church discipline."[2] The question was: could the Jews be counted as Dutch? As the dignified Portuguese phrases on the old tombstones testify, the Jews were not part of the Dutch nation, but belonged rather to another people still clinging to the culture and ways of the Iberian Peninsula which had long since disowned them. Quite definitely, the English might argue, if they chose, that there was no reason to guarantee the same freedom of worship in private houses that the Jews had been enjoying under Dutch rule.

In 1665, the Duke's Laws were put into effect. Certain provisions governing religion were applicable only to Long Island and Staten Island at first, but, after 1674, they were extended to include the entire province. These regulations provided that "no person should be molested, fined, or imprisoned, for differing in judgment in matters of religion, who professes Christianity."[3] Now it might be argued that there was no intention to exclude the Jews from the Articles of Capitulation, but in the laws established only a year later, the Jews were quite definitely debarred from the privileges accorded all Christian sects.

On the other hand, the laws did not officially place the Jews under a ban nor authorize persecution on grounds of belief. From the absence of any records to the contrary, we have a right to assume that Judaism enjoyed the same toleration of private worship as had prevailed during the last years of Dutch rule.

It is interesting to note that the instructions concerning religion, issued to a succession of English governors, seesawed between a grant of religious freedom to Christian sects alone and a grant of religious freedom that embraced every faith. As far as the Jews were concerned, it made a great deal of difference whether or not all religions were recognized, although it must be confessed that we of today cannot detect any change in the treatment accorded them under one set of instructions or another.

In 1674, after a brief period of Dutch occupation, Edmund Andros was sent over as the new governor of the colony. His instructions concerning religion were so sweeping that Jews, too, were embraced within their broad terms. "All persons of what Religion soever," were to be allowed to live without "any disturbance or disquiet whatsoever, for or by reason of their differing opinions in matter of Religion," provided that they did not disturb the public peace or molest others "in ye free exercize of their religion."[4]

This enlightened statement of universal toleration was replaced by a more limited formula in 1683, when Thomas Dongan succeeded to the governorship. This time he was instructed to accord freedom of religion to all who "profess faith in God by Jesus Christ."[5] Accordingly, the Jews were again overlooked.

But in 1686, Dongan received another set of instructions. In accordance with the new policies, all men "of what Religion soever" were to be permitted to live in the province and follow their beliefs.[6] Perhaps it was not without significance that James, the avowed Catholic, had ascended the throne of England; and apparently concerned for the welfare of his fellow Romanists, he had advised Dongan (likewise a Catholic) to follow the ways of universal toleration.

An account of the state of religion in New York, which Dongan wrote in 1687, has been preserved. In his description of the various sects, the governor stated that

the Church of England, the Dutch Calvinists and Lutherans, and the French Calvinists, each had their own
ministers. Then he remarked: "Here be not many
of the Church of England; few Roman Catholicks;
abundance of Quakers preachers men and women especially; Singing Quakers; Ranting Quakers; Sabbatarians;
Antisabbatarians; Some Anabaptists, some Independents;
some Jews; in short of all sorts of opinions there are some,
and the most part, of none at all."[7] The casual manner in
which the Jews were listed, suggests that they were
accepted without question as on a par with the other
curiosities of religion.

Despite the liberal note of toleration that was sounded
in New York, there were abundant evidences of religious
discord. The Duke's Laws set up a union of church and
state, but just what religion was established depended
upon the wishes of each community. Every parish was to
build a church and maintain a Protestant minister by
taxes, besides electing a board of overseers through the
vote of a majority of the householders.[8]

The colonial governors, however, were not content to
let events take their course. It was their desire to foster
the almost nonexistent Church of England in the province.
Strangely enough, James II, himself a Catholic, sent
secret instructions to Governor Dongan that the *Book of
Common Prayer* should be used at every service and that
marriages should be celebrated according to the rites of the
Anglican Church.[9]

The Assembly, during the rule of Governor Fletcher,
passed an equivocal sort of bill which the governor chose

to interpret as a charter for the establishment of the Episcopal Church in the County of New York and three of the neighboring counties. Moreover, against the will of the people, who were largely dissenters, he succeeded in forcing an Anglican minister upon New York.[10]

The governors showed a special malice in attempting to counteract the rising power of the Presbyterian Church. On one occasion, two prominent ministers of that denomination, Mackemie and Hampton, were arrested because they preached without a license from Governor Cornbury while on a visit to New York. The governor's position was indefensible—a thoroughgoing misapplication of the law— but, nevertheless, both of the unoffending clergymen were imprisoned for six months before their names were cleared.[11]

There is no need to describe here the annoyances suffered by the various religious denominations of the colony. The Quakers, Presbyterians and Moravians had especially unpleasant experiences, but men of other sects also were compelled to submit to the whims of an intolerant government. One must not, therefore, suppose that the Jews were the only religion with grievances, although some of their problems were peculiarly their own.

For one thing, the Jews had no synagogue. As had been the case under Dutch rule, they were obliged to worship in private houses, a condition that they found unsatisfying. They therefore renewed petitions for the right to erect a synagogue, but for some time their efforts met the same unfavorable response which the Dutch authorities had accorded them.

In 1685, they requested Governor Dongan "for liberty to exercise their Religion"—the right of public worship. The governor referred the petition to the mayor and aldermen of New York, and they returned an emphatic "No." The only public worship to be tolerated was that of "those that professe faith in Christ, and therefore the Jews Worship not to be allowed."[12]

Despite this rebuff, the Jews did not have to wait very long before their dream of a synagogue was realized. According to one authority, the synagogue was already in existence in 1692. This source was a Frenchman, M. Lamothe-Cadillac, who wrote a description of the English colonies. He named the sects which were included in the population of New York, and among them he listed the Catholics and the Jews. "Each sect," he added, "has its Church and freedom of religion."[13] We know for a fact that the first Catholic church in New York was not established until 1786,[14] and this error on the part of the French writer weakens our faith in his accuracy regarding a Jewish synagogue in New York in 1692.

But if there was no Jewish house of prayer in 1692, one existed in 1695. Our information this time comes from the Rev. John Miller, chaplain to His Majesty's Grenadiers stationed in New York. He was a man with an unquenchable thirst for facts, and, while he was living in New York, he made it his hobby to amass all available data about the place in the form of detailed descriptions and maps. In 1695, with a great collection of documentary material, he sailed for home. While at sea the ship was captured by a French privateer. In an outburst of patriotism the unhappy clergyman flung his beloved papers overboard so that no valuable information might fall into the hands of the enemy.

During his imprisonment, Miller seemed to have regretted his hasty act, and he busied himself in piecing together all his scraps of recollection. All the things he had discovered were set down once more. The description which he wrote as a prisoner of war existed in manuscript form until it was published in 1843.[15]

Included in the papers thus placed at the service of posterity was a map of New York City drawn from memory, of course. This chart indicated a site on Beaver Street as "the Jewes Synagogue."[16] Miller asserted that there were, in all, six churches in New York County. He gave the number of Jewish families in the city as about twenty, and he said that their minister was Saul Brown. It is worth noting that he estimated the total number of families in New York as 855. Accordingly, if his figures are correct, the Jews numbered something over two per cent of the population of New York during the closing decade of the century.[17]

An old deed from the year 1700 offers further proof, if needed, that a synagogue existed in New York at that time. This particular document conveyed a house on Mill Street, bounded on the east by the house of John Haperding, "now commonly known by the name Jews' Synagogue."[18]

In our own day, scholars have been puzzled by the fact that Chaplain Miller's map, which is otherwise accurate, locates the synagogue on Beaver Street, while five years later it is found on Mill Street.[19] When we consider, however, that the Jews rented a house for their services, there is nothing strange in their moving from one place to another in the course of five years.

The synagogue was the first one to be established in the English colonies. One of the oldest churches found in New York, it was there before the first Catholic parish had been organized or the first Baptist church built, and it even antedates the erection of the original Trinity Church. Today the same congregation still exists under the name of Shearith Israel, worshiping in a beautiful edifice on Central Park West. Shearith Israel means "the Remnant of Israel." When the congregation was founded, almost three hundred years ago, it represented the tiny remnant that had found its way to New Amsterdam; but today it is surrounded by the biggest Jewish community the world has ever seen.

During the entire colonial period, it was impossible for the congregation to secure a charter. Incorporation was a privilege enjoyed by the Church of England, although four Dutch churches were also accorded that right. No other denominations were allowed to obtain charters.[20] As a result, the Jewish congregation could not own property in its own name. When the members bought a lot for a synagogue in 1728, it was necessary to have four men purchase it individually as trustees. They, of course, gave bond as a guarantee "to secure the land forever for the use of the Jewish Congregation." As the years passed and one by one the trustees died, the community was embarrassed over the problem of the ownership of the synagogue, which could not be vested in the community by law. Who would be the legal owners, they asked, when the last trustee died? The issue was not satisfactorily settled until 1784, after the last trustee was gone and the Revolutionary War had been fought. Only then was the congregation permitted to incorporate.[21]

The first religious leader of the congregation, as far as we can ascertain, was Saul Brown, known as the Jewish minister, who, while *hazzan*,[22] fulfilled many of the functions that are today associated with rabbis. Brown moved to New York from Rhode Island and, in 1685, figured in a case involving the Jewish right to enter the retail trade.[23] He petitioned Governor Dongan for the privilege of carrying on a retail business, and the governor referred the issue to the council. These worthies decided that no Jew might sell at retail within the city, although, if the governor's permission could be secured, they might carry on as wholesale merchants.[24]

This incident represented a severe setback for the civil rights of the Jews. To be sure, the Amsterdam directors of the Dutch West India Company had stated explicitly that the Jews might not keep shop; but, right or no right, they began to sell goods to the general public under Dutch rule without suffering the ill will of the authorities. Instead of meeting with prosecution and fines, the Jews were admitted to the coveted burgher right.

One can only speculate as to the cause of the change in the attitude of official New York which brought about the exclusion of Jews from a field they had been occupying for almost thirty years. Were there too many Jewish merchants? Was their competition a severe trial for other storekeepers? There must have been some compelling reason for the city fathers to renounce an established policy and invoke the Dutch law which for so long had been a dead letter. But as though this were not bad enough, they went even farther and made the wholesale trade of Jews dependent upon the governor's whim, something he might forbid at his pleasure.

Quite possibly the ban against participation in the retail field had something to do with the prominence of Jews in the import and export trade of New York. I daresay, however, that a more significant factor was their numerous family and commercial connections with merchants in the important centers of Europe and the West Indies.

It is impossible to learn just how long Jews were forbidden to sell at retail, as we have no record of the withdrawal of the ban. We do know from other sources, however, that within forty years Jews were conducting shops without hindrance. There was, for example, Solomon Myers, who was made a freeman of the city of New York in 1724. The old list tells us that he was a shopkeeper;[25] evidently the Jews in that trade enjoyed a legitimate status at the time. Peter Kalm, the Finnish university professor who visited New York in 1748, remarked that the Jews were "allowed to keep shops in town."[26]

Another field that was closed to Jews by the Dutch was that of handicrafts. The eighteenth century, however, witnessed the entry of a number of Jews into skilled trades. If we turn once more to the list of freemen, we find that, in

1716, Abraham Pereira, the tallow chandler, was admitted to the rolls.[27]   Again and again, we discover allusions to other Jewish artisans in the records.   During the half century after Pereira was admitted, a Jewish peruke-maker,[28] a baker,[29] a tailor,[30] and a brazier[31] were all invested with the rights and privileges of freemen.   One of the outstanding silversmiths of New York during the middle of the eighteenth century was Myer Myers, who was finally elevated to the office of president of the Silver smiths' Society.[32]   In this way, we have conclusive proof that the last of the forbidden occupations was open to Jews.

It is interesting to note that, during the early English period, the authorities recognized the *hazzanim* as on a par with the ministers of other denominations.   They were accordingly exempt from military service and other obligations incumbent upon ordinary lay citizens.[33]

One disability imposed by the Dutch West India Company upon the Jews of New Amsterdam never seems to have been tested during all the years of English rule. This was the requirement that the Jews look after their own poor.   All through the colonial period, the members of the congregation assumed this duty.   For instance, in the report of the synagogue's expenses for the year 5490 (1729-1730), we find the item: "For *obras Pias*[34] to the poor of this city and outside, and for sending persons to their destination £53 4 1."[35]   Poor strangers were boarded in the house of the *shammash*[36] at community expense,[37] and even the physicians' bills of the destitute were taken care of by the officers of the congregation.[38]

During the colonial period, the Jewish community never turned to the municipal authorities for assistance in taking care of their needy. Instead of looking upon this obligation as a disability, they regarded it as a religious act,[39] and they took pride in the fact that Israel looked after its own. The mediæval synagogue, like the mediæval church, was an eleemosynary institution. In New Amsterdam, the care of the poor orphans of the town was transferred from the deaconry to a special court only in the time of Peter Stuyvesant.[40]

Another function of the synagogue was its school, founded in 1755 and placed under the control of the *hazzan*.[41] It was decided in 1762 to employ a regular master, and Abraham Is. Abrahams was hired at a salary of twenty pounds per year plus perquisites. The school at that time was not merely a Hebrew school, but "a publick school" (in the English sense) with "English Reading Writing & Cyphering" in the curriculum.[42]

For one youth, at least, education did not halt there. This was Isaac Abrahams, probably, the schoolmaster's own son, who was granted the degree of A.B. by King's College in 1774, the only Jew graduated from that institution before the Revolution. At commencement, Abrahams delivered a Latin oration, "On Concord."

But this was not the only Jewish tie of which the college, later to become Columbia University, could boast. Perhaps it was no idle gesture for them to select as the motto of its original seal the Hebrew words, *Ori El*.[44] When, in 1762, the authorities of the young institution were soliciting funds in England, one of the five canvassers who

served was Moses Franks of London, a New Yorker by
birth.[45]

By the second quarter of the eighteenth century the
make-up of the congregation had undergone a marked
change. Originally its members had been altogether of
Spanish-Portuguese descent. Later on, there had been
quite an influx of German Jews until, in 1730, the Ashkenazim were a majority of the congregation. No wonder
some of the grandees were concerned for the Sephardic
purity of the ritual.[46]

The coming of these Jews, who spoke the Judeo-
German dialect, was part of a great mass movement from
Europe. Each of the colonies welcomed settlers from
foreign lands to share with the predominantly British
element in the upbuilding of the wilderness. As a result,
the problem of naturalization arose. In New York, the
question was further complicated by the presence of the
original Dutch population transferred by right of conquest
from another flag. The articles of surrender, however,
declared the inhabitants to be free denizens.[47] Denization
was a form of quasi-naturalization that carried with it
certain privileges. Apparently the Jews then living in
New Amsterdam were included within the act.

The newly established Assembly applied itself to the
problem of naturalization. In 1683, it passed an act
naturalizing all foreigners resident in the colony at that
time. Looking into the future, it further provided that
later settlers of alien birth, if Protestants, might be naturalized through the act of the Assembly.[48] As Jews were

affected by this law, those who were lucky enough to reach New York by 1683 were naturalized automatically, like their neighbors, while the later arrivals were excluded from the privilege on religious grounds.

The interests of the newcomers among the Jewish inhabitants of New York were neglected by the Assembly, but were materially advanced by the act of Parliament passed in 1740 which for the first time provided a uniform policy for the regulation of naturalization throughout the British colonies in America.[49] In New York between 1741 and 1748, twenty-four Jews were naturalized.[50]

In colonial times, naturalization included civil rights, but did not imply the right of suffrage, with which it is associated today. The franchise was a privilege possessed by only a limited group, the people of means. According to the act of 1699, voters in provincial elections had to possess real property to the value of forty pounds, in freehold, or, according to the rule which applied to Albany and New York, they had to be freemen of corporations.[51]

We get some idea of the small minority which was given the right to vote for the members of the Assembly by the example of a fiercely contested election held in New York City in 1735. Although coaches accompanied by drums and music were used to bring out practically every voter, scarcely eight hundred votes were cast in a community of ten thousand people.[52]

The government was worried by the possible evil results of permitting Catholics to vote, and an act was passed in 1701 to prevent them from exercising the franchise. "From henceforth and for ever hereafter, no Papist, no Popish Recusant . . .," it provided, "shall be Suffered to give his Vote . . . for any Officer or Officers whatsoever."[53] Nevertheless, the Jews were undisturbed by law, and the issue of their place in the electorate did not arise for a good many years.

Jews were also accorded fair treatment in the courts as witnesses. They were permitted to omit the words, "on the true faith of a Christian," and, as far as we know, during the seventeen-twenties their reliability as witnesses was never impugned. We have some hint of this state of affairs from an order, issued by Governor Burnet subsequent to the death of George I, declaring that Jews might omit the acknowledgment of Christian faith, taking the abjuration oath, as was the rule in giving sworn testimony before a court.[54] Although both the right of the Jew to vote and the recognition of his evidence seemed firmly established, they were rudely shaken at the same time in a famous case involving a disputed election which arose in 1737.

The affair took on some of the aspects of a battle royal and kept the Assembly busy for a month before the issue could be decided. It seems that Adolph Philipse, late speaker of the Assembly and member of the well-known family whose name is linked with the Philipse Manor of Yonkers, ran against Cornelius Van Horne for the office of New York City's representative in the Assembly. Philipse won; but there were charges of improper conduct on the part of the sheriffs in the management of the election, and Van Horne petitioned to the Assembly for a hearing before Philipse should be admitted to his seat.[55]

During the proceedings, Murray, the counsel for Philipse, asked the permission of the Assembly to call in some Jews to testify. Both parties withdrew while the question was discussed, and then the members of the house voted that Jews might not serve as witnesses "in the controversy now pending."[56]

William Smith, the author of a history of New York, represented Van Horne at the hearing. He raised a storm over the fact that the election lists revealed that various Jews had voted for Philipse, and he denied their right to enjoy the franchise. In vain Murray argued that the law gave the suffrage to all freeholders of competent estates, without making any exception for the purpose of excluding Jews. Smith insisted that Jews had no right to vote — first, because they were disfranchised in England, and, second, because of the responsibility for the crucifixion of Jesus of which he accused them.[57] As he delivered his fiery harangue, declaring that the curse of blood guilt still rested upon Jews, making them unworthy of political rights, we are told that the assemblymen wept and the rabble was ready to engage in a pogrom.[58]

No disorders occurred, but the Assembly did its duty. It passed a resolution, "that it not appearing to this House, that Persons of the *Jewish* Religion, have a Right to be admitted to vote for Parliament Men, in *Great-Britain*, it is the unanimous Opinion in this House, that they ought not to be admitted to vote for Representatives in this Colony."[59]

Another noteworthy decision in the case recognized the right of nonresident freeholders to the franchise in accordance with English precedents. We recall this contest especially, however, as a double defeat for the Jews and a backward step for the cause of progress. While Catholics had been disfranchised by law, the Jews were now deprived of their vote by resolution. Their status as witnesses was less desperate. True, their evidence was barred in this case, but no effort was made to exclude their testimony permanently. Perhaps the least important outcome of the hearing was the fact that Philipse's election was confirmed.[60]

Granted the conditions in colonial New York, no setback for the Jews could be permanent. As has been pointed out elsewhere, neither the act of 1701 nor the resolve of 1737 was repealed up to the Revolution, but their enforcement was left to local officers who were not necessarily diligent on behalf of the law.[61]

When the inquiring Professor Kalm came from abroad in 1748, he made it his business to mingle extensively with the "many Jews settled in New York." To him they were an interesting folk, because at that time no Jewish communities existed under the Swedish flag. Accordingly, he described his visit to their synagogue in New York, and wrote of the Jews' ships and country seats. What is most arresting in his account is the statement: "They [the Jews] enjoy all the privileges common to other inhabitants of this town and province."[62] That, we repeat was in 1748.

It may be that Peter Kalm's word concerning the

political status of the Jews should not be considered final.
He may not have been aware of the disfranchisement put
into effect eleven years before. On the other hand, that
same regulation may have been a dead letter by the time
he arrived.

But enough of surmise. Beyond dispute is a poll-list
of the Assembly election of 1761 which has been preserved
to our own day. On that list you will find among the
voters of New York the names of several Jews.[63]

Thus did the Jew of New York finally come into his
own as a citizen, attaining those rights of which he has
never since been deprived. It was not necessary for him
to await the revolutionary State Constitution, that was
born in the stormy year of 1777, with its declaration that
"the free toleration of religious profession and worship
shall forever hereafter be allowed within the State to all
mankind."[64] Within a century of the passing of Stuyvesant's rule, the Jew of New York had been granted full
civil and political emancipation.

CHAPTER VII

PENN'S EMPIRE ON THE DELAWARE

FOR countless centuries the Delaware had made its untroubled journey among the forests from the mountains to the sea. Indians roamed and dwelt and fought along its banks. The historic period begins with the coming of the white man — the Swedes and Finns in early days, and later the Dutch and the English.

The Viking element, who enjoyed their brief moment of power, should be regarded as men brimming with that Lutheran zeal which led their king, Gustavus Adolphus, to fight and die for the cause. Sweden was not then the hospitable country towards Jews that it is now. With rare exceptions, no Jews might live in the major cities of the kingdom nor conduct public worship until the year 1782.[1]

When Johan Printz, the rotund governor, arrived to take command in 1643, his instructions included such matters as religion. In order that God should be paid "proper honor, laud and praise," he was directed to promote the Swedish Lutheran service, but he was also to allow the colonists from Holland to worship according to the Dutch Reformed way.[2] There was not much room for dissent here.

We do not know of any Jews who came in with the

Swedes. How could they when the gates of the home country were barred? It was another story with the coming of the Dutch, who also laid claim to the region. As soon as they took over New Sweden, in 1655, the Jews appeared.

Something of the story of the attempt made by the authorities of New Amsterdam to keep Jewish traders from the fur-producing regions around the Delaware has already been told.[3] On November 29, 1655, the Jews petitioned for the right to buy furs in the newly annexed territory centering about the South River, as the Delaware was known. Stuyvesant and his council maintained the position that the Jews were not to purchase their pelts in the area; but they recognized the fact that Jewish dealers, who had already shipped goods for barter into the South River country, would be injured if the ban were immediately enforced. Accordingly, the council voted to allow the traders to send out one or two of their number who might dispose of the stock before returning to New Amsterdam.[4]

The two agents of the Jewish fur trade of New Netherland appear to have been Isaac Israel and Isaac Cardoso. Isaac Israel, who was one of the Jews of New Amsterdam, is mentioned elsewhere in the records. On April 3, 1656, he was made defendant in a complaint by Jacob Barsimson, the first Jew in New Amsterdam, who charged that Israel had struck him in Abraham de Lucena's cellar.[5] Isaac Cardoso, despite his old Sephardic name recently borne by a member of the United States Supreme Court, is not well known to searchers among the records.

At any rate, on December 29, 1655, some months before the encounter with Barsimson in the cellar, we find Israel and Cardoso at Fort Casimir (near the present New Castle, Delaware) when a delegation of Indian sachems appeared. The chiefs were dissatisfied with the prices they received for their skins, which were no doubt low enough, and they asked for presents in addition — a sort of bonus, it seems. Their demands were modest, and fifteen of the residents in Fort Casimir, who agreed to the terms, collected some sort of contribution for the redskins. Not so Isaac Israel and Isaac Cardoso. They "refused to give their consent and prepared to leave the river and give up their trade, than to assist, with other good inhabitants, in maintaining the peace of this highway." So wrote Jean Paul Jacquet, the Dutch vice-director of the Delaware, in his minutes.[6]

This was hardly fair to Israel and Cardoso. True, they had not conciliated the Indians, but they had good reason. This was the last trip they could make to the South River. They had no incentive to build up good will with the sachems whom they and their fellow Jews of New Amsterdam never expected to see again.

But if the reader recalls the progress which the Jews made in breaking down the various disabilities imposed by the Dutch, he will not be suprised to learn that the restrictions on the Indian trade also disappeared. Three months after the Fort Casimir episode, the Jewish merchant of New Amsterdam, Joseph d'Acosta, was allowed to send goods to the South River.[7] Thus ended the ban on Jewish fur trading.

In April, 1656, one month after the end of the restrictions, we hear that Israel was back in the Delaware country.[8] There is a slight but intriguing possibility that he became a member of the high council. We are told that in 1663 "the Hon[ble] Councillor Israel" directed the trading at Passajongh.[9] Unfortunately, the first name is lacking. We know there were non-Jews in eighteenth-century Pennsylvania by the name of Israel.[10] We know likewise that Jews were not accorded office during the Dutch period. Still, it is interesting to conjecture whether this councilor was Isaac Israel, the Jew of New Amsterdam.

There is reason to believe that numbers of Jews traveled back and forth between the Hudson and the Delaware Rivers bartering for furs. We come across Isaiah (more likely Isaac) in 1657, when he had a dispute with certain Swedes which was finally aired before Jean Paul Jacquet.[11] No doubt, there were others too, who were not immortalized by occasional brawls.

One more reference to the Dutch period and we are finished with it. This concerns Pieter Plockhoy, the quixotic Dutch Socinian Mennonite who dreamed dreams of a peaceful and harmonious community made up of the members of his sect. Financed by a loan from the burgomasters of Amsterdam,[12] twenty-five families crossed the ocean and settled on the banks of the Horekill, now Lewes Creek, in 1662. They lived under a peculiar dispensation.

Though they were religious folk, "for the maintenance of peace and concord" they determined that all members

of the clergy should be excluded.[13] In order to preserve
harmony, they decided to keep out not only Catholics
and "usurious Jews," but also "all intractable people,"
which meant "English stiff-necked Quakers; Puritans;
fool-hardy believers in the Millenium and obstinate
modern pretenders to revelation."[14]

This exclusive community came to a swift and tragic
end. Two years after its establishment, British troops
under Sir Robert Carr came into the Delaware country
to conduct a campaign of bloodshed and spoil. They
plundered the pacific Mennonite settlement and seized
everything they possessed "to a very naile."[15]

With that, the curtain was rung down on the prologue
of Swedish and Dutch rule. What followed was the great
inflow of immigration which was to characterize the
British control of the country between the Hudson and
the Delaware for a century and more.

The British invaders, though they came with fire and
sword, introduced throughout the Delaware valley a religious toleration which had been lacking among the
Mennonites of the Horekill and elsewhere under the
Dutch. In his covenant with the inhabitants who were
transferred to the new regime, Carr, the conqueror, act-
ing under orders,[16] guaranteed freedom of conscience for
all.[17]

Our attention is now directed to the area west of the
Hudson and east of the Delaware which we know today
as New Jersey. This tract was turned over to two lords
proprietors, Lord John Berkeley and Sir George Carteret.
They were anxious to settle their extensive holding with

almost any type of colonist — Dutch from New York, Puritans from New England, and whatever other diverse elements that might be attracted. Accordingly, a "concessions and agreement" was issued in 1664 which guaranteed that the inhabitants should not be molested because of differences in religion unless they disturbed the civil peace, any law of England to the contrary notwithstanding.[18]

The spirit of religious freedom must have been in the air. A remarkable document appeared which was drawn up and signed on March 3, 1676, called "The concessions and agreements of the proprietors, freeholders and inhabitants of the province of West New-Jersey." It served as a constitution to direct the destinies of the new colony. Chapter XVI is of particular interest for us. It declares "that no men, nor number of men upon earth, hath power or authority to rule over men's consciences in religious matters." Therefore, no one was to be disturbed "for the sake of his opinion, judgment, faith or worship towards God." Everyone was to enjoy his own judgment freely in matters of religious worship throughout the province.[19]

A bit of literary detective analysis of this declaration suggests the legal training of Lincoln's Inn and the ideal of religious liberty that marked one of the proprietors — none other than William Penn. Penn shared with a number of other Quakers an interest in the ownership of West Jersey,[20] and one can well imagine a man of his philosophy and zeal leaping at the opportunity to implant such principles in the blueprint for the community

across the seas. This compact is aflame with his doctrine
that the state had no right to invade the conscience of
the individual.

Penn was one of the great figures of his century. Son
of an admiral of the royal navy, Quaker, statesman, lawgiver and colonizer, he was a man whose background included the court circles of the Restoration and whose
spirit plumbed the depths of mysticism. In early man-
hood, outraged by the sufferings inflicted upon Quakers
for conscience sake, he had cast his lot with the Society
of Friends.[21]

His strong sentiments against religious persecution
went far beyond the confines of his own sect. "What
ground can there be why some, and not all, should be
tolerated?" he asked.[22] In his protest against the sufferings of the Quakers, he pointed out that oppression did
not create uniformity,[23] and he eloquently exclaimed:
"Force makes hypocrites; 't is persuasion only that makes
converts."[24]

Penn wrote widely on the religious questions which
were close to his heart — such matters as the use of
oaths, the need for tolerance and the futility of persecution. At times he discarded his humane philosophy
towards other faiths, as when he wrote harshly of Catholics.[25] His attitude towards the Jews was also characteristic of the age.

He felt "tender compassion" for this people whose long
captivity and unparalleled miseries were the result of
their denial of Jesus as the Christ, he wrote in a special
tract intended to convert the seed of Abraham. This

pamphlet, dated 1695, was called "A Visitation to the Jews." One finds an impassioned spirit in its pages, as when the author fairly shouts at the Jews: "You cannot deny but that there was such a Man as *Jesus*, and that he was put to Death by your Fathers."[26]

In the New Jersey situation, Penn was tangled up with the confusion of complex ownership, diffuse responsibility and diverse population. If he wished to establish an asylum for his harried Quakers, he must look elsewhere. Fortunately for Penn, he had against King Charles a claim for a considerable sum, amounting to sixteen thousand pounds. It was a simple matter for the royal hand to assign all the land west of the Delaware and north of Maryland to him in settlement. Penn was now free to launch his "holy experiment," his example to the nations, in the fields of Pennsylvania.

He set up a state based on true Quaker idealism, without oaths and without force. The Indians, who were cozened elsewhere, were treated with kindness. That was something worthy of praise. Just the same, for all its high aims, much of the scheme was impractical and some of the principles were contradictory. This becomes apparent when we study the religious disabilities that were set up in Pennsylvania.

Perhaps one might have expected a government sponsored by William Penn to erase completely distinctions based on credal differences. When one looks at the "Laws Agreed Upon for Pennsylvania," which were signed and sealed by government and freemen in England, May 5, 1682,[27] an element of conflict is observed.

First, in article 2, we note the liberal prerequisites for a freeman. Landowners and artisans alike — who paid scot and lot — even former indentured servants who took up fifty acres of land and cultivated twenty of them — were to be freemen capable of voting and being elected to the provincial council or General Assembly.[28] But article 34 declares that voters and officials, including members of the Assembly, should "be such as profess faith in Jesus Christ."[29] There is no reconciling the breadth of the one article, without the slightest religious qualification, and the requirement of Christian faith in the other.

The principle of complete religious toleration is brought out in article 35. It assured "all persons . . . who confess and acknowledge the one Almighty and Eternal God, to be the Creator, Upholder, and Ruler of the world," that they would not be molested nor compelled to frequent or support any form of worship whatever, provided they lived peaceably.[30] This recognition of the right to be undisturbed was accorded Jews but denied agnostics.

To return to the requirements for voting and holding office, Pennsylvania was an instance where Catholics enjoyed privileges which Jews did not share. This legislation favorable to Catholics appears to have been an oversight which was eventually corrected. In 1693, we find the members of the Assembly subscribing to tests which no Romanist could accept.[31] Isaac Sharpless, a historian of the Friends, has said: "While freedom of worship was permitted to all, it was intended to make Pennsylvania's government one of and for Orthodox Protestant Christians only."[32]

But as it turned out, Jews and Catholics were not the only ones excluded from the ranks of freemen. Under Governor William Markham, in 1696, the new frame of government came to designate as freemen eligible for voting or holding office those who had resided in the province for two years and owned fifty acres of land or property valued at fifty pounds.[33] Ownership of land as a requirement took care of a considerable number of farmers, but managed to disfranchise the city mechanics and artisans. This was just what the Philadelphia Quaker plutocracy wanted in order to keep power in its own hands. Only one taxable male in ten in that city was able to meet the suffrage requirements in the year of freedom, 1776.[34]

Whatever limitations may have existed in Pennsylvania as regards democratic institutions, Philadelphia and its hinterland attracted settlers by the thousands, not only from the British Isles but also from German states. The twentieth century, accustomed to looking back on colonial America with a patronizing eye, is little impressed by the fact that Philadelphia had forty thousand inhabitants in 1776.[35] Yet the Quaker city not only boasted the largest population in the colonies, but its numbers exceeded those of any city in Great Britain or Ireland, save London itself.[36]

Though over a long period some form of tropism has attracted Jews to metropolitan centers, Philadelphia during the greater part of the eighteenth century was the exception which proved the rule. Jews did not stream into the province of Pennsylvania. Nor were they discouraged by a persecuting spirit abroad in the colony, for while the Jews could not expect to enjoy full political rights, they were otherwise undisturbed.

Still, there were a few Jews in Philadelphia who made their appearance some time after the turn of the eighteenth century. The earliest to achieve any eminence was Isaac Miranda, whom James Logan, one of the biggest political figures of the day, described in 1723 as an "apostate Jew or fashionable Christian Proselyte."[37] Miranda became in time deputy judge in the court of vice-admiralty.[38]

The first evidence of an actual settlement of Jews in Philadelphia comes from the travel diary of a German visitor, the youthful Commissary Philipp von Reck, who had been associated with the Salzburgers' migration to Georgia. He found the city, when he visited it in 1734, "a seat of all religions and sects." In his catalogue of denominations, we find not only the more familiar varieties but also groups difficult to identify, such as Dümplers, Sabbatarians, Boehmites, Schwenckfelders and Trichtfelders. The list concludes with the Well-Wishers (*Wohlwünscher*), the Jews, and the heathens.[39] What a company!

The life of the Jewish community of Philadelphia had numerous facets, but its beginnings go back to the traditional effort to gain a cemetery. The first burial ground was acquired in 1738, when Nathan Levy purchased a tract of land as a family lot.[40] The cemetery was soon so well filled that an addition was necessary, but when Levy appealed to Richard Peters, secretary of the proprietaries in 1747, he was put off.[41] Four years later, he protested against the "sportsmen" who practiced their marksmanship in the cemetery and thereby destroyed a tombstone. He offered a twenty-shilling reward for information which would lead to the conviction of the vandals.[42] At a later time we learn that the cemetery was from the first regarded by the Jews as "a trust for a burial place for the interment of Hebrews."[43]

The organization of Congregation Mikveh Israel came after the cemetery. The year of its inception is believed to have been 1747.[44] We know that it had progressed far enough by the year 1761 for the erection of a *Shuleh* to be discussed.[45] However, the actual building of the synagogue was postponed till the latter days of the Revolution when Philadelphia had become a city of refuge for Jews from other communities exposed to the ravages of war.

The Jews of Philadelphia did not live in seclusion, but participated in the gay social life of the colonial city. An older writer, in describing the assembly first organized by the socially-minded Joseph Shippen and others in 1749, has said that the "elite and fashionables" were enrolled for the dance on the basis of their "ancestral bearings and associations."[46] The subscription was three pounds. Notwithstanding all the emphasis on snobbery and wealth, certain Jews were able to gain admittance to this select company.

We observe in the membership two, and more probably three, Jewish names. These were David Franks and

Samson Levy, who were merchants of the time. Joseph
Marks, the third man,[47] cannot be identified as a Jew
with finality. Marks was the name of several men of the
Jewish community, notably Henry and Levy Marks who
were mentioned in the will of Michael Gratz in 1765.[48]
But there were also many non-Jews called Marks in
colonial Pennsylvania.

David Franks, subscriber to the assembly and partner
of Nathan Levy of cemetery fame,[49] was the outstanding
figure in the mercantile field. He was born in New York,
but, following his removal to Philadelphia, became the
most prominent Jew of the city. Married to Margaret
Evans, a Gentile lady,[50] he permitted his children to be
brought up as Christians.[51] This, no doubt, made his
entree into Philadelphia society easier.

Like certain other practical men of affairs, he could see
no reason why social vision should interfere with business.
Accordingly, in 1761, we find his name, along with those
of Samson Levy and Joseph Marks who were his comrades in the glamorous assembly, affixed to the protest
made by a group of merchants against a proposed duty
on the importation of Negroes.[52] The intent of the measure was to discourage the slave trade, but these Jewish
merchants were among those who wished to see the
traffic continue.

Franks had very close ties with the British authorities, for he was identified with the provisioning of His
Majesty's troops in America. He displayed his loyalty
to the crown during the dark days following Braddock's
defeat, when he belonged to the Independent Troop of

Horse of Philadelphia.[53] He showed his fidelity even more pointedly when he suffered and paid dearly for his devotion to the king during the American Revolution.

Philadelphia was the seat of culture, one of the great educational centers of the new world. Not a few of the institutions of the city bore the imprint of Benjamin Franklin, who was the founder of the College of Philadelphia, later to be known as the University of Pennsylvania. With him as sponsor, this institution was hospitable to all faiths. As the recent historian of the University puts it, "there was little mention of religion" to be found in its constitutions.[54]

The preparatory school associated with the College was called the Academy. We have the names of five Jewish boys who were enrolled there in the decade before 1770.[55] Only one of these lads, Moses Levy, completed the college course and received the degree of A.B., in the class of 1772.[56] He was the sole Jewish graduate of the institution in pre-Revolutionary days.

Philadelphia was not the only Jewish settlement in Pennsylvania. Although the province never attracted a considerable Jewish population, it had a scattered one. The Jews found in the hinterland were vitally interested in the fur trade which was carried on in the wilderness, and numbers of them were early settlers in some of the new towns established among the forests.

Lancaster was one of these outposts. Founded in 1730, it was still something of a frontier community when Richard Locke, an English minister, passed by in 1747.

He reported on his journey to the Society for the Propagation of the Gospel in Foreign Parts and described the make-up of the population. Under the caption of "Heathen and Infidels," he stated that the Quaker and Indian populations were below the average, and he added, "here are ten families of Jews."[57]

Easton was settled in 1750 and one of its eleven founders proved to have been Myer Hart, a Jew. He was no doubt a figure of some importance, being for a time the only merchant in the town and, accordingly, the biggest taxpayer.[58]

One might add another community of Jews to the list, if one were of a credulous turn of mind. This was Schaefferstown in Lebanon County. In 1843, I. Daniel Rupp compiled a local history which claimed that the place was originally settled in 1732, or earlier, by German Jews who had both synagogue and rabbi. He asserted that the settlers later scattered, leaving behind their cemetery, the wall of which was still standing in the historian's day.[59] In lieu of any further evidence, it appears most likely that the first comers to the neighborhood belonged to a German Christian sect which observed certain Mosaic practices also found among Jews.[60]

Trade with the Indians in the eighteenth century was more than a matter of bartering and haggling over furs with local savages. The Jews of Pennsylvania had both imagination and vision which inspired them to initiate vast projects in the field of western trade and land development. One of the most prominent men in the movement was Joseph Simon, the leading merchant of Lancaster. His son-in-law was Michael Gratz,[61] who came, with his brother Barnard, from Langendorf in Upper Silesia to Philadelphia, and who was the father of Rebecca Gratz of *Ivanhoe* fame.[62]

These three men and their associates proceeded like merchant venturers to take over a large share of the western country which was just then being opened. Their operations branched out of Pittsburgh;[63] through their land intersts they played a part in the founding of Wheeling[64] and Louisville;[65] and their enterprises expanded until they obtained control of much of the trade in the Illinois country.[66]

A vast collection of Gratz papers awaits sifting. In addition, other unpublished manuscripts in various libraries in the United States and England contain references to the roles played by Jewish merchants of Pennsylvania in the winning of the west. Let one example suffice. David Franks, the prominent Philadelphia purveyor to the British forces in North America, serviced the lonely British garrisons of the Mississippi Valley over a period of years. A letter from him to General Thomas Gage, the commander-in-chief, written on February 5, 1771, inquired whether the firm of Levy and Franks should undertake to send provisions from "the Illinois" to the "Troops station'd at the Natchese & Iberville on the Mississippy."[67]

In colonial days it was a far cry from the banks of the Delaware to the forests about the little outpost at Natchez, and yet this Philadelphia firm was ready to ship supplies over the long and hazardous route beyond the mountains. The factor of Jewish enterprise in eighteenth-century pioneering should attract scholarly research. Studies should reveal the part that Jews played in linking the Ohio and Mississippi valleys to the Atlantic seaboard. It was probably more significant, and certainly more romantic, than the colorful operations of the widely publicized Jewish counting houses by the Newport waterfront.

As we have seen, Jews appeared in the region below Philadelphia when it was under Dutch rule. There is nothing to be said about the Jews in the "Three Lower Counties" after Penn launched his holy experiment, for few if any settled there. In 1704 the section was separated from Pennsylvania to become Delaware. Its laws on freemen and voting were modeled on those of Pennsylvania.[68]

New Jersey, on the other hand, with its position between the Delaware and Hudson rivers, attracted a number of Jewish settlers. It became a royal province in 1702 when the proprietors of East Jersey and West Jersey turned over their control to the crown. Incidentally, one of the thirty-two proprietors of West Jersey was a London Jew named Benjamin Levy.[69] As a royal colony, New Jersey extended liberty of conscience to all except Papists.[70]

The Quakers were a numerous element in West Jersey, and, what with their refusal to bear arms and to take oaths, they became a subject of heated controversy. In 1718, "Several Inhabitants of and Traders to" New Jersey petitioned the crown to override Governor Hunter who had allowed Quakers to assume office by making a solemn affirmation instead of taking oath. One of the twelve men who declared that this concession did great damage to themselves was Moses Levy, described as "a Jew here."[71] Two facts call for comment. First, a Jew was permitted to join in the petition; second, and perhaps more important, when his rights were not circumscribed, he sought to limit the amount of religious liberty enjoyed by others.

A SILVER TANKARD

made by Myer Myers, President of the Silversmiths' Society of New York,
showing the coat-of-arms of the Livingston family.

A LAW
OF
MARYLAND
Concerning
RELIGION.

Oraſmuch as in a well-governed and Chriſtian Commonwealth, Matters concerning Religion and the Honour of God ought to be in the firſt pla e to be taken into ſerious conſideration, and endeavoured to be ſettled. Be it therefore Ordained and Enacted by the Right Honourable *CÆCILIUS* Lord Baron of *Baltemore*, abſolute Lord and Proprietary of this Province, with the Advice and Conſent of the Upper and Lower Houſe of this General Aſſembly, That whatſoever perſon or perſons within this Province and the Iſlands thereunto belonging, ſhall fro m henceforth blaſpheme GOD, that is curſe him; or ſhall deny our Saviour JESUS CHRIST to be the Son of God; or ſhall deny the Holy Trinity, the Father, Son, & Holy Ghoſt; or the Godhead of any of the ſaid Three Perſons of the Trinity, or the Unity of the Godhead, or ſhall uſe or utter any reproachful ſpeeches, words, or language, concerning the Holy Trinity, or any of the ſaid three Perſons thereof, ſhall be puniſhed with death, and confiſcation or forfeiture of all his or her Lands and Goods to the Lord Proprietary and his Heirs.

And be it alſo enacted by the Authority, and with the advice and aſſent aforeſaid, That whatſoever perſon or perſons ſhall from henceforth uſe or utter any reproachful words or ſpeeches concerning the bleſſed Virgin *MARY*, the Mother of our Saviour, or the holy Apoſtles or Evangeliſts, or any of them, ſhall in ſuch caſe for the firſt Offence forfeit to the ſaid Lord Proprietary and his Heirs, Lords and Proprietaries of this Province, the ſum of Five pounds Sterling, or the value thereof to be levied on the goods and chattels of every ſuch perſon ſo offending; but in caſe ſuch offender or offenders ſhall not then have goods and chattels ſufficient for the ſatisfying of ſuch forfeiture, or that the ſame be not otherwiſe ſpeedily ſatisfied, that then ſuch offender or offenders ſhall be publickly whipt, and be impriſoned during the pleaſure of the Lord Proprietary, or the Lieutenant or Chief Governor of this Province for the time being: And that every ſuch offender and offenders for every ſecond offence ſhall forfeit Ten Pounds Sterling, or the value thereof to be levied as aforeſaid, or in caſe ſuch offender or offenders ſhall not then have goods and chattels within this Province ſufficient for that purpoſe, then to be publickly and ſeverely whipt and impriſoned as before is expreſſed: and that every perſon or perſons before mentioned, offending herein the third time, ſhall for ſuch third offence, forfeit all his lands and goods, and be for ever baniſht and expelled out of this Province.

And be it alſo further Enacted by the ſame Authority, advice, and aſſent, That whatſoever perſon or perſons ſhall from henceforth upon any occaſion of offence, or otherwiſe in a reproachful manner or way, declare, call, or denominate, any perſon or perſons whatſoever, inhabiting, reſiding, trafficking, tra-ding, or commercing within this Province, or within any the Ports, Harbours, Creeks or Havens to the ſame belonging, an Heretick, Schiſmatick, Idolater, Pu-ritan, Presbyterian, Independant, Popiſh Prieſt, Jeſuit, Jeſuited Papiſt, Lutheran, Calviniſt, Anabaptiſt, Browniſt, Barrow iſt, Antinonian, Roundhead, Separatiſt, or other name or term in a reproachful manner relating to matter of Religion, ſhall for every ſuch offence forfeit and loſe the ſum of Ten ſhillings Sterling, or the value thereof, to be levied of the goods and chattels of every ſuch offender and offenders. the one half thereof to be forfeited and paid unto the perſon & perſons of whom ſuch reproachful words are, or ſhall be ſpoken or uttered, and the other half thereof to the Lord Proprietary and his Heirs, Lords and Pro-prietaries of this Province: But if ſuch perſon or perſons who ſhall at any time utter or ſpeak any ſuch reproachful words or language, ſhall not have goods or chattels ſufficient and overt within this Province to be taken to ſatisfy the penalty aforeſaid, or that the ſame be not otherwiſe ſpeedily ſatisfied, that then the perſon and perſons ſo offending ſhall be publickly whipt, and ſhall ſuffer impriſonment without Bail or Mainpriſe untill he, ſhe, or they, reſpectively, ſhall ſatisfie the party offended or grieved by ſuch reproachfull Language, by asking him or her reſpectively forgiveneſs publickly, for ſuch his offence, before the Magiſtrate or chief Officer or Officers of the Town or place where ſuch offence ſhall be given.

And be it further likewiſe enacted by the authority and conſent aforeſaid, that every perſon and perſons within this Province, that ſhall at any time hereaf-ter prophane the Sabbath, or Lords day, called Sunday, by frequent ſwearing, drunkenneſs, or by any uncivil or diſorderly Recreation, or by working on that day when abſolute neceſſity doth not require, ſhall for every ſuch firſt offence forfeit two ſhillings ſix pence Sterling, or the value thereof; and for the ſecond offence five ſhillings Sterling, or the value thereof: and for the third offence, and for every time he ſhall offend in like manner afterwards, Ten ſhil-lings Sterling, or the value thereof: and in caſe ſuch offender or offenders ſhall not have ſufficient goods or chattels within this Province to ſatisfy any of the aforeſaid penalties reſpectively hereby impoſed for prophaning the Sabbath or Lords day called Sunday as aforeſaid, then in every ſuch caſe the party ſo offending ſhall for the firſt and ſecond offence in that kind be impriſoned till he or ſhe ſhall publickly in open Court before the chief Commander, Judge or Magiſtrate of that County, Town, or Precinct wherein ſuch offence ſhall be committed, acknowledge the ſcandal and offence he hath in that reſpect given, againſt God, and the good and civil Government of this Province: and for the third offence and for every time after ſhall alſo be publickly whipt.

And whereas the inforcing of the Conſcience in matter of Religion hath frequently fallen out to be of dangerous conſequence in thoſe Commonwealths where it hath been practiſed, and for the more quiet and peaceable Government of this Province, and the better to preſerve mutual love & unity amongſt the is before declared and ſet forth, that no perſon or perſons whatſoever within this Province, or the Iſlands, Ports, Harbors, Creeks, or Havens thereunto be-longing, profeſſing to believe in Jeſus Chriſt, ſhall from henceforth be any ways troubled, moleſted, or diſcountenanced, for, or in reſpect of his or her Re-ligion nor in the true exerciſe thereof within this Province or the Iſlands thereunto belonging, nor any way compell'd to the belief or exerciſe of any other Re-ligion againſt his or her conſent, ſo as they be not unfaithfull to the Lord Proprietary, or moleſt or conſpire againſt the civil Government, eſtabliſhed or to be eſtabliſhed in this Province under him and his Heirs. And that all and every perſon and perſons that ſhall preſume contrary to this Act and the true intent & meaning thereof directly or indirectly, either in perſon or eſtate, wilfully to wrong, diſturb, or trouble, or moleſt any perſon or perſons whatſoever within this Province, profeſſing to believe in Jeſus Chriſt, for or in reſpect of his or her Religion, or the free exerciſe thereof within this Province, otherwiſe then is pro-vided for in this Act, that ſuch perſon or perſons ſo offending ſhall be compelled to pay treble damages to the party ſo wronged or moleſted, and for every ſuch offence ſhall alſo forfeit Twenty ſhillings Sterling in Money, or the value there of, half thereof for the uſe of the Lord Proprietary and his Heirs, Lords and Pro-prietaries of this Province, and the other half thereof for the uſe of the Party ſo wronged or moleſted as aforeſaid; or if the party ſo offending as aforeſaid, ſhall refuſe or be unable to recompence the party ſo wronged, or to ſatisfy ſuch fine or forfeiture, then ſuch offender ſhall be ſeverely puniſhed by publick whipping and impriſonment during the pleaſure of the Lord Proprietary or his Lieutenant or chief Governor of this Province for the time being, without Bail or Mainpriſe.

And be it further alſo enacted by the authority and conſent aforeſaid, that t e Sheriff or other Officer or Officers from time to time to be appointed and au-thorized for that purpoſe of the County, Town, or Precinct where every particular offence in this preſent Act contained, ſhall happen at any time to be com-mitted, and whereupon there is hereby a forfeiture, fine, or penalty impoſed, ſha l from time to time diſtrain, and ſeize the goods and eſtate of every ſuch perſon ſo offending as a oreſaid againſt this preſent Act or any part thereof, and ſell the ſame or any part thereof for the full ſatisfaction of ſuch forfeiture, fine, or penalty as aforeſaid, reſtoring to the party ſo offending, the remainder or over plus of the ſaid goods or eſtate, after ſuch ſatisfaction ſo made as aforeſaid.

CHAPTER VIII

BLASPHEMY UNDER THE CALVERTS

COLONIAL Maryland should have been the abode of peace and harmony. The *Ark* and the *Dove*, two ships which sailed out of Cowes with the first settlers, in November, 1633, had scriptural names symbolic of reconciliation.

Moreover, the founder of the new colony was Cecilius Calvert, Lord Baltimore, a Roman Catholic, member of the most persecuted sect of the day in England. He was fully aware of the fact that his coreligionists not only were robbed of their civil rights, but were also compelled to endure the brutal invasion of the sanctuary of the spirit. They might not live within ten miles of London, nor journey more than five miles from home without a special license. Those who refused the sacrament in the Anglican fashion sometimes lost their property as punishment, and occasionally brave priests, who dared say the mass in secret, were put to death as martyrs.[1]

When Calvert became lord proprietor of Maryland he recognized the great care which he must exercise in the field of religion. There must be no grounds for outcry against Papist persecution, and he therefore instructed the governor and commissioners to observe the utmost circumspection in religious matters. Catholics should conduct their devotions in private; the authorities should "treat the Protestants with as much mildness and favor as Justice will permit." In this way they might obviate "any just complaint" in Virginia or England.[2]

It was an auspicious beginning, but the religious history of Maryland during the colonial period offers a paradox. One school of historians sees the Catholic foundation of the province as the original source of American religious liberty, but blames the Puritans and Anglicans for wrecking something beautiful and pure. A second group denies the thesis that Maryland was ever the religious Utopia of the seventeenth century, and as they marshal their arguments they might include the puzzling story of Jacob Lumbrozo, the "Jew doctor" who was prosecuted for blasphemy. This physician, who migrated to Maryland in 1656,[3] was described as being "late of Lisbone in the Kingdome of Portugall."[4] He was without question one of the most engrossing characters of the time.

A wealth of material in the court records enables us to sketch a full-length portrait of the man. He had a winning personality, a glib tongue that was at home in the English language, and a cultured address. His friends included some of the most important people in the colony.[5] Lumbrozo was known as the Jew doctor,[6] but his talents extended also in other directions. He was farmer, innkeeper and businessman. He traded with the Indians[7] and bartered imported goods in exchange for planters' tobacco.[8]

Despite his charm, his versatility and his social connections, Lumbrozo was a thoroughgoing rogue. One may read accounts of his knavery in the court records for pages at a time. He was the most consummate scoundrel, the most picturesque villain, to appear among the gallery of conventional, respectable Jews who lived in America during colonial days. History played an ironical little trick when she selected a man of Lumbrozo's kidney to play the role of loyal Jew threatened with a martyr's fate.

As we have already noted, Lumbrozo came from Lisbon, and his Portuguese origin is a matter worthy of comment. For a hundred and fifty years the Jewish religion had been banned in that country. All Jews who would not accept the Catholic faith had long since pursued the bitter road of exile. It was widely known that all the roots of Judaism had not been destroyed for, frequently, *Christãos novos* were exposed as loyal to the faith of their forefathers, and those who were hardened offenders were handed over to the civil authorities by the Holy Inquisition for execution in the great square of Lisbon.

It is noteworthy that Lumbrozo did not have to mask his religion in Maryland. This was despite the fact that Jews were excluded from freedom of religion in a province which boasted a law code fortified by the curious Act Concerning Religion. Before studying how Lumbrozo got trapped by one of its ferocious provisions, it is well to familiarize ourselves further with the religious and political background of seventeenth-century Maryland.

The Calverts had a difficult problem in maintaining a religious equilibrium in their troubled colony. From the very start there was a Protestant majority, and that meant trouble for any attempt to secure Catholic rights. Difficulties increased as the Roundheads secured their ascendency in the civil war at home and the turmoil spread to Maryland.

Baltimore continued his policy of conciliation. He even named William Stone, a Protestant planter of Virginia, as his governor and invited the persecuted Puritans there to find a refuge in Maryland. Before taking office, Stone and his council had to swear that they would molest no one professing to believe in Jesus Christ, and "in particular no Roman Catholic" in respect to religion.[9] It is clear that the province welcomed all Christians.

The Puritan newcomers proved themselves a troop of malcontents dabbling in sedition and insurrection. Their tumults may have forced Lord Baltimore to take special steps to safeguard the Catholic minority. At any rate, it was at his direction that the famous Act Concerning Religion was brought before the General Assembly in 1649.

This law, a favorite subject of controversy among historians, aimed to make Maryland an oasis for all professing Christians, but did not provide any particular change in the traditions already existing in the colony. What is more, it was no milestone along the road of religious freedom. Although hailed as "one of the proud boasts of Maryland,"[10] it contained provisions that no modern democracy would tolerate.

The act declared, near the beginning, that whoever should "blaspheme God, that is Curse him, or deny our Saviour Jesus Christ to be the sonne of God, or shall deny the Holy Trinity. . . , or shall use or utter any reproachfull Speeches, words or language concerning the said Holy Trinity. . . shall be punished with death and confiscatōn or forfeiture of all his or her lands and goods to the Lord Proprietary and his heires." Furthermore, reproachful words or speeches concerning Mary and the apostles were to be punished by heavy fines or public whippings and imprisonment. Banishment was the penalty for the third offense.[11]

The following section attempted to deal with men who vilified those of other persuasions. Fines were imposed for using such epithets as heretic, idolator, Puritan, Presbyterian, Jesuit, Roundhead, and the like.

The act further provided: "Whereas the inforceing of the conscience in matters of Religion hath frequently fallen out to be of dangerous consequence in those commonwealthes where it hath been practiced," no believer in Jesus Christ should be molested in his religion or compelled to acknowledge any other faith.[12]

The ban on name-calling was motivated by good intentions, and the freedom of conscience for all Christians was an enlightened policy marred only by its exclusion of Jews and infidels. But the ban on any slight to the apostles, Mary, Jesus and God threatened to suppress any discussion not consonant with orthodox theology.

Let me hasten to add that the provision against blasphemy was not unique at the time. Some writers have observed a Puritan quality in it, because the year before the Act Concerning Religion became law, the English Long Parliament had prescribed the death penalty for those who denied a belief in God or the Trinity.[13] According to the Massachusetts General Laws of 1648, any person, whether Christian or pagan, who blasphemed the members of the Trinity or reproached "the holy religion of God as if it were but a politick device to keep ignorant men in awe," should be put to death.[14]

A similar severity characterized the Virginia code of 1611 which was fathered by Governor Dale, a man without Puritan leanings. This code imposed the death penalty for the following offenses: speaking "impiously or maliciously, against the holy and blessed Trinitie;" blaspheming "Gods holy name;" and speaking in "derision or despight of Gods holy word."[15] It is more accurate to blame the spirit of the times than the evil genius of Puritanism for this type of legislation. As we shall presently see, the Maryland law on blasphemy had a special significance for us.

Meanwhile, despite the aim of the Act Concerning Religion to promote tranquillity among the varied faiths in its midst, Maryland was to enjoy little peace during the coming year. After all, it was the seventeenth century and the Puritan communities resented any condominium with Catholics. They ordered things differently in Massachusetts and in England.

There was an uprising against the government which countenanced the "Roman Papish Religion;" Stone was removed from office;[16] men were killed in the Battle of the Severn;[17] and the victorious Puritans finished by disowning the rule of the Calverts and ousting Catholics from a share in government.

The assembly which met in October, 1654, now free of Catholics,[18] passed a revised version of the Act Concerning Religion, which excluded the Papists from the protection of the laws of England and restrained them from the practice of their faith. Other Christians might worship as they pleased, provided that they did not abuse this right by injuring their fellows or practicing licentiousness.[19]

The new law on religion dealt with blasphemy in a surprisingly mild fashion. Common swearers, blasphemers and cursers who used imprecations against God or man were to be admonished by the magistrate and for a second offense were subject to whatever penalty the court might determine.[20] Quite a contrast to capital punishment!

Puritan rule did not prove lasting. While Maryland Jesuits had to flee to Virginia and endure great hardships, as Catholic sources tell us,[21] Lord Baltimore was in England struggling to regain his proprietary. He used all energy to convince Cromwell of the justice of his cause,[22] and he finally recovered his title to Maryland.

Among the instructions Baltimore sent his new governor, Josias Fendall, on October 23, 1656, was one restoring the original Act Concerning Religion. "*All Persons who profess to believe in Iesus Christ*" were given full freedom of religion. Moreover the authorities were commanded to employ "the penalties mencōned in the said Act . . . vpon any offendors against the same or any part thereof."[23] Thus was the barbaric punishment for blasphemy restored to the Maryland statute books.

It was not long before the blasphemy law found a victim — our acquaintance, Jacob Lumbrozo.

The crisis arose as a result of Lumbrozo's association with Richard Preston, Jr., son of one of the leading men in Maryland. Preston, Sr., was among the persecuted Puritans of Virginia who had settled in Maryland on invitation. A leader in the revolt which dislodged his erstwhile Catholic hosts, he served as speaker of the Assembly in 1654,[24] and as commissioner under Governor William Fuller.[25]

The Preston family sympathized with Quakerism, and in the course of time they abandoned the Puritan cause to join the Society of Friends. Very likely their conversion was brought about by the visit to Maryland of two Quaker missionaries, Josiah Coale and Thomas Thurston, who were entertained by the Prestons in the summer of 1658.[26] At any rate, the younger Preston, the following February, "declared" the facts in a deposition to be true rather than submit to oath.[27] This was quite in accord with Quaker practice. The occasion was the presentation of evidence against Lumbrozo.

The more important of the Prestons' summer visitors seems to have been Josiah Coale. Rufus Jones has described him as "one of the finest spirits among the entire band of 'publishers of Truth' in the colonies."[28] He attempted to preach the Quaker message to whites and Indians alike, and he was not the kind who submitted to man-made laws which outraged his principles.[29]

A clash with the provincial authorities was inevitable. Both he and Thurston refused to take the pledge of fidelity and urged their followers to do likewise. In addition to this offense, they were charged with seducing "many of the people unto erroneous & blasphemous Tenetts."[30] (Apparently the disciples of George Fox were outside of the Maryland scheme of toleration because of their aggressive proselytizing.) The trouble-makers were accordingly arrested and expelled from the colony.[31]

Before this happened, Coale spent some time in Lumbrozo's company.[32] This was probably his first encounter with a follower of Moses and, if he was like some of his contemporaries, he longed to win lost Jewish souls. At that very time a pair of Quaker missionaries were boldly trying to make converts among the Jews living in the ghettos of Catholic Italy.[33]

Coale seems to have seized the opportunity to cross-examine Lumbrozo on a very delicate subject,—the Jewish attitude towards Jesus. Lumbrozo answered his queries with frankness, but he outraged some of his hearers, and as a result ran afoul of the law on blasphemy.

The affair ultimately came before the provincial court which sat at St. Mary's on February 23, 1658/9. Josias Fendall, the governor, presided, and the board consisted of five men.[34] Lumbrozo was "charged by his Lps Attorney for uttering words of blesphemy agst Our Blessed Sauior Jesus Christ."[35]

On this occasion the depositions of two witnesses were read. One of them, Richard Preston, Jr., described the searching questions Coale directed to Lumbrozo: Were the Jews looking for a messiah? Yes, answered Lumbrozo. Who was crucified at Jerusalem? He was a man. How were his miracles performed? By the art of magic. How then were the disciples able to bring about similar miracles after the crucifixion? He might have taught them his art, said "the Jew Doctor."[36]

The second deposition read at the hearing was made by John Fossett, a man about forty-four years old. He related that he also had discussed the character of Jesus with Lumbrozo at the Preston home, probably on the day of the Coale interview, but there is no direct evidence to this effect.

According to Fossett's statement, he had insisted that Jesus was more than mere man, witness the resurrection. Lumbrozo cynically replied that his body had been stolen by disciples. No man ever performed such miracles as Jesus, said Fossett. They might have been done by sorcery, was the answer. Then Fossett accused Lumbrozo of considering Jesus a "Negromancer." "To wch s^d Lumbrozo answered nothing but laughed."[37]

Lumbrozo appeared in court to face the charges and corroborated what appears between the lines of the two depositions, namely, that he was prodded into expressing his opinions on Jesus. He testified that he was forced "by them to declare his Opinion, & being by profession a Jew he answered to some particular demands then urged, & as to that of miracles done by Art magick, he declared what remains written concerning Moses & the Magicians of Egipt: But sayd not any thing scoffingly or in derogaōn by him, Christians acknowledge for their Messias."[38]

The court decided that Lumbrozo was to remain in the sheriff's custody "until hee put in security Body for

Body" to answer the charge of blasphemy at the next court session. His accusers, moreover, were to appear in person against him.[39] That is the last we hear about the affair.

It so happened that at this time Governor Fendall proclaimed an amnesty in connection with the installation of Richard Cromwell as Lord Protector. The governor chose this occasion to pardon all persons who "stood indicted conuicted or Condemned to dye."[40] This may have been how Lumbrozo escaped further prosecution.

One may doubt whether he would have suffered death in any event. His influence and position were too strong for that — unless a popular outcry had been raised against him, something which was absent. As a matter of fact, as a Jew, his lack of legal status in the province was thoroughly ignored.

We know that Lumbrozo was an important member of the community who enjoyed all the privileges of his Christian neighbors. Some time before the blasphemy charges were raised, he witnessed a promissory note.[41] In 1663, he was permitted to serve on the jury of the provincial court.[42] The very next day he acquired letters of denization by the same formula as was employed for Catholic or Protestant aliens.[43] During this same period Lumbrozo changed his given name from the Jewish Jacob to the equally Jewish John without leaving an explanation for posterity.[44]

Lumbrozo's facility in expression and argument must have been generally recognized, for he appeared in court a number of times as attorney. One such occasion was in February, 1662/3, before his denization, when he argued for his two servants, John and Margery Gould, in an action of defamation which they had brought against Giles and Elizabeth Glover. Lumbrozo charged that Mrs. Glover had abused Margery by crying: "Play the whore in the Corne feeld againe." He attempted to clinch his case by quoting snatches of rhyme like the following:

"Shee liues for euer in eternall shame
    that liues to see the death of her good name."

Following the testimony of one witness, the case was continued at the request of the defendants until the next meeting of the court.[45] That is the last heard of the action.

There was nonetheless a sequel, and a fantastic one at that. Three months after championing the cause of the Goulds, Lumbrozo was himself suing his servants and erstwhile friends for defamation. They were accused of spreading the tale that he had offered John Gould half his possessions, "boath land and hogs and all that he had," if he might enjoy special privileges with Margery. Margery testified how Lumbrozo had attempted to force her, while he furnished scriptural prooof that his intentions were honorable. Daniel Johnson, the defendants' attorney, dared Lumbrozo to carry his case to the provincial court, but the latter, deciding that discretion was the better policy, withdrew his suit and paid the costs.[46]

Lumbrozo was involved in an even more unsavory

matter two and a half months later when he was arrested for producing a criminal abortion upon Elizabeth Wild, his maidservant. This had taken place, it was claimed, after he had made the reluctant girl submit to him by force.

Lumbrozo managed to escape from this dilemma by marriage, which disqualified the girl as witness against him. Naturally Elizabeth repudiated the statements she had previously made. The jury indicted them both,[47] but the records report no further proceedings.

One more sordid charge against Lumbrozo must be mentioned. Thomas Allcock, who lost his wife and child in an Indian attack, had Lumbrozo arrested in November, 1665, for receiving goods stolen from his house at the time of the murders. The trial was set for January 2, 1666, before the provincial court at St. Mary's.[48] Serious as this affair was, there is no mention of any further action. Lumbrozo may have been dead when the case was called in January. By May, Elizabeth was not only a widow but the wife of another man.[49] John, Lumbrozo's son, was posthumously born to her.[50]

Strange, is it not, that this bizarre individual was the single Jewish personality who played a part in the history of the province of Maryland? Down until the eighteenth century there were no identifiable Jews, despite some names of men who might have been Jewish but who were probably Spanish and Catholic. The story of Jewish rights before the Revolution is only a matter of scraps and bits which must be set against the background of a ferocious anti-Catholic trend.

A new epoch, serving as a prologue to the bigotry to come, was ushered in when Maryland became a royal province in 1691. The governor was instructed (like others in charge of colonies directly attached to the crown) to afford "a liberty of conscience to all persons except Papists." This continued until 1703 when, strangely enough, the words "except Papists" were omitted in the instructions. For the twelve years that followed there appeared to be complete religious freedom for all men.[51]

Then the oppression of Catholics set in, and there were no half measures. Papists were suspected of the foulest treason, and the Assembly listened to hysterical accusations that they would combine with the French and Indians beyond the frontier and with Negro slaves at home to destroy the state.[52] Catholics were disfranchised[53] and their priests might not say mass.[54] Catholic parents were even forbidden to win back erring Protestant children to the faith.[55]

A special head tax on imported Irish Catholic servants was invoked to limit the Romanist population. In 1717, the tax was set at forty shillings, the same figure as for Negro slaves, and was continued until the period of the Revolution.[56] (British convicts arrived in droves tax free.)[57] There was a similar tax, known as the *Leibzoll*, exacted from the Jews of Germany at this same period.[58] Moses Mendelssohn, the philosopher, was charged the same entry fee at the gates of Dresden as a Polish cow.[59]

An even more vicious measure which has some Jewish interest, passed the lower house on May 18, 1756.[60] It provided that German or French Catholics landing

in Maryland must pay a tax of five pounds. If they
were priests or Jesuits, the exaction was two hundred
pounds.[61] In order to determine whether newcomers
were Catholics, they were compelled to sign the test and
take the oath of abjuration, something that no loyal
son of the Church would do.[62] The bill, however, proposed that Jews entering Maryland might take the
special oaths prescribed for their benefit by the Naturalization Act of 1740.[63]

The measure was defeated in the upper house and
never became law.[64] It has significance, however, because
it proves that the sensibilities of the Jews were recognized
by Maryland in the eighteenth century, despite the
barbarous treatment of Catholics.

A passage in the provincial records furnishes a clue
to prove that Jews were permitted to sojourn in Maryland
and conduct business there. It tells us how Sampson
Levy, an early Jewish resident of Baltimore,[65] was able
to obtain a judgment against the widow Susanna Risteau,
in the provincial court in 1755.[66]

The right of residence and the privilege of earning
a livelihood which Jews possessed did not afford them
complete equality. There was no such thing as religious
toleration. As a non-Christian people, they would not
have been permitted to conduct public worship. There
never were enough Jews, it so happened, to question
the provisions of such a law. Few as they were, however,
they were regarded as members of an inferior order
of citizens, ineligible to vote or hold office.

The Revolution came and brought religious and civil

equality to the hunted Catholics. But the Jews of Maryland had to wait impatiently while their numbers increased greatly before they could secure recognition. Only after the passage of another half century did they succeed in their struggle for emancipation.

Maryland is sandwiched in between two colonies which played dominant parts in colonial history and in the drama of the Revolution. These were the populous and influential provinces of Pennsylvania and Virginia. In Pennsylvania, as we have seen, Jews were established, in Philadelphia and the outlying towns alike, as city merchants and Indian traders. Far different was the situation in colonial Virginia where there was only a faint trace of Jews throughout all its eventful history.

Perhaps one reason for the absence of Jews was the rural economy of both the tidewater area and the hinterland of piedmont and mountains. Even Williamsburg, the capital and largest center, had a population not far above the thousand mark. And Jews, it must be remembered, preferred towns.

The few Jews settled in the Old Dominion were scattered during the entire colonial period, if we may judge by some of the names that have survived in the records. We may go as far back as John Levy who acquired land in James City County in 1648.[67] The historian of Albemarle County declared that Michael Israel, who patented eighty acres of land in 1757, was a Jew; but he failed to cite his authority.[68] One final example of a probable Jew in Virginia was Hezekiah

Levy, who was a member of the Fredericksburg Masonic Lodge to which George Washington belonged.[69]

The Virginia tradition included the established Anglican church whose clergy was supported by the inhabitants whether they liked it or not. Judging from the agitation conducted by Presbyterians and others, there were strong objections raised. These came to a head in 1779 when Thomas Jefferson authored the classic Statute of Virginia for religious freedom, which completely emancipated the consciences of the commonwealth's citizens. Jefferson composed it in such fashion that it comprehended "within the mantle of its protection, the Jew and the Gentile, the Christian and Mahometan, the Hindoo and infidel of every denomination."[70] Both he and his state won immortality in the battle for religious freedom.

CHAPTER IX

SOUTH CAROLINA FROM SHAFTESBURY
TO SALVADOR

CAROLINA owes its origin to the time in 1663 when eight English noblemen, on profit bent, secured a grant of land between Virginia and Spanish Florida. This great tract they proposed to colonize. How else could they make money?

It was not as easy to secure settlers for the southern wilderness as for the more inviting stretches of New England and the Middle Colonies. The proprietors must have recognized that their best prospects were among the dissenters, for their first charter proclaimed that, along with public worship according to the forms of the Anglican Church, the proprietors were ready to make such concessions as they saw fit to nonconformists of good behavior.[1]

A second charter, dating from 1665, went a step farther. It guaranteed that no person should be molested or punished for differences in belief or practice if given indulgence by the proprietors.[2] Neither document required settlers to be Christians or Protestants, but decisions in matters of religion were left completely in the hands of Carolina's owners.

The first faltering policies were terminated in 1669, when Lord Ashley assumed leadership and began to steer

a more determined course. Ashley, later to become the
Earl of Shaftesbury, was an inscrutable politician who
belonged to a different school from the typical courtier
of the Restoration age. He was endowed with a keen mind
and independent judgment, and had a broad sympathy
for religious toleration.

One of the most productive friendships in the history
of English thought developed between him and the
philosopher, John Locke. Out of a fortuitous meeting
in Oxford in 1666 the two men were drawn together,
and Locke became the statesman's confidant and physician. One may see Ashley's influence at work in Locke's
writings.[3] This is particularly true of his *Epistola de
Tolerantia*, which someone has called the most original
of Locke's works,[4] with its plea for the recognition
of absolute liberty.[5]

When Ashley became the head of the enterprise, it
was only natural for him to make his close friend, John
Locke, chief secretary of the company of the lords
proprietors.[6] Accordingly, Locke put on paper "my
lord's" ideas and his own, and the net result was *The
Fundamental Constitutions for the Government of Carolina*
which Locke wrote in his own hand.[7]

The *Constitutions* which were prepared in 1669, with
their seignories and baronies, their landgraves and
caciques, seem to the uninitiated a melange of archaic
concepts. Sixteen of the articles concern matters of
religion, and they make rewarding reading.

The *Constitutions* set up the Church of England
as the established faith, the only one to be supported

by taxes.[8] In the very next article they provided that "seven persons agreeing in any religion shall constitute a church." There are extensive reasons given why this form of liberalism should prevail:

1. The natives were heathens whose lack of Christianity gave the newcomers "no right to expel them or use them ill."

2. It would be unreasonable to keep out any of the prospective settlers who would be of different religous opinions.

3. There should be civil peace and a compact with all men whatever their backgrounds, to avoid offense to God and scandal to the true religion.

4. "Jews, Heathens and other dissenters from the purity of the Christian religion" should obtain a chance to acquaint themselves with its doctrines and "by good usage and persuasion ... be won over to embrace ... the truth."[9]

This article offered as cordial a welcome to Jews as Roger Williams himself might have extended, even if the object was to win them over to Christianity.

The *Constitutions* did not obligate a man to embrace a particular denomination, but they required him to have some religion. Each person above the age of seventeen had to identify himself with a religious group or else forfeit the protection of the law.[10] Atheism as such was under a ban, but all religions were to be respected. "Abusive language against any religion" was forbidden, "that being the certain way of disturbing the peace, and of hindering the conversion of any to the truth."[11]

So much for the religious philosophy of Locke's

Constitutions. The truth is that this fabric of government was never accepted by the settlers of Carolina. Five times the proprietors sought the adherence of the Assembly, but their efforts proved futile on each occasion.[12] A final version of the *Fundamental Constitutions* was proffered as late as 1698 in somewhat abridged form. The same religious conditions as before were in evidence, but the Jews as such were not mentioned.[13]

Shortly afterwards the division of the province into North and South Carolina was achieved. For some time the settlements to the north had suffered because of remoteness from the government at Charleston. In fact, it was easier for them to ship their tobacco by way of Virginia. Isolation bred separatism, until finally the official break was completed in 1712 when Edward Hyde became first governor of North Carolina.[14]

There were practically no Jews in North Carolina during the colonial period.[15] Such as came there lived under a regime with a hateful established church whose treatment of dissenters was harsh. Of more interest to Jews was their struggle for complete emancipation after freedom and statehood had been achieved.[16] This was not entirely realized until 1868 when Jews were permitted to hold office under the state constitution, a product of Reconstruction days.[17]

South Carolina's record, on the other hand, has been outstanding, with its treatment of the Jews more uniformly favorable than that of any other colony where they settled in numbers. Few indeed were the rebuffs faced, while the story of the rights enjoyed by the Jews establishes South Carolina as the first community in the modern world where Jews might vote. It was also the first government where a Jew was elected to office by his Christian neighbors.

The first Jew mentioned was living in South Carolina in 1695, fifteen years after the founding of Charleston. In that year the Yamassee tribe, which was friendly to the English, took four Indians from Spanish Florida their prisoners and brought them to Charleston, where Governor John Archdale had them questioned. The governor wrote: "They could speak *Spanish*, and I had a *Jew* for an Interpreter, so upon examination I found they profess'd the Christian Religion as the Papists do." They were accordingly rescued from the prospect of slavery and sent to St. Augustine.[18] As for the unnamed Jew, he was assumedly Sephardic, and therefore well qualified to translate such Spanish as was spoken by the Indians.

The early Jewish arrivals were a tiny segment of the heterogeneous population of South Carolina, which showed a marked diversity from the beginning. Most conspicuous among the dissenters were the Huguenots who entered the province in large numbers following the revocation of the Edict of Nantes in 1685.[19] By 1700 they numbered one-twelfth of the population.[20] For our study the place of the Huguenots in South Carolina life is important. In their political struggles they served as shock troops in the battle for the rights of aliens. If we search for a clue to explain the enjoyment of civil rights by the Jews of South Carolina on a large scale, it is found in the part played by these French-speaking foreigners.

Unfortunately for the peace of mind of the Huguenots themselves, they plunged into partisan politics. In France these Protestants had fought for the cause of Calvinism; under English rule they associated themselves with the political fortunes of the Anglican Church.[21] It so happened that in South Carolina the dissenters and the Church of England party were pretty evenly matched, so that the Huguenots occupied a key place in the party strife.[22]

Quite understandably the Huguenots as foreigners were in an exposed position and became the butt of agitation by the dissenters. The latter went so far as to question the validity of French marriages and the legitimacy of the offspring of Huguenots. What is more, their opponents insisted that since the French settlers were aliens, their estates would revert to the proprietors upon death.[23]

Of course, the Huguenots appealed to the proprietors in England for support and received a reply that stiffened their resistance. The French settlers, said the authorities overseas, "have Equall Justice wth English men and Injoy the Same Privilidges."[24]

The Huguenots must have listened with satisfaction when Governor Joseph Blake, a Puritan, addressed the Assembly on February 23, 1697, and urged that the lawmakers unify the population by passing various measures that would improve the standing of aliens by securing their estates.[25] A joint committee of both chambers set to work immediately[26] and, by the time the Assembly adjourned on March 10, the act they proposed had become law.[27]

The statute declared that religious persecution had forced some aliens to settle in South Carolina and these people had proved themselves law-abiding and industrious. "All Aliens, male and female, of what nation soever, which now are inhabitants of South Carolina," it declared, should have all the rights of anyone born of English parents.[28]

It is asserted that since certain settlers had come in the hope of securing freedom of conscience, all Christians (Papists excepted) should enjoy full freedom of worship. They were not, however, to disturb the public peace or interfere with the religious services of others.[29]

It should be noted that freedom of conscience was granted only to Protestants, but the full rights of British subjects in all other respects were extended to every alien who applied by petition to the governor within the next three months. Those who became naturalized in this way were required to swear allegiance to the king.[30]

Included with the text of the law were the names of sixty-four men who had already petitioned the General Assembly for the benefits now accorded. The list has a distinct Huguenot flavor except for the four names at the end. The conclusion is as follows: "Simon Vallentine merchant, — [undecipherable] merchant, Jacob Mendis merchant, and Avila merchant."[31]

There is every reason to believe that these were four Jewish merchants, some of whom — probably all — were of Spanish and Portuguese descent. The first of them, Simon Valentine, may be positively identified. Under the name of Simon Valentyn Vander Wilde, a Jew, he was recorded in New York as receiving his burgher right in 1682.[32] His South Carolina naturalization papers too have been preserved. They read in part as follows:

GREETEING

KNOW Yee that Simon Valentine Mercht: an alien of ye Jewish Nation borne out of the Crown of England hath Taken his oath of allegiance to our Sovereign Lord William ye Third . . . And is fully . . . Qualified and Capacitated to have use and Enjoy all the rights Priviledges Powers and Immunityes Given . . . any Alien then Inhabitant of South Carolina . . .

The document is dated May 26, 1697 — two and a half months after the law was enacted — and is signed by the governor, John Blake.[33]

We have a shred of information about Abraham Avilah, one of the other three merchants whose names accompanied Valentine's on the petition. In 1698, Avilah empowered Valentine to serve as his attorney.[34] This lends further probability to the hypothesis that Avilah was Jewish.

The act of naturalization was truly a historic event. Many years were to elapse before 1740 when Parliament would pass its law to naturalize foreign Protestants and Jews in the colonies. We recall that when a similar attempt to naturalize Jewish aliens in England was made in 1753, the act was revoked following furious demonstrations of popular resentment. Note 1697, the year of Jewish naturalization in South Carolina, as a milestone in Jewish history.

A second important right secured by the Jews of South Carolina was the franchise, which was also highlighted by the political battles of the Huguenots. For the mass naturalizations did not end the party struggles, which continued as bitterly as ever.

From the very earliest times, the qualifications of voters had been defined in exceptionally broad terms. The *Fundamental Constitutions* had declared merely that no one owning less than fifty acres of freehold[35] should be able to participate in the election of a member of Parliament, as the General Assembly is there called. In 1692, the Assembly extended the franchise to anyone who would swear that he was worth ten pounds. Although the text has been lost,[36] we know what became of the measure. The proprietors vetoed it, claiming the bill was so loosely worded that even the pirates of the Red Sea would have been qualified to vote in Carolina.[37] If the pirates of the Red Sea might vote, why not the Jews in the province?

The voting situation became a crucial issue as the outgrowth of one of the fights which flourished between the dissenters and the Church of England party. In 1702 there was quite a commotion in the Assembly when the dissenters claimed that Governor James Moore had organized a military expedition against St. Augustine in order to enslave Indians for private gain.[38] At the time, half the members walked out, so that a quorum was lacking to approve the debts incurred during the campaign.[39] Later there was a riot, or rather a brawl, which resulted in one casualty, a woman's miscarriage.[40]

This was all very trivial. But in the tense atmosphere of South Carolina it was deemed sufficiently serious to demand redress from the proprietors in England. Accordingly, one hundred and fifty inhabitants of Colleton County, including Assembly members, gathered together on June 26, 1703, and signed a long address of grievances which they sent to London by John Ash, one of the dissenter leaders. They hoped thus to gain the support of the lords proprietors in the battle against the Anglican party.[41] After describing the course of Governor Moore's troubles and the abortive riot in Charleston, they went on to tell of the election procedures in the province.

They felt that foreigners had infringed on the "fundamental rights & unquestionable Privileges belonging to *English-men*," for no alien, unless properly qualified, should have the right to vote. Yet in the Berkeley County election of November, 1701, aliens, free Negroes and servants had participated.[42]

But things were even worse in the election of 1703.

> For at this last Election, Jews, Strangers, Sailors, Servants, Negroes, & almost every *French* Man in Craven & Berkly County came down to elect, & their Votes were taken; & the Persons by them voted for were returned by the Sheriff, to the manifest wrong & prejudice of other Candidates.[43]

The protest concluded with a passionate appeal for that relief which could not be found in Carolina. "When

Foreigners & Strangers shall make our laws," it declared, ". . . when, in a word, Force is made the Arbiter of all differences, . . . it is surely a time, if ever there be one, for a people to complain."[44]

It goes without saying that the Jewish issue was dragged into the controversy because the Jews were not lined up with the dissenters. Had they voted on the other side, the ballots to which they were entitled by law would have been respected and not denounced. Because they were anxious to confound the governor's followers, the dissenters had to impeach the character of all associated with him.

This same procedure was pursued in a rabid pamphlet, entitled *Affairs in Carolina*, which was begun by John Ash, the representative of the dissenters in London. Death intervened before the work was finished, but Ash got far enough to accuse Simon Valentine, the Jew naturalized in 1697, of serving as go-between for Governor Moore in a shady deal. It concerned the collection of money from John Martin to foster illegal trade with the French at a time when a state of war existed between the two nations.

Ash admitted that he could not prove his charges in a court of law.[45] Mr. Alexander Salley, who edited his pamphlet, stated that the abuse and bias of the brochure rendered it unreliable as a historical source.[46] Ash makes clear, however, which side Valentine (and other Jews) espoused in the great provincial struggle.

After Ash's death, Joseph Boone continued agitation in England on behalf of the dissenters, first before the proprietors and then before the House of Lords.[47] He presented a memorial to that body which described the role of the Jews in the election in almost the same language as Ash had employed.[48] At this time, he engaged England's outstanding public relations counsel of the day, Daniel Defoe. The author of *Robinson Crusoe* turned out a pamphlet called *Party-Tyranny* for the benefit of the two houses of Parliament.[49] There, too, appears the account of the Jewish voters.[50]

While the dissenters were carrying their futile protests to England, the Anglican group at home made reprisals in their own way. In 1704, they passed an act to exclude dissenters from the Assembly by requiring all nonconformist members to receive the sacrament of the Lord's Supper according to the usage of the Church of England. At the same time, Anglican assemblymen were excused from the sacrament altogether.[51]

On November 4, 1704—six months later—the Anglicans had their revenge. They set up a church establishment (quite in harmony with the provisions of the *Fundamental Constitutions*),[52] they passed a new naturalization law, and they authorized new standards for suffrage.

The new naturalization regulations added two restrictions not found in the act of 1697. First, a candidate for naturalization must take the oath of allegiance to Queen Anne and that of abjuration to the house of Stuart "on the Holy Evangelists or otherwise according to the form of his profession." The "otherwise" was the loophole which provided for such exceptions as Jews. The second provision was more significant in that it would not permit naturalized subjects to serve in the Assembly.[53]

The new suffrage requirements demanded that voters be twenty-one years of age, own fifty acres of land or be worth ten pounds, and reside in their precincts for three months.[54] This law allowed aliens to vote as before.

The act to keep dissenters out of the Assembly did not have a long life, for it was based on party vengeance. Repeal was brought about on November 30, 1706.[55]

The election law, however, was not replaced until September 19, 1721. The new statute declared that "every free white man . . . professing the Christian religion" who was at least twenty-one years of age, able to meet the property requirements, might vote after a year's residence in the province.[56]

The same act did not include Christianity among the qualifications for membership in the Assembly, nor was there any Christological phrase in the oaths taken by those elected. But each successful candidate had to be sworn "on the holy evangelists."[57] In addition, each member was expected to take "the usual oaths" and conform to other regulations which were beyond fulfillment by any believing Jew.

There is no evidence to indicate that the Jews were under consideration when this new legislation became effective. There were so few of them in the colony at the time that, in 1723, a full account of the state of religion in South Carolina did not see fit so much as to mention the Jews.[58]

The fact was that a long period elapsed before Charleston might be described as having a Jewish community. We know already of the four Jews who were naturalized in 1697. Barnett Elzas, who wrote on the Jews of South Carolina, found only two additional Jewish names in Charleston during the next thirty-five years.[59] During the thirties of the eighteenth century a thin trickle of Jewish immigrants flowed in and, beginning with 1750, Jewish names occur more frequently in Elzas' catalogue.[60] Many of the newcomers came from England, some of them belonged to the malcontents who abandoned Savannah, and a few, no doubt, sailed to Charleston from the West Indies.

In 1750 the community was large enough to establish a congregation, known as Beth Elohim,[61] which acquired a synagogue during its first decade of existence.[62] Probably this house of prayer was a converted dwelling. At any rate, it was the second synagogue on the North American continent, the first being in New York. In South Carolina there never seems to have been an attempt to bar Jews or any other sect, save Catholics, from worshiping as they pleased.

Isaac Da Costa, who came over from London in 1750, was representative of the community in two important fields of activity: religion, and trade. He was *hazzan* of the congregation, while serving as shipping agent and merchant, dealing in European and Indian goods.[63]

Moses Lindo, probably the most unusual of the Jewish merchants, laid claim to an education at the Merchant Taylor's School in London.[64] He became an expert in indigo and asserted that he had been summoned before Parliament to testify on the qualities of the Carolina product.[65]

In 1756, he removed to Charleston[66] where he exercised his talents as sorter of the indigo which was now being grown in ever increasing quantities, since the British government offered a bounty for the colonial crop.[67] Seventy-four prominent men of South Carolina signed a testimonial which declared Lindo to be the only man qualified to grade the indigo properly, and Governor Thomas Boone (at Lindo's own request) made him "Surveyor and Inspector-General of the Indico" of South Carolina.[68]

There are other examples of Lindo's flair for histrionics. One was his correspondence with the authorities of the College of Rhode Island, to which he promised a munificent endowment if Jewish students were made welcome.[69] Another was the dispatch of a large water sapphire or topaz, purchased for a trifle, to the queen of England, since he deemed one of lesser rank unworthy of so precious a stone.[70] Lindo died in 1774.[71]

Turning from business to the social life of Charleston, we find little if any discrimination against Jews. Moses Solomon became one of the members of St. Andrew's Society, a Scottish social and philanthropic organization to which men of other stocks gained admission.[72] And Isaac Da Costa, the *hazzan*, in 1759, was made treasurer of King Solomon's Lodge, No. 1, the oldest regularly constituted lodge in the Masonry of South Carolina.[73]

There was even a Jewish officer, named Joseph Levy,

commissioned lieutenant in the South Carolina Regiment of Foot in 1757. During the Cherokee War of 1760 and 1761, we find Lieutenant Levy enrolled in Colonel Middleton's South Carolina Regiment.[74] This conflict was a training school for some of the state's heroes of the Revolution. Henry Laurens, William Moultrie, Francis Marion, Isaac Huger and Andrew Pickens were officers who served as comrades in arms with Levy.[75]

During these years the political pattern of South Carolina had been changing. The election law of 1721, which required voters to be Christian, came to be replaced by one in 1745 which raised the property qualifications,[76] and by one in 1759 which made Protestantism a requirement.[77] Maybe the arrival of a contingent of Acadian exiles was responsible for this.[78] Were Jews being deprived of the vote during this period? There is no evidence that they were prevented from casting their ballots, and when we note that one Jew, Francis Salvador, was actually elected to office, we may be sure that any restriction on voting had become a dead letter.

Salvador, who was born in England, belonged to one of the most prominent Jewish families in the country.[79] His grandfather, Francis Salvador, Jr., had been associated with the effort to send Jews to Georgia at the outset of Oglethorpe's undertaking.[80] Young Salvador — he was probably only twenty-six at the time[81] — landed in Charleston, 1773,[82] and set himself up as a planter on some of his family-in-law's land in the Ninety-Six district.[83]

The neighborhood was seething with agitation against Parliament and King George, and Salvador, newcomer though he was, played an active part in the patriot cause. Perhaps he recognized that out on the Carolina frontier a man was rated at his own worth, while across the sea in England all his family's prestige and influence could not wipe away the stigma of being a Jew. At any rate, his district made him their representative to the First and Second Provincial Congress in 1774. There he was named to various committees concerned with the conduct of the war.[84] He was the first Jew in American history, and probably the first Jew in the modern world, to serve in an elective office.

Early in the Revolution, Salvador was slain in a border clash with Indians who had taken the warpath under British instigation.[85] His career was not so much a tribute to the man himself as it was a symbol of the atmosphere of good will which prevailed in South Carolina.

The state of religion that existed there on the eve of the Revolution was almost idyllic, if we may judge by the picture which William Gerard de Brahm painted. De Brahm established a German community at Bethany, Georgia, and built the fortifications of Charleston. His service as surveyor for South Carolina, Georgia and East Florida gave him the background for a descriptive work with the bizarre title of *Philosophico-Historico-Hydrogeography of South Carolina, Georgia, and East Florida.*[86]

Said De Brahm of Charleston:

> The city is divided in two parishes, has two churches, St. Michal's and St. Philip's, and six meeting houses, vidt an Independent, a Presbyterian, a French, a

German, and two Baptist; there is also an assembly
for Quakers, and an other for Jews; all which are
composed of several nations, altho' differing in
religious principels, and in the knowledge of salvation,
yet are far from being incouraged, or even inclining
to that disorder which is so comon among men
of contrary religious sentiments in many other parts
of the world, where that pernicious spirit of controversy has laid foundation to hatred, persecution,
and cruel inquisition, in lieu of ascertaining thereby
how to live a godly life. A society of men (which
in religion, government, and negotiation avoids
whatever can disturbe peace and quietness) will
always grow and prosper: so will this City and Province, whoose inhabitants was from its beginning
renound for concord, compleasance, courteousness,
and tenderness towards each other, and more so
towards foreigners, with out regard or respect of
nation or religion."[87]

This tradition is more glorious than anything in South
Carolina's annals about the craft of a Marion or the
brilliance of a Calhoun, or all the heroism of her sons
during the dark days of the War Between the States.

CHAPTER X

OGLETHORPE'S WARD'S:
LONDON PHASE

THE founding of Georgia was a characteristic expression of the surgent humanitarianism which
marked the eighteenth century. James Oglethorpe, scion
of an old Jacobite family, who fought at Belgrade and
entered Parliament, was suddenly hurtled into fame as
chairman of a committee which disclosed the shocking
conditions existing in the jails of England where rapacious
keepers despoiled those imprisoned and subjected them
to inhuman cruelties.[1] "If this be Law," he said in his
report to the House of Commons, May 12, 1730, "all
England may be made One extended Prison."[2]

Oglethorpe's outcry evoked a sympathetic response
on the part of the British upper classes. He was encouraged to advance a step farther by proposing that something be done to remove a body of newly released debtors
to some far-off spot where they might begin life afresh.
He spoke to his friend, Viscount Percival, of transporting
some of the thousands of starvelings from the streets of
London to America, where farmers and fighters were alike
needed along the French and Indian frontier. Percival
thought it a good scheme.[3]

At that time there were a number of philanthropic

movements afoot in England with the object of serving
Indians, Negroes, and even whites in the New World.
The Rev. Thomas Bray had organized his Associates
for the promotion of Christian knowledge and the propagation of the Gospel in foreign parts. Berkeley, remembered as the bishop-philosopher who prophesied the
westward course of empire, dreamed also of a Christian
college in "the sea girt Bermuda islands" and got the
promise of a government subsidy of twenty thousand
pounds.[4]

Somehow Oglethorpe managed to merge the various
well-meaning groups into one unit which aimed at a
debtor settlement in Carolina. What is more, he secured
control of various liberal endowments, including half
of the government pledge to Berkeley, all for that
precious scheme of his.[5] He entered into protracted
negotiations with the crown and finally, on June 9, 1732,[6]
he secured George II's signature on the charter for "the
Colony of Georgia in America."[7]

In matters of religion the charter was reasonably
liberal. "There shall be a liberty of conscience allowed
in the worship of God to all persons . . . except papists,"
declared the patent.[8] Aside from the current animus
against Catholics in England, we must remember that the
Spaniards were in near-by St. Augustine and Frenchmen
lurked in Mobile. All Catholic settlers would be suspect
as spies.[9]

Nothing was said about propagating the Christian
religion. This was curious, as the phrase occurred in
the charters of other colonies and as the trustees in charge

of Georgia's destinies, men of a religious bias and a philanthropic bent, were drawn from the ranks of Dr. Bray's Associates and Oglethorpe's committee on jails.[10]

The trustees consisted of the twenty men, listed in the charter, who were organized as a corporation.[11] Since the undertaking was a philanthropic venture, none of them was to derive a profit directly or indirectly from their service. Their policies were guided by a spirit of paternalism, a common trait in uplift work. They regarded the settlers as wards of the corporation rather than as individuals responsible for their own governance.[12]

The various trustees differed from each other in the regularity of their attendance at meetings and in the zeal with which they pursued their goal — the relief of the destitute. Other than Oglethorpe himself, the most outstanding member of the body was John Lord Viscount Percival, who was made first earl of Egmont in 1733. By the Georgia charter he was first president of the corporation.[13]

Egmont belonged to a type of peer that was all too rare in the age of Walpole, for he was honorable and conscientious both in public and private life. He was deeply engrossed in the whole Georgia venture and gave considerable time to it. His *Diary*, a faithful mirror of the court life of the period, also gives us a thorough account of the deliberations of the trustees. It furnishes us a far more adequate picture than the brief minutes which were kept.[14]

The sponsors of the new movement sought to achieve

PROCESSING INDIGO IN SOUTH CAROLINA IN THE EARLY DAYS

JAMES EDWARD OGLETHORPE

their main purpose, that of regeneration, by means of a businesslike efficiency. The trustees themselves undertook to sift the ranks of the prospective colonists. Catholics were excluded as a matter of course, but the authorities were strict even with Protestants who were anxious to migrate. Some of the applicants were turned down because they were capable of earning a living at home, others because they failed to get their creditors' consent to sail.[15]

The special darlings of the trustees were the Salzburgers, simple Lutheran peasants, who had been driven from their peaceful valleys by the fury of the ruler, Anton of Firmian, the Catholic archbishop. All Protestant Europe felt compassion for these victims of persecution,[16] and the corporation decided to remove some of them from Frankfort to Georgia and to give them land and free maintenance for a whole year.[17]

Adequate support from government and people alike was required to carry out the ambitious Georgia venture. Accordingly, the trustees, in Professor Crane's words, conducted "a remarkable publicity campaign, designed to 'sell' Georgia to Parliament, to charitable folk, and to intending colonists."[18] With the object of winning the socially-minded of the time, they arranged for the publication of propaganda material in newspapers and in highly colored pamphlets.[19] But they also proceeded to commission a long list of men, in sympathy with the movement, to solicit subscriptions.[20] The canvassing personnel included all ranks of society, from vicars to viscounts and lords. Jews also participated.

Three members of the London Jewish community, Anthony Da Costa, Francis Salvador, Junior, and Alvaro Lopez Suasso, made application to serve as fund-raisers for Georgia. The trustees probably figured that these men would be able to tap resources in Jewish circles which might not be so responsive to other solicitors. At any rate, they seem to have acted in haste, for they subsequently deeply regretted their action on September 21, 1732, of giving sealed commissions to the Jews.[21] The observant Egmont was taking the waters at Bath when this occurred, and so we lack the full details of what transpired. But we do know that, if he had been present, he would have fought the step.[22]

The three newly commissioned fund-raisers were socially prominent and influential bankers who were members of the Spanish-Portuguese community. Francis Salvador was to have a grandson of the same name who would become a patriot hero of South Carolina and perish early in the Revolution.[23] At just that moment, the two other members of the committee were linked to the unsavory breach of promise suit of Philip Da Costa against his cousin, the widowed Kitty Villareal, which was receiving the widest publicity.[24] Kitty's brother was Anthony (alias Moses),[25] and her solicitor was Alvaro Lopez Suasso,[26] who was the brother of Baron Suasso.[27]

Meanwhile, the preparations for establishing the new settlement of Georgia were proceeding apace and Oglethorpe was able to sail from Gravesend, on November 17, with over one hundred prospective colonists aboard the frigate *Ann*.[28] But Da Costa, Salvador and Suasso were not consumed with eagerness to serve the wretched victims of the English jails or the equally unhappy fugitives from Salzburg. They were seeking the solution of a problem that was closer to their hearts — the growing numbers of destitute German and Polish Jews in London who were a drain on the charity funds of the Sephardic community. In addition, the Jewish aristocrats with their Marrano strain resented the very presence of their Ashkenazic brethren, who might have been uncouth in their sight, but who none the less had never compromised their Jewish loyalties.[29] Why not export some of this unwelcome overflow to Georgia?

There were practical difficulties in the way. The trustees were selecting the immigrants carefully and, though German Protestants were invited, in view of the spirit of the time, German Jews would not be equally welcome. It seems probable that the Jewish committee inquired of the corporation whether Jews might also go to Georgia if their own people paid the cost and the trustees assumed no burdens. At any rate, we find Egmont describing the meeting of December 7, 1732, in his *Diary* as follows: "We then had a debate . . . whether we should send any Jews over if they went on their own expense; against which Mr. Vernon and I argued and gave our reasons, but Mr. Towers and Heathcot were for it, so the matter is referred to future consideration."[30]

Both James Vernon and Percival had strong religious convictions. At a later date, Vernon complained that Towers, Heathcote and others were worldly men who showed too little regard for the religious design of the colony.[31] We may appreciate that to the godly the presence of Jews would be a profanation of the Protestant sanctuary of Georgia.

The Jewish canvassers were supposed to place the funds they raised at the disposal of the corporation. In view of the prospective exclusion of the Jews from Georgia, however, they doubtlessly felt justified in allocating the monies collected in such a way that needy Jews might get to Georgia whether the trustees liked it or not.

Meanwhile, on Janurary 17, 1732/3, the trustees considered the problem of the settlement of the Jews anew. This time, Egmont reported, they came to an agreement "that no Jews should be sent," and "the deputations given them to collect should be revoked."[32]

There was more discussion on the same subject two weeks later. Egmont summed up the general sentiment as follows: "We do not think it proper to make a settlement of Jews, and therefore thought it proper to recall those deputations, having heard that they designed their collections for their own use, besides the report of our sending Jews has prevented several from subscribing to us."[33] This last point, no doubt, proved a conclusive argument in determining the exclusion of the Jews.

Benjamin Martyn, secretary of the corporation, was directed to convey the bad news to Messrs. Suasso, Salvador and Da Costa, which he did in a formal letter. It abounded in circumlocutions, but had none of the Chesterfieldian courtliness we associate with missives

of the eighteenth century. He stated he had learned
that, since the canvassers had received their commissions,
"certain Expectations have from thence been raised
contrary to their Intentions, Which may be of ill consequence to their said Designs. Therefore to obviate any
Difficulties, that may attend the same," the trustees
desired the three gentlemen to return their commissions
to Mr. Martyn.[34]

The letter was reinforced by a visit from Martyn
himself[35] which failed to intimidate the Jews. Their response was a request that they might "at least" keep their
commissions until Oglethorpe's return from Georgia.[36]
There the matter rested for the time being.

The trustees were not yet aware that a shipment of
German Jews was already en route to Georgia.[37] And
before Oglethorpe was to leave his newly-founded town
on the river, where the "Landskip" was so agreeable,[38]
still another cargo of Jews would arrive.

After the lapse of two centuries, one can afford to
be philosophical about this conflict between the Jewish
leaders and the corporation. The trustees lived in an
England where Jews were suffered but not respected;
they regarded Georgia as a purely Christian philanthropy;
and they feared a Jewish infiltration would injure the
assets of the colony. The Jews, on the other hand,
were hemmed in by an unreasoning prejudice. Could
they be blamed for side-stepping these barriers when
they themselves bore the costs?

And so forty-three Jews were smuggled out of England
in Janurary, 1732/3. We have no description of their

sailing or their arrival written on the spot, but we do possess the account of the master of their ship, a man named Hanson, as he reported the matter to the trustees the following December, almost a year later.

Now Hanson acquired no fondness for his miserable passengers. He considered them a poor lot, the type that the Jews sent out "to ease their synagogue of them," to use Percival's words.[39] This pretty accurately accounts for the type of Ashkenazim who were then a financial burden on the London community. It does not, however, altogether rule out a sprinkling of Sephardim in the group.

Perhaps the hostile ship captain, Hanson, was not exaggerating when he declared that Oglethorpe was so displeased over the arrival of the Jews that he consulted the lawyers of Charleston "whether he could not send them back, which they advised him he could not," to use Egmont's account. Then "Mr. Oglethorp gave them plots in the town of Savannah."[40] There was nothing like the assignment of land to make a settlement permanent.

A few months after the arrival of the Ashkenazim — on July 11, to be exact—a second group of Jews landed at Savannah. Benjamin Sheftall, who was one of the party, kept a Hebrew record of their experiences, which was translated in part and published in Isaac Leeser's *Occident* over a century ago.[41] The document appears genuine. Certain of its statements have been confirmed by the publication of other material which was not available in Leeser's time.

Sheftall described their hazardous voyage, from the time that their vessel sustained injury in the Thames, through their narrow escape from shipwreck off the coast of North Carolina, down to the time when the forty Jewish immigrants set foot on Georgia soil with their precious *Sefer Torah*.[42] Almost all were Sephardim, although Sheftall was said to be of German descent.[43] He made a list of their names[44] and proudly told his children that these settlers at least had paid their own passage across the ocean.[45]

The outstanding member of the troop was a Portuguese physician named Samuel Nunez. Mordecai Noah, the New York editor and politician who a century later sought glory in the abortive Ararat venture, claimed him as an ancestor and told a dramatic tale of the good doctor's escape from Lisbon and the arm of the Inquisition. It seems that Nunez invited the agents of the Holy Office to his home for a banquet, and then shanghaied them on board a brigantine which also carried the Nunez family and their jewels to safety in England.[46] This is a good story even though probably compounded of family moonshine.

But the truth of Nunez's advent in Georgia is almost as striking as the legend about his departure from Portugal. Oglethorpe described the incident in a letter to Vernon in England, and we have it at second hand in the version given by Egmont in his *Diary*. While the general was away in Charleston, "the people were fallen to drinking of rum,"—I am using Percival's words—"whereby we had lost twenty persons, and their sickness was grown contagious, so that those who attended them, nurses, etc., were all dead, but a ship of forty Jews arriving with a physician, he entirely put a stop to it, so that not one died afterwards."[47] This story verges on the miraculous.

The first tidings of the coming of the Jews to Georgia reached England some time before the trustees were made aware of the exploit of Nunez. It is not clear, however, which shipment of immigrants first came to their attention and moved them to write Oglethorpe as follows on October 18:

> The Trustees have heard with concern of the arrival of Forty Jews with a design to settle in Georgia. They hope they will meet with no sort of encouragement, and desire, Sir, you will use your best endeavours that the said Jews may be allowed no kind of settlement with any of the grantees, the Trustees being apprehensive they will be of prejudice to the Trade and Welfare of the Colony.[48]

A month later news arrived that the skill of Nunez had halted the pestilence. The trustees were no longer so bitter, for, after all, the Lisbon physician had rendered signal service. They still hoped a way might be found to get rid of the Jews in a decent manner, and they wrote Oglethorpe:

> Sir
>
> The Trustees are very much pleased with the Behaviour of the Jewish Physician and the Service he has been to the Sick: As they have no doubt but you have given him some Gratuity for it they hope you

have taken any other Method of rewarding him than
in granting of Lands.[49]

Perhaps they already suspected what they had not yet
had time to learn. Nunez and his shipmates were in
possession of plots of land.[50]

Another month went by in London. On December 15,
the trustees met once again, and this time they listened
to Captain Hanson as he recounted the story of the first
cargo of Jews. It was an unpleasant tale of disagreeable
experiences with the forty-three impoverished voyagers
whose reputations he blackened. "Many of them ran
from their Christian creditors, and none of them would
work when they came there," he declared in Egmont's
account. The concluding statement was as follows: "They
cheated the said Captain, besides eating his provision, so
that he reckons he is about three or four hundred pounds
a loser by them."[51]

As the trustees listened to his embittered report, they
must have pictured a swarm of penniless, ungrateful
spongers descending upon fruitful Georgia like so many
locusts. There was no way for them to learn the other
side of the story, how the Salzburgers and the Anglican
minister, Samuel Quincy, praised them. This was all
to come later.

Action was needed in the crisis. (Who knew? More
Jews might be en route!) The trustees bethought themselves of the commissions once so lightly issued to Messrs.
Suasso, Salvador and Da Costa which had never been
returned. They accordingly resolved, said Egmont,
"to re-demand those commissions."[52]

At the next meeting, which was held a week later, on December 22, the trustees drafted an emphatic letter — virtually an ultimatum — demanding the immediate return of the commissions which had already been annulled. They declared that the commissions had been misapplied to raise monies that enabled certain Jews to go to Georgia. This was not only contrary to the intentions of the corporation, but might be of ill consequence to the colony itself. If the gentlemen did not return their commissions along with a financial statement, their conduct would be advertised to the world.[53] It was an angry communication. "We all resented the Jews proceeding in that matter," wrote Egmont in his *Diary*.[54]

When the trustees met on January 5, 1733/4, they learned of the answer from the three Jews, who stubbornly clung to their repudiated authority. The letter, said Egmont, made "a civil, but trifling excuse for sending some of their nation to Georgia without our knowledge."[55]

The trustees, in reply, wrote that the letter which had been received, "do's not appear satisfactory," and they renewed their old demands, while adding a new one.

> The Trustees do likewise require that the said Messrs Alvaro Lopez Suasso, Francis Salvador Junr, and Anthony Da Costa, or Whoever else may have been concern'd in sending them over, do use their Endeavors, that the said Jews be removed from the Colony of Georgia, as the best and only Satisfaction they can give to the Trustees, for such an Indignity offer'd to Gentlemen acting under his Majesty's Charter.[56]

Two weeks later, on January 19, Martyn, the secretary, was able to report that he had carried the letter to the three canvassers. This time they gave way and returned the commissions, a whole year after the original demand. The trustees then voted to postpone further consideration of the Jewish question until Oglethorpe himself came home.[57]

As time passed, however, they began once more to worry about the Jews. On March 13, the common council of the trustees, a smaller group than the main body, resolved that Thomas Towers should draw up a statement dealing with the Jewish settlement in Georgia. This was to be presented at the next regular meeting,[58] but no further action is reported in the records.

Meanwhile, they sent Oglethorpe a request for an account of the Jews who had settled in his colony, but this communication failed to reach the general while he was in Georgia. He sailed from Savannah ten days after it was written and found a welcome in London like the triumph of a victorious Roman general.[59] He gave the trustees a report on Georgia, and we may be sure that when he touched on the role of the Jews in Savannah his estimate was favorable, for the trustees never committed another hostile act against them.

We notice a certain parallel between the coming of the Jews to Georgia and New Netherland. In both instances they encountered violent opposition. In the one case, however, we recall that the hostility centered in the colony, while in the other the coming of the Jews was fought by the authorities back home until they finally discovered that the Jews were assets.

There was one member of the corporation, Captain Thomas Coram, who remained dissatisfied with the way the Jewish inroad had been handled. He was a hot-tempered, poorly educated old man who once lived at Taunton, Massachusetts. For all his irascibility, he had a good heart, we are told.[60] But he was very difficult to handle, thanks to "his restiveness under opposition and his freedom of expression," in Worthington C. Ford's words.[61]

On March 27, Coram wrote his associates about "two pernicious mistakes" that had been made in Georgia. He was forced to protest in writing, he said, because, due to his want of eloquence, his good intentions had been disregarded in the past. First, he objected to the peculiar law which excluded female offspring from the inheritance of land. Secondly, he was outraged by the unsanctioned settlement of Jews. (More of them were on the way, he asserted.)

> Unless you speedily take some vigorous resolutions to suppress effectually the two great evils aforesaid [he wrote], Georgia will soon become a Jewish colony. All the Christians there will. . . fall off and desert it, as leaves from a tree in autumn . . . except some few carpenters, sawyers, smiths, &c. whom the Jews will find most necessary and useful . . . All Christian benefactions for that colony will soon cease. [He therefore urged his fellow members to avert] the ruin of the colony of Georgia as the reproach and scandal of the trustees.[62]

Coram's written word was as ineffective as his speech. The Jews stayed on, and the inheritance law was not repealed for a time at least. Over a year later, Egmont wrote that Coram had "left our Board in disgust, and prates against us."[63]

In September, 1738, the emigration from Georgia was under way. Coram believed this meant the doom of the colony, and he exulted. It was a pleasure to know, he wrote, that the trustees were seeing his prophecy fulfilled; the inhabitants of Georgia were deserting like leaves from a tree in autumn.[64]

Alas for Coram's triumph, it was short-lived. The migration proved only a passing phenomenon and, once the causes were removed, Georgia resumed its progress.

CHAPTER XI

OGLETHORPE'S WARDS:

GEORGIA PHASE

TWO months after the establishment of the colony of Georgia, General Oglethorpe reported only four hundred inhabitants in Savannah.[1] The two ships of Jews which arrived before the community was five months old brought a total of eighty-three passengers.[2] This was a considerable addition to the population and, although with the passing of time the percentage of Jews declined, they remained too large an element in Georgia's early history to be ignored.

One of the most important steps taken during the early months of Savannah's existence was the assignment of plots of land to the settlers, and visitors must have been impressed when they saw a succession of township lots belonging to Jews on the west side of the town.[3]

The division of land among eighty-five settlers, on July 7, 1733, allowed each one a tract for his house, a plot for his garden, and a farm which amounted to fifty acres.[4] There were no Jewish names on the original list, but twelve of the Portuguese Jews who arrived on July 11 were permitted to share in the allotment.[5] Despite the prejudice of England and the bitter hostility of the trustees, these newcomers were placed on an equal footing with the other inhabitants of Georgia.

The Jews who were named in this document represented only the second group of arrivals, but we know from two other good authorities that the German Jews also enjoyed the benefit of the land grants. First, there is Captain Hanson's irascible report to the trustees that Oglethorpe gave the Jews from his ship plots in the town of Savannah.[6] Secondly, we have testimony from another contemporary source, the *Journal* of the godly John Martin Bolzius, minister of the Salzburgers who settled the town of Ebenezer. (Not only his *Journal*, but also his letters home are a rich mine of information on the Jews who lived in Georgia.)

As we read his description of the coming of these Salzburger exiles to Georgia, we can imagine their feelings as they set foot on this alien soil. As far as the German Protestants were concerned, the language of the English settlers was as incomprehensible as the words of Tomochichi and his Indians. Only the Jews could offer them a welcome in a speech they understood — not the proud Sephardim, of course, but the Ashkenazic Jews who had left the same Germany that they had.

The day after the Salzburgers landed, a Jewish man and his wife entertained them at breakfast where the main dish was a good rice soup.[7] The couple subsequently performed many acts of kindness for which they would take no pay, and the grateful Lutherans set to work clearing the Jews' land of trees and tilling their soil as an expression of appreciation.[8] Let no one say that Jew and German have always been at war!

The human-interest story confirms the fact that the

German Jews were permitted to acquire land. There was another little incident, which seemed to corroborate Hanson's count of forty-three Jewish passengers. Bolzius reported that twelve families of Jews joined them at services.[9] Obviously they were not twelve families of Spanish Jews, but a dozen German households who hungered for the familiar speech of their homeland even though what they heard was an exposition of evangelical Christianity. Elsewhere Bolzius furnished the interesting item that only two of the Jewish families spoke Yiddish.[10]

The pious Salzburgers misinterpreted this gesture of friendliness, and Bolzius wrote in his *Journal*: "We hope we shall preach the Gospel of *Jesus Christ* to these people not without result."[11] A more realistic view was taken by the Rev. Samuel Quincy who had been sent over by the trustees to minister to the English settlers. He wrote concerning the German Jews to Henry Newman, secretary of the Society for the Promotion of Christian Knowledge: "Their kindness show'd to M[r]. Bolzius and the Saltzburgers was Good temper and humanity of the people, and not to any inclination to Change their Religion, as I can understand."[12]

For a time Bolzius had high hopes. He sent for literature written by Professor Johann Callenberg of Halle,[13] who was the guiding spirit at work for the conversion of the Jews of Germany.[14]

The missionary tracts did not work as Bolzius had expected, however, for he later wrote that his efforts to convert the Jews had made them abusive and that they were more stubborn than ever.[15] It is true that one

TRUSTEES OF GEORGIA RECEIVING THE INDIANS

painted by Verelst

Rev. John Martin Bolzius

Jew did express a desire to be baptized, but there is every reason to believe that he was a member of the Portuguese community who was won over by English zealots.[16]

The Jewish farmer who entertained the Salzburgers with the good rice soup was by no means the only one of his people who was attached to the soil. A number of the poor ones also farmed, but, according to Bolzius, the practice of agriculture had little appeal for the Jews. Though they had "indeed pledged themselves to the Trustees . . . to cultivate the land," the well-to-do among them had entered trade. Bolzius added that "others, however, who do not have the riches for it are really badly off."[17] What was the bargain made by the Jews with the trustees which compelled the poorer element to become reluctant planters? Nothing is said of it in Egmont's *Diary* or the records of the trustees.

During the first year of the Jews' settlement some question arose about their rights as landholders. Could a Jew, for instance, lease land and make improvements? This was the problem about which Thomas Causton, keeper of the colony's stores, wrote Oglethorpe on January 22, 1734. It was probably straightened out to the satisfaction of the Jews involved.

One of the Jewish planters, named Abraham de Lyon, had experience as a vigneron in his native Portugal,[18] and his particular skill was much in demand, for the trustees desired to improve viticulture.[19] The trustees, in fact, were so much impressed by reports of his skill that they undertook to give him financial aid. More on that subject later.

There is an enthusiastic account of a visit to the
De Lyon vineyard written by Colonel William Stephens,
who became Secretary for the Trust in Georgia in 1737.[20]
Although the season was December, when there were
no grapes to be seen, Stephens reported that nothing
had given him so much pleasure since his arrival in
Georgia. He quoted "Persons of unquestionable Credit"
who had described huge bunches of grapes "as big as
a Man's Thumb, almost pellucid," which had grown
on the vines in abundance.[21]

The great hopes for the fine vintages which Georgia
would ultimately produce were shared by Samuel Wesley,
oldest brother of the illustrious John. A close friend and
admirer of Oglethorpe, he wrote a poem in the general's
honor which dipped into the future to sample the wines
which Georgia would sell in the markets of Europe. A
sample of his versifying follows:

> Now bid thy Merchants bring thy wine no more
> Or from th' *Iberian* or the *Tuscan* Shore:
> No more they need th' *Hungarian* Vineyards drain,
> And France herself may drink her best *Champain*.
> Behold! At last, and in a subject Land,
> Nectar sufficient for thy large Demand.[22]

Perhaps the spirit of the doggerel would distress some of
the teetotallers among Methodists today.

The newly manifested sympathy of the trustees
towards De Lyon was also expressed in their dealings
with other Jews — Dr. Nunez, for instance. According
to Bolzius, the "old Jew" was appointed physician
by the trustees to treat the people at their own expense.

The German cleric did not seem particularly impressed by Nunez's skill, for while Bolzius acknowledged he spoke Latin fairly well, he added: "He may, however, understand his *artem medicam* badly."[23]

The trustees also made purchases from the Jewish merchants who were established at Savannah and carried on the type of importing and exporting business characteristic of the age. As early as January, 1736, the Corporation was in debt to Messrs. Minis and Solomons to the extent of £ 215.[24]

No longer might the Jews of Georgia complain of a barrier of prejudice and discrimination, and Bolzius was moved to write: "Even the Jews, of whom several families are already in the country, enjoy all privileges the same as other colonists.[25] Among other things, he noted that they had permission to carry "muskets like the others in military style."[26] Perhaps the happy situation in which the Jews now found themselves was to a large extent the result of the reputations they had acquired. The Rev. Samuel Quincy characterized them as follows: "They all in general behave themselves very well, and are industrious in their business."[27]

There were enough Jews for a synagogue, but many years were to pass before one was built. There were two reasons for this neglect. One was the lack of religion that characterized society in general in early Georgia. The other was the deep gulf which separated the two Jewish elements in the population.

No one could question the ungodly spirit which was abroad in Georgia. Successive Anglican ministers who were sent out made the unpleasant discovery that the "best people," including the political leaders, were infidels.[28] Bolzius was shocked by the way the English settlers, without regard for the holiness of the day, hobnobbed with Jews on Sunday. He wrote: "They [the English] drink, play, walk, and pursue all worldly amusements with them [the Jews]; indeed they desecrate Sunday with the Jews, which no Jew whatever would do on his Sabbath to please the Christians."[29]

More than that, Savannah had to wait almost twenty years for its first church of any denomination to be built.[30] The Jews were quite understandably influenced by the apathy in matters religious which prevailed. Besides there was some doubt whether the Jews would have been granted the right to build a synagogue if they and applied for the privilege.[31] A pretty kettle of fish it would have been had the Jews of Savannah owned a house of worship while the Christians neglected to build! How explain that to the powers in London?

Perhaps the Jews might have surmounted the general religious indifference that existed in the community and built a synagogue, were it not for the serious divisions which existed among themselves. The German and Portuguese Jews had little in common. It was not only that they differed in language, in economic status and social background: their religious forms were also at variance and, more than that, their religious attitudes.

The Rev. Samuel Quincy undertook to analyze the two groups. The Germans, he said, were "rigid observers of their Law," but the Portuguese, following their profession of Christianity in Portugal and Brazil, were "more lax in their way, and dispense with a great many of their Jewish Rites,"[32] including, according to Bolzius, the custom of eating kosher meat.[33]

It is conventional to say that the Sephardic Jews were of a nobler mold than their Ashkenazic brethren. According to Quincy this was not so, for he reported that the Germans were "thought the better Sort of them."[34] On the other hand, John Wesley, the founder of Methodism, who spent two unhappy years in Georgia, put in a good word for his Jewish neighbors. He wrote in his *Journal*, on April 4, 1737: "I began learning Spanish, in order to converse with my Jewish parishoners, some of whom seem nearer the mind that was in Christ than many of those who call him Lord."[35]

The bitterness that marked relations between the two groups of Jews was a scandal that even came to the attention of the Christian community. A Jew in Savannah complained to Bolzius in 1738 "that the Spanish and Portuguese Jews persecuted the German Jews [there] so much that no Christian could persecute another like that."[36]

How then could they be expected to worship together and unite in building a synagogue? It appears that the Spanish Jews fought any attempt to work together in petitioning for the purpose.[37] Bolzius wrote in 1739: "The German Jews think themselves entitled to have a synagogue built, and are willing to have the Spanish ones share in its use. The latter, however, do not consent but want the priority."[38]

It must not be thought that, because of the absence of a synagogue, Jewish worship was lacking. Each group had sufficient men for a *minyan* and conducted services according to its own ritual. Bolzius reported in 1738 that the German Jews met in an old miserable cabin "where the men and women are completely separated. A youth who understands a good many languages, particularly Hebrew, is their reader and is paid by them."[39] From Benjamin's Sheftall's account of the coming of the Sephardic contingent, we learn that they determined to open a synagogue in July, 1733. Accordingly, a house on Market Square was rented, and "divine service was regularly performed for years."[40]

The unfavorable religious climate which existed in Georgia was no fault of the trustees, who tried their best to promote godliness, particularly of the Anglican variety.[41] They sent reasonably liberal instructions to the president of Savannah County in 1741, directing him to promote divine worship in accordance with the rites of the Church of England, but to "allow a Free Toleration of all Protestant Dissenters of every Denomination." Moreover, all who pursued their private opinions peaceably were to enjoy freedom of conscience without scrutiny.[42]

The trustees favored the Salzburgers[43] and encouraged the Scottish Presbyterians.[44] The Moravians, on the other hand, were not hospitably received because of their opposition to military service, and at length they withdrew to Pennsylvania.[45] In practice, the Catholic religion was under a ban, since the Spanish frontier was too near for it to be suffered. Judaism, as we have seen, was undisturbed.

Georgia may have been indifferent to religion, but there was a fierce passion seething in the cauldron of politics. Men resented the remote control of the trustees; they resented the mismanagement of an important functionary, Thomas Causton, the storekeeper; they resented likewise the conduct of Oglethorpe himself. A great outcry was raised over the unfortunate land regulations, the unique ban on rum in the colony, and the prohibition against Negro slavery which the trustees believed would destroy the opportunities for white labor.[46]

A lengthy protest, drawn up and signed by freeholders in 1738, catalogued their woes in a pamphlet entitled "A True and Historical Narrative of the Colony of Georgia." It pointed out that "only a very few of the General's Favorites" plus the contented Salzburgers declined to sign. The sponsors themselves would not permit widows and orphans to participate as they were not considered proper judges. "The *Jews*," they declared, "applied for Liberty to sign with us; but we did not think it proper to join them in any of our Measures."[47]

It is true that the malcontents would not accept Jewish participation in their movement, but none the less they did not hesitate to cite an instance where a Jew was dealt with unfairly when they thought it would buttress their cause. Reference has already been made to the fact that the trustees had advanced some money to Abraham de Lyon for the purpose of promoting viticulture. They voted him two hundred pounds, which they sent to General Oglethorpe, then in Georgia, with instructions to give the vigneron that sum on receipt of the proper guarantees. Quite characteristically, Oglethorpe followed orders only as far as he saw fit. According to the pamphleteers, he offered De Lyon only twenty or thirty pounds, because the "Perpetual Dictator"[48] had other uses for the money. As a result, it was claimed that the vinegrower abandoned his project of importing forty thousand vines for sale to planters.[49]

As a matter of fact, Oglethorpe actually advanced half of the trustees' loan to De Lyon.[50] Still, a hundred pounds were withheld. We may, indeed, be sure that if the enemies of Oglethorpe had had the correct information the fury of their attack would not have been lessened.

What gave the political agitation such force was the unhappy economic conditions which prevailed in Georgia. To the harried settlers the fields of South Carolina with slaves doing the heavy work seemed far more attractive than the hardships at home. Accordingly, around 1739 and 1740, a heavy tide of emigration developed in which the Jews played a prominent part. At one time, the exaggerated report reached England that every last Jew had gone.[51]

In the midst of this crisis the trustees were forced to capitulate on such issues as rum, slaves and land ownership. The flow of migration now streamed back from South Carolina, Jews included. By the time 1752 came around and the charter of the trustees expired, the province was getting on its feet again. Georgia now became a royal colony.[52]

Under the new dispensation very much the same system prevailed as in other colonies of the king. As far as religion was concerned, the instructions sent the governor authorized liberty of conscience for every well-behaved person, except Papists.[53] Meanwhile, Geogia moved in the direction of church establishment.

The trend was evident in a law of 1758 which provided for the division of the colony into parishes and the establishment of religious worship "according to the Rites and Ceremonies of the Church of England." Furthermore, church wardens and vestrymen were authorized to levy taxes for the repair of their churches and other religious purposes.[54] A prime mover for this act was the converted Italian Jew, Joseph Ottolenghe, who became a zealot of the Anglican Church.[55]

On the whole, the nonconforming denominations were not disturbed, but much of the religious controversy that did develop centered on the matter of burials. The Jews of Savannah, for example, began to worry about the limits of their cemetery. In 1762 they sent a petition to the Lower House which recalled the fact that, when the earliest Jewish settlers had been given a burial plot, its extent was not adequately defined. The Jews therefore petitioned for a specific allotment which would include both the section already in use and an extension of it. They further desired, once this grant should be obtained, to surround it with a fence.

No action was taken by the House; the petition was tabled.[56]

Meanwhile the dissenters were having trouble over their funerals. Samuel Frink, the rector of Christ Church, it seems, used to demand a fee for the tolling of his church bell at the time of the last rites. On such occasions, even when the bell remained mute, Frink expected this exaction to be paid.[57] At length, John Zubly, who was minister of the Presbyterian Church of Savannah, rebelled at Frink's tyranny, and on March 27, 1770, he petitioned the Upper House for a part of the Savannah common to be used by dissenters as a cemetery.[58] After hearing the arguments of Zubly and the intolerant Mr. Frink, the lawmakers postponed further discussion of the bill until June 1. No session was reported on that day and of course the measure died.[59]

The Jews were rash enough to choose this season to revive their own cemetery claims, seven years after their previous petition had failed. The new suit followed the same approach. It reminded the Lower House that in 1733 General Oglethorpe had given their forebears a lot for the burial of the dead. The House was asked to confirm the original allotment and to assign the Jewish community as much land as was deemed proper.[60] On April 6, 1770, the lower chamber passed an act which granted the Jews part of the common for burial purposes.[61]

This was just a week after the Upper House had finished with Zubly's bill for dissenters, and the furor over the nonconformists' claims had not yet died down, we may be sure. When the Jews' bill was sent to the Upper House for action, the opponents of the measure took steps to defeat it.

The day after the affirmative action of the Lower House certain freeholders of Savannah presented a memorial to the Upper House protesting against the Jews' proposal. The tenor of this document reflected an unkindly feeling towards Jews which perhaps existed in wide circles.

"The few Inhabitants of Savannah who professed the Jewish Religion," it stated, could not prove by any record that Oglethorpe had ever allotted them a burial ground. The memorialists were apprehensive that, if the bill became law, it would have "very detrimental Consequences," as the site desired would block the extension of the town in a southerly direction. Its acquisition by the Jews would also depreciate property values, "as they apprehend no Person would choose to buy or rent an House whose Windows looked into a Burial Ground of any kind particularly one belonging to a People who might be presumed from Prejudice of Education to have imbibed Principles entirely repugnant to those of our most holy Religion."[62]

The Upper House took cognizance of the conflicting sentiments concerning the Jewish cemetery and they decided to refer the bill to a committee of the whole House,[63] which met on April 11. Several amendments were made. The same tactics that had killed Zubly's bill were now used against this cemetery measure. Discussion of the revised bill was postponed until the session on

June 2.[64] It appears that there was no meeting on that date, however, and so the bill died.

One of Zubly's letters voices the anger he felt at the time he was defeated in his attempt to secure a burial ground.[65] We may only surmise the bitterness in the Jews' hearts.

There was no use waiting indefinitely for the authorities to grant them a section of the common land for the enlargement of the cemetery. In August, 1773, Mordecai Sheftall gave them a five-acre plot for that purpose. It was conveyed to ten trustees, all merchants — two in Savannah, two in Charleston, two in New York, two in Newport and two in London. Sheftall provided that the land should serve forever as a burial place "for all persons *whatever* professing the Jewish religion," and as a site for a future synagogue.[66]

Some years had elapse befored the Savannah community was ready for a synagogue. In 1774, however, the Jews found themselves sufficiently numerous to form a congregation which met in the home of Mordecai Sheftall.[67]

It would be a pleasant task to wipe out the bad impression of community relations conveyed by the cemetery episode with a retelling of the well-known story of the founding of the Union Society in 1750. Unfortunately this tale of the Protestant, Catholic and Jew who banded together to take care of the orphans in their midst is not history but legend. The earliest reference to the tradition appears in an oration made in 1833,[68] and, despite the good intentions of the speaker, an address made after the lapse of eighty-three years is without any value as source material.

There was indeed a bright side to Jewish life in Georgia. Religion was no bar to their holding of office, and we know that Daniel Nunez, son of the Portuguese physician of early days, was made waiter of the port of Savannah in 1765 by a vote of both houses of the Assembly,[69] while Moses Nunez served as searcher of the port in 1768.[70]

We find the name of Moses Nunez included among the list of officeholders taking the oaths of allegiance and supremacy. The old oaths required each man to swear "upon the faith of a Christian."[71] This was enough to disqualify any believing Jew. Yet Jews held office. We may assume that the same practice, of exempting Jews from the unacceptable sections of oaths, that prevailed in eighteenth-century New York,[72] was in force in Georgia.

Two other Jewish names are included among the officeholders who took the oaths of allegiance and supremacy to George III between 1766 and 1774. One of the men was David Emanuel, who was installed as justice of the peace for St. George Parish in 1766.[73] The other was James Lucena, who filled the same post in the Parish of Christ Church in 1773.[74]

All this time James Oglethorpe was still living in England. He had played an important part in establishing Georgia during the rule of the trustees; he had witnessed the steady progress of the colony under its royal governors. In the period of the American Revolution he was actually something of a sympathizer of the rebellious colonies.[75] He lived even to call on John Adams when the latter came as American minister to the Court of St. James.[76]

One wonders if Oglethorpe, as he scanned the news from Georgia in 1766, let his eyes fall on the name of David Emanuel, justice of the peace for St. George Parish. Perhaps he recalled those early days when the Jews had first appeared, and the trustees tried in vain to drive them out. Perhaps — a most unlikely "perhaps," indeed — he closed his eyes and foresaw the day in 1801 when the impossible happened and David Emanuel became governor of Georgia, the first Jew to hold such an office in the history of the United States.[77]

CHAPTER XII

L' ENVOI

IT IS almost two centuries now since the United States
emerged from the chrysalis of colonial life. The nation
is no longer a string of colonies fringing a narrow coast
line, for it not only straddles a continent, but is also
one of the great powers dominating the world. Whatever
may be said of the might and wealth of America, the glory
of this land is in the moral force of its political philosophy
which today represents an ensign of hope to a world
wearied by the shibboleths of fascism and reaction.

This spiritual element is not a thing newly created.
Much as technics have advanced since the days of
Washington, the essential American ethic remains un-
changed since the richly creative eighteenth century.
The retorts of the colonial laboratory distilled the doctrine
of the rights of man as master of his own conscience,
recognizing that one's religious dogma was a personal
matter between oneself and the Master of the universe.
It declared that an individual's religious loyalties were
not in conflict with the exercise of his duties as citizen,
and this divorce between civil rights and religious beliefs
is a characteristically American contribution to the
world's progress.

We in the United States have established a standard,

have created an ideal. And yet it would be dishonest to paint the interplay between the various racial and religious components of our nation with a Utopian brush. In many quarters there is a sharp contrast between the formulation of America's social philosophy and that same philosophy in action. In fact, it would be fair to say that two conflicting principles have been at war for America's soul. We may aptly quote Goethe's Faust:

Zwei Seelen wohnen, ach! in meiner Brust;
Die eine will sich von der andern trennen.

These two contrasting forces have been tribal fanaticism and neighborly understanding. One has worked through the lynching, the tar bucket and the hooded mob. It has preached suspicion and hate of Negro and Jew, of Catholic and alien. Nourished on greed and envy, it has contributed no heroes to the national pantheon and has inspired no monuments of stone.

Its influence, however, has persisted through the years. In colonial days, the fanatical anti-Catholic spirit of the thirteen colonies so alienated the French majority of Canada that they remained loyal to the King during the Revolution, and, as a result, the Maple Leaf banner flies over the Dominion instead of the American flag. A century ago, agitators in various cities inflamed mobs to burn down Catholic churches and convents. And today we see old patterns of hate whipped into new forms, until certain areas of American life are torn by a religious bigotry from which the Jew has by no means escaped.

The opposite genius of the American people has
functioned through the ringing tones of the Declaration
of Independence, the Constitution and the Bill of Rights.
Its symbol has been the Statue of Liberty, its instrument
the public school. It has been defined by a host of heroes
whose names include Washington and Jefferson, Lincoln
and Franklin D. Roosevelt. This is the America we love,
for whose security our men go out to die. This is the
America which is the hope of mankind.

An old newspaper account describes the celebration
of Independence Day in Philadelphia when the Constitutional Convention was gathered there in 1787. Because
of the import of the day and the prominence of the
delegates assembled, a special observance was in order.
Accordingly, a great parade was organized, and the
committee on arrangements noted that this was the
first time Philadelphia had seen "the clergy of different
Christian denominations with the rabbi of the Jews,
walking arm in arm."[1] That same quality has carried
through in American life. Not only have Jewish and
Christian ministers marched arm in arm through the
years, but the laymen have also gone forward together
as citizens devoted to a common cause. Nowhere has
this been more in evidence than marching down the road
into Germany and storming the defenses of Okinawa.

When the colonies first recognized the Jew as a man
and an equal, they made a covenant in the heavens
for justice and brotherhood. That covenant is still
remembered.

May it never be forgotten.

NOTES TO CHAPTER I.

[1] Infra, 49 f.
[2] Cecil Roth, *A History of the Jews in England*, 57.
[3] Ibid., 166.
[4] Ibid., 171.
[5] H. S. Q. Henriques, "Proposals for Special Taxation of the Jews after the Revolution," *Transactions of the Jewish Historical Society of England*, IX, 48.
[6] Roth, 176.
[7] Ibid., 179 f.
[8] Ibid., 182 f.
[9] Ibid., 215 ff.
[10] *Statutes of the Realm*, V, 246.
[11] *Journals of the House of Commons*, VIII, 468.
[12] Ibid., VIII, 480.
[13] Herbert Friedenwald, "Material for the History of the Jews in the British West Indies," *P. A. J. H. S.*, V, 63 f.
[14] Ibid., V, 64.
[15] N. D. Davis, "Notes on Jews of Barbados," *P. A. J. H. S.*, XVIII, 133 ff.
[16] Wilfred S. Samuel, *Jewish Colonists in Barbados*, 9, note b.
[17] Friedenwald, *P. A. J. H. S.*, V, 97.
[18] Samuel, 9.
[19] Charles Gross, "Documents from the Public Record Offices," *P. A. J. H. S.*, II, 169.
[20] Law of 1711. Friedenwald, *P. A. J. H. S.*, V, 90.
[21] Ibid., V, 89 f.
[22] George F. Judah, "The Jew's Tribute in Jamaica," *P. A. J. H. S.*, XVIII, passim.
[23] Rosendale, "An Act Allowing Naturalization of Jews in the Colonies," *P. A. J. H. S.*, I, 94.
[24] Ibid., I, 96.
[25] Ibid., I, 96 f.
[26] J. H. Hollander, "Naturalization of Jews Under the Act of 1740," *P. A. J. H. S.*, V, 108 f.

NOTES TO CHAPTER II.

[1] *Harvard College in the 17th Century*, 200.
[2] Except at Glasgow for a brief period.
[3] *Harvard College in the 17th Century*, 200.
[4] *Magnalia Christi Americana*, I, 560.
[5] Ibid., I, 205.
[6] Andrews, *The Colonial Period of American History*, I, 487.
[7] Shurtlieff, *Records of Massachusetts*, III, 159.
[8] *Records of Quarterly Courts of Essex County, Massachusetts*, IV, 87.
[9] Ibid.
[10] *First Report of the Record Commissioners of the City of Boston*, 29.
[11] Friedman, *Jewish Pioneers and Patriots*, 281 ff.
[12] A variant of Baruch.
[13] *Records of the Suffolk County Court*, II, 624.
[14] Professor Zechariah Chafee, Jr., who apparently did not know that Gideon was a Jew living in Boston, cites the case as an example of a non-resident plaintiff making an appeal for justice (*Records of the Suffolk County Court*, I, xci).
[15] *Massachusetts Historical Collections*, IV, 9, 159.
[16] Cobb, *The Rise of Religious Liberty in America*, 230 ff.
[17] "Charter of Massachusetts Bay," *Publications of the Colonial Society of Massachusetts*, II, 19.
[18] Ibid., II, 22.
[19] *The Hutchinson Papers*, I, 174.
[20] Dow and Edmonds, *Pirates of the New England Coast*, 1630–1730, 34 ff.
[21] Four Boston Jews contributed to the building of a new synagogue in New York. D. de Sola Pool, *The Mill Street Synagogue*, 71.
[22] Friedman, *Early American Jews*, 8.
[23] *Massachusetts Historical Society Collection*, Series 5, XI, 95.
[24] Friedman, 156.
[25] Ibid., 155.
[26] *Report of the Boston Record Commissioners*, XXIX, 234.
[27] Ibid., VIII, 151 f.
[28] Friedman, 7.
[29] Moore, "Judah Monis," *Massachusetts Historical Society Proceedings*, LII, 285 ff.
[30] Friedman, "Judah Monis," *P. A. J. H. S.*, XXII, 1.
[31] Moore, LII, 288.
[32] Lebowich, "The Jews in Boston till 1875," *P. A. J. H. S.*, XII, 102.
[33] Ibid., XII, 102 ff.

³⁴ "Harvard College Records," Part I, *Publications of the Colonial Society of Massachusetts*, XV, 93.

³⁵ Moore, LII, 291.

³⁶ Ibid., LII, 294.

³⁷ Ibid., LII, 301 f.

³⁸ Friedman, "Judah Monis," *P. A. J. H. S.*, XXII, 21 f.

³⁹ Friedman, *Early American Jews*, 39.

⁴⁰ Willard, "Naturalization in the American Colonies," *Massachusetts Historical Society Proceedings*, 1858–1860, 342.

⁴¹ Franklin Dexter (ed.), *Itineraries of Ezra Stiles*, 52.

⁴² Infra, 51 ff.

⁴³ Percy A. Scholes, *The Puritans and Music*, ch. II.

⁴⁴ McKinley, *Suffrage Franchise in the English Colonies*, 389 f.

⁴⁵ Session of Gen. Court, Sept. 18, 1649, *Public Records of Connecticut*, I, 197.

⁴⁶ Gen. Court of Election, May 16, ibid., I, 207.

⁴⁷ Gen. Court, July 11, ibid., I, 261.

⁴⁸ Nov. 9, *Connecticut Colonial Records*, I, 343.

⁴⁹ Josiah Benton, *Warning Out in New England*, 63.

⁵⁰ Court of Elec., May 17, *Public Records of Connecticut*, I, 351.

⁵¹ Benton, 85 ff.

⁵² His name is frequently mentioned in the records: See *Connecticut Hist. Soc.*, VI, 121, 154, 166, 180, 195, etc.

⁵³ Ibid., VI, 135.

⁵⁴ Ibid., XXI, 196.

⁵⁵ *Connecticut Colonial Records* — N. E.: Records of the Court of Assistants, 1669–1701, 7, Ms. in Connecticut State Library.

⁵⁶ *Public Records of the Colony of Connecticut*, II, 144.

⁵⁷ Infra, 87 f., 89 f., 94 f.

⁵⁸ *Public Records of the Colony of Connecticut*, II, 144.

⁵⁹ Infra ch. VIII, passim.

⁶⁰ *Public Records of the Colony of Connecticut*, VI, 526.

⁶¹ Franklin B. Dexter, *Biographical Sketches of the Graduates of Yale College*, III, 700.

⁶² Infra, 48 f., 52, 54 f.

⁶³ From the *Itinerary*, quoted in *Diary of Ezra Stiles* (Dexter, ed.), I, 283.

⁶⁴ Ibid.

⁶⁵ *Public Records of Colony of Connecticut*, VII, 554.

⁶⁶ Ibid., XIII, 360.

⁶⁷ Ibid., VII, 107, 237, 257,

⁶⁸ *Connecticut Public Acts*, Oct., 1842, p. 41.

⁶⁹ Article 6, *Revised Laws of New Hampshire*, 1942, 6.

NOTES TO CHAPTER III.

[1] *The Colonial Mind*, 62.

[2] James Ernst, *Roger Williams*, 244.

[3] Ibid., 245.

[4] Ibid., 429.

[5] Clarence Saunders Brigham, *The Fourth Paper Presented by Maj. Butler*, xxii.

[6] Ibid., 19.

[7] Ibid.

[8] Ibid., 18.

[9] *Records of the Colony of Rhode Island*, I, 374 ff.

[10] Report of George Carr, *Calendar of State Papers, Colonial Series, 1661–1668*, 343.

[11] Infra, 77, 79 f.

[12] Letter to Classis of Amsterdam, August 14, 1657, *Ecclesiastical Records of the State of New York*, I, 400.

[13] Ernst, 443.

[14] Samuel Arnold, *History of Rhode Island*, I, 103.

[15] Poore, *The Federal and State Constitutions*, part II, 1596 f.

[16] *Records of the Colony of Rhode Island*, II, 110, 113.

[17] Letter of 1654–5, *Publications of Narragansett Club*, VI, 278 f.

[18] Howard Preston, *Rhode Island and the Sea*, 7.

[19] Preston, Chapin and Moriarty, *Letter Book of Peleg Sanford*, passim.

[20] Wilfred Samuel, "Review of the Jewish Colonists of Barbados," *Transactions of the Jew Hist. Soc. of England.*, XIII, 63 ff.

[21] "Lyons Collection" *P. A. J. H. S.*, XXVII, 416.

[22] Samuel Oppenheim, "The Jews and Masonry," *P. A. J. H. S.*, XIX, 10 ff.

[23] Melvin Johnson, *Beginnings of Free Masonry in America*, 44 ff.

[24] Facsimile in *Lyons Collection P. A. J. H. S.*, XXVII, facing p. 175.

[25] Samuel, "Review of the Jewish Colonists in Barbados in the Year 1680," *Transactions of the Jew. Hist. Soc. of England*, XIII, 26.

[26] Supra, 7.

[27] *Records of the Colony of Rhode Island*, III, 160.

[28] "Barbados," *Jewish Encylopedia*, II, 523.

[29] John Austin, *Genealogical Dictionary of Rhode Island*, 290, 292. Dyer's will also identifies his father as William Dyer (husband of Mary). See Henry Waters, "Genealogical Gleanings in England," *New England Historical and Genealogical Register*, XLIII, 144.

[30] Warrant of the Duke of York to Sir Allen Apsley, Brodhead, *Documents Relative to the Colonial History of the State of New York*, III, 214.

[31] Commission of William Dyer as collector at New York, ibid, III, 221 f.

[32] Proceedings against Mr. Dyer, ibid., III, 289.

[33] Court of Assizes at New York to the Secretary of State, ibid., III, 287.

[34] Report discharging Mr. Dyer, Sept. 30, 1682, ibid., III, 321.

[35] Certificate of Dyer's appointment, Jan. 4, 1683. *Records of Massachusetts Bay*, V, 530.

[36] Simon Bradstreet to Edward Randolph, Dec. 8, 1684: Toppan, *Edward Randolph*, III, 337; Dyer to Sir Leoline Jenkins, Sept. 12, 1684: Fortescue (ed.), *British Colonial Papers*, 1681–1685, 685.

[37] Letter from Gov. Dongan of New York to Blathwayt, May 12, 1686: Goodnick, *Edward Randolph*, VI, 166, n. 282.

[38] Dyer to Sir Leoline Jenkins, Sept. 12, 1684: *British Col. Papers*, 1681–1685, 685.

[39] Transcript of suit, Lyons Collection, *P. A. J. H. S.*, XXVII, 175 f.

[40] *Rhode Island Col. Records*, III, 243.

[41] Sidney Rider (ed.), *Charter and Acts and Laws of Rhode Island, 1719*, 3.

[42] Joseph Felt, *Ecclesiastical Hist. of New England*, II, 395.

[43] *Rhode Island Col. Records*, II, 184.

[44] Ibid.

[45] *Col. Period of American Hist.*, IV, 61.

[46] Introduction to *Charter and Acts and Laws of Rhode Island, 1719*, [15] f.

NOTES TO CHAPTER IV.

[1] It is significant that when the New York Jewish congregation was erecting its synagogue in 1729, four Boston Jews contributed, while nothing was forthcoming from Newport (D. de Sola Pool, *The Mill Street Synagogue*, 71 f.). Thirty years later, after the Newport Jewry had revived, the New Yorkers sent them £149 in cash for their synagogue building project, besides other gifts (ibid., 40).

[1a] "Ezra Stiles" in *Dict. of Am. Biography*, XVIII.

[2] George Alexander Kohut, *Ezra Stiles and the Jews*, passim.

[3] *Literary Diary of Ezra Stiles*, III, 77.

[4] Ibid., I, 399 f.

[5] So described on the title page of his sermon, *The Salvation of Israel*, published in Newport in 1773.

[6] Franklin Dexter (ed.), *Itineraries of Ezra Stiles*, 384.

[7] *Diary*, I, 11 n.

[8] Ibid., I, 11.

[9] Samuel Arnold, *History of Rhode Island*, II, 333 n.

[10] Mss. of 1774 Census of Newport, R. I., State Archives, Providence.

[11] Max Kohler, "The Jews in Newport," *P. A. J. H. S.*, VI, 75.

[12] "The Graves at Newport," XXXIX, 375.

[13] Anita Lebeson, *Jewish Pioneers in America*, 92.

[14] Elizabeth Donnan, *Documents Illustrative of the History of the Slave Trade*, III, Section on Rhode Island, passim. A good sample is on 21 f.

[15] Arnold, *History of Rhode Island*, II, 447 n.

[16] *Commerce of Rhode Island*, I, 88–92, 97–100.

[17] Naturalization may have taken place early in 1741. Huhner, "Naturalization of Jews in New York under the Act of 1740," *P. A. J. H. S.*, XIII, 6.

[18] John Bartlett, *Records of Colony of Rhode Island*, V, 307 f.

[19] Ibid., V, 375 f.

[20] Bruce Bigelow, "Aaron Lopez," *New England Quarterly*, IV, 757.

[21] Ibid., IV, 772.

[22] *Commerce of Rhode Island*, I, 92.

[23] *New England Quarterly*, IV, 764.

[24] *Diary*, III, 24.

[25] Harold Korn, "Documents Relative to the Estate of Aaron Lopez," *P. A. J. H. S.*, XXV, passim.

[26] *Diary*, III, 24.

[27] *Records of the Colony of Rhode Island*, XV, 262, 267.

[28] Stiles is our only source for these facts. *Itineraries*, 52.

[29] Lopez Ms. papers, Newport Historical Society.

[30] Ibid.

[31] *Itineraries*, 52 f.

[32] Ibid., 52.

[33] Ibid., 53.

[34] Perhaps Stiles confused the issues in the Philipse-Van Horn contest. Vide infra, 111 ff.

[35] *Itineraries*, 53.

[36] Arnold, II, 495.

[37] Ibid.

[38] Lloyd to Lopez, March 29, 1762. Lopez Mss. of Newport Historical Society.

[39] Written September 13, 1762. Lopez Mss.

[40] Written August 13, 1762. Lopez Mss.

[41] Huhner, "Naturalization of Jews in New York," *P. A. J. H. S.*, XIII, 6.

[42] Lee M. Friedman, *Jewish Pioneers and Patriots*, 144.

43 *Diary*, I, 377.
44 Ibid., I, 391 f.
45 Walter Bronson, *The History of Brown University*, 3 f.
46 Ibid., 506.
47 Ibid.
48 Ibid., 36.
49 Ibid., 31.
50 Ibid., 48.
51 Reuben Guild, *History of Brown University*, 224 f.
52 N. Taylor Phillips, "Family History of David Mendez Machado,"
P. A. J. H. S., II, 52.
53 Leon Huhner, "The Jews of South Carolina from the Earliest
Settlement to the End of the American Revolution," *P. A. J. H. S.*,
XII, 44 f.
54 Guild, 223.
55 That.
56 Their.
57 The.
58 The letter is from the Brown Archives in the John Carter Brown
Library of Providence.
59 Charles Robinson, *Register of the Merchant Taylors' School*.
60 Letter to the writer from Merchant Taylors' School, Sandy Lodge,
Northwood, Middlesex, England, October 14, 1940. It has been suggested that the Lindo brothers may have attended the Merchant
Taylors' School under assumed names.
61 Walter Bronson, *The History of Brown University*, 98.
62 Ms., Brown University Archives.
63 Bronson, 98.
64 Ibid.
65 Ibid., 98 f.
66 Ibid., 99.
67 Ibid., 511.

NOTES TO CHAPTER V.

1 E. B. O'Callaghan, *History of New Netherland*, II, 540.
2 Reproduction of Danckers' etching of New Amsterdam about
1650. Frontispiece to *New Amsterdam and Its People*, by J. H. Innes.
3 Alexander Flick (ed.), *History of the State of New York*, I, 298.
4 Edward Channing, *A History of the United States*, I, title of chapter XVIII.
5 J. F. Jameson, *Narratives of New Netherland*, 337 ff.

⁶ *Documents Relative to the Colonial History of the State of New York*, I, 123.

⁷ F. J. Zwierlein, *Religion in New Netherland*, 6.

⁸ Ibid., 2.

⁹ Letter of the Revs. Megapolensis and Drisius to classis of Amsterdam, Oct. 6, 1653. *Ecclesiastical Records of New York*, I, 318.

¹⁰ Letter to Stuyvesant, Mar. 12, 1654. *Documents . . . of New York*, XIV, 252.

¹¹ Letter of the Revs. Megapolensis and Drisius to classis of Amsterdam, Oct. 6, 1653. *Ecclesiastical Records*, I, 317.

¹² Ibid., I, 318.

¹³ Letter to Stuyvesant, June 14, 1656. *Documents . . . of New York*, XIV, 351.

¹⁴ Letter to Stuyvesant, Mar. 12, 1654. Ibid., 252.

¹⁵ Petition to Governor and Council, Oct. 24, 1656. *Ecclesiastical Records*, I, 359.

¹⁶ Act of classis of Amsterdam, Apr. 10, 1657. Ibid., 374.

¹⁷ Letter of the Revs. Megapolensis and Drisius to classis of Amsterdam, Aug. 5, 1657. Ibid., I, 393.

¹⁸ Act of classis of Amsterdam, Apr. 10, 1657. Ibid., 374.

¹⁹ Letter of the Revs. Megapolensis and Drisius to classis of Amsterdam, Sept. 10, 1659. Ibid., 449.

²⁰ Patent of Maspeth. O'Callaghan, *History of New Netherland*, I, 425. Zwierlein, *Religion in New Netherland*, 155 f.

²¹ Zwierlein, 144 ff.

²² Ibid., 144.

²³ Letter of the Revs. Megapolensis and Drisius considered by Stuyvesant and Council, Jan. 15, 1656. *Documents . . . of New York*, XIV, 336 f.

²⁴ Council Minute, Feb. 1, 1656. *Ecclesiastical Records*, I, 343 f.

²⁵ Minutes of Council, Nov. 8 and 11, 1656. *Documents . . . of New York*, XIV, 369 f.

²⁶ Brodhead, *History of the State of New York*, I, 637.

²⁷ O'Callaghan, *History of New Netherland*, II, 348 ff.

²⁸ Brodhead, I, 526.

²⁹ Zwierlein, 242 f.; *Documents . . . of New York*, XIV, 526.

³⁰ Letter from directors to Stuyvesant, Apr. 4, 1652. *Documents . . . of New York*, XIV, 172.

³¹ Letter to Stuyvesant, Mar. 21, 1651. Ibid., 135.

³² Letter to director of West India Company from Department of Amsterdam, June 6, 1653. G. H. Cone, "The Jews of Curaçao," *P. A. J. H. S.*, X, 150.

³³ Letter from Vice-Director Rodenburch to directors, Apr. 2, 1654. Ibid., 152.

[34] Letter from the Rev. Megapolensis to classis of Amsterdam, Mar. 18, 1655. J. F. Jameson, *Narratives of New Netherland*, 392.

[35] Infra, 94.

[36] Samuel Oppenheim, "Early History of the Jews of New York," *P. A. J. H. S.*, XVIII, 3.

[37] Council Minutes, Sept. 7, 1654. *Records of New Amsterdam*, I, 240.

[38] Oppenheim, 69 f.

[39] Ibid., 43 ff. See also Leon Huhner "Whence Came the First Jewish Settlers of New York?" *P. A. J. H. S.*, IX, 74–85.

[40] H. Wätjen, *Das holländische Kolonialreich in Brasilien*, 172.

[41] Letter to the classis in Amsterdam, Mar. 18, 1655. Jameson, 392.

[42] Council Minutes, Sept. 10, 1654. *Records of New Amsterdam*, I, 241.

[43] Council Minutes, Sept. 10, 1654. Ibid., 244.

[44] The ship's sailors also had claims against the Jewish travelers, but they consented to wait until the arrival of a ship from Holland. See Council Minute, Oct. 26, 1654. Ibid., 259. Probably the other claims were also settled, if at all, when the funds arrived.

[45] Ibid., 370.

[46] Letter to classis, Mar. 18, 1655. Jameson, 392.

[47] Letter of Sept. 22, 1654. Oppenheim, *P. A. J. H. S.*, XVIII, 4 f.

[48] Letter to classis of Amsterdam, Mar. 18, 1655. Jameson, 392.

[49] The office combined the duties of sheriff and prosecutor.

[50] Council Minute, Mar. 1, 1655. *Records of New Amsterdam*, I, 291.

[51] Letter of March 18, 1655. Jameson, 392 f.

[52] Apr. 4, 1652. *Documents . . . of New York*, XIV, 172.

[53] Oppenheim, *P. A. J. H. S.*, XVIII, 15.

[54] Ibid., 9. It was common for the Sephardim of Amsterdam to describe themselves as Portuguese without adding the qualifying word *Jew*.

[55] Ibid., 9 ff.

[56] Ibid., 13.

[57] Ibid., 9.

[58] Ibid., 8.

[59] Ibid., 19 f.

[60] Ibid., 21.

[61] *Ecclesiastical Records of New York*. I, 343 f.

[62] Letter of June 10, 1656. Oppenheimer, *P. A. J. H. S.*, XVIII, 21.

[63] Letter of June 14, 1656. Ibid., 33.

[64] Ibid., 75 f.

[65] Zwierlein, 247.

[66] Act of Council, Aug. 19, 1655. *Documents . . . of New York*, XII, 92 f.

[67] Resolution of Council, Aug. 28, 1655. Ibid., 96.

[68] Act of Council, Aug. 28. Ibid., 95 f.
[69] Act of Council, Aug. 30. Ibid., 96.
[70] Oppenheim, *P. A. J. H. S.*, XVIII, 26.
[71] Act of Council, Nov. 5, 1655. Ibid., 25.
[72] Council Minute, Apr. 11, 1657. *Records of New Amsterdam*, VII, 154.
[73] Court Minute, Mar. 1, 1655. Ibid., I, 290 f.
[74] June 14, 1656. O'Callaghan, *Laws*, 194.
[75] Mar. 15. *Records of New Amsterdam*, II, 63.
[76] "Netherlands," in *Jewish Encyclopedia*, IX, 229.
[77] June 14, 1656. O'Callaghan, *Laws*, 194.
[78] Minute of Apr. 11. *Records of New Amsterdam*, VII, 154.
[79] The Jewish system of dietary laws.
[80] Another example of regard for Jewish sensibilities was the recognition that a Jew summoned on the Sabbath did not have to appear in court. Ibid., II, 396, 397.
[81] Ibid., VII, 259, 261.
[82] "Oath *More Judaico*," *Jewish Encyclopedia*, IX, 367 f.
[83] *Records of New Amsterdam*, I, 306 f., 313 f.; II, 2 f.; *et passim*.
[84] Mrs. S. Van Rensselaer, *History of the City of New York in the Seventeenth Century*, I, 435.
[85] Ibid., 438.
[86] Ibid., 41, 365.
[87] O'Callaghan, *Laws*, 89 f.
[88] Letter to Stuyvesant, Jan. 27, 1649. Ibid., 92.
[89] Oppenheim, *P. A. J. H. S.*, XVIII, 27 ff.
[90] Dec. 23, 1655. Ibid., 29 f.
[91] Jan. 15, 1656. Ibid., 30.
[92] It is noteworthy that only nineteen of the many Christians in the city paid the same tax as these five Jews, and but five contributed greater sums. Probably the Jews were assessed more heavily than their neighbors. *Records of New Amsterdam*, I, 367 ff.
[93] Oppenheim, *P. A. J. H. S.*, XVIII, 31 f.
[94] June 10, 1656. Ibid., 21.
[95] June 14. Ibid., 33.
[96] *Records of New Amsterdam*, II, 261 f.
[97] O'Callaghan, *Laws*, 298.
[98] Ibid., 299 ff.
[99] Council Minute, Apr. 11, 1657. *Records of New Amsterdam*, VII, 154.
[100] Council Minute, Apr. 20, 1657. Oppenheim, *P. A. J. H. S.*, XVIII, 36.
[101] Elizabeth Donnan, *Documents Illustrative of the History of the Slave Trade to America*, III, 421.

NOTES TO CHAPTER VI.

[1] Articles of Capitulation, *Documents Relative to the Colonial History of the State of New York*, II, 250.

[2] Ibid., 251.

[3] *Ecclesiastical Records of the State of New York*, I, 572.

[4] *Documents . . . of New York*, III, 218.

[5] Brodhead, *History of the State of New York*, II, 660.

[6] Instructions to Governor Dongan, May 29, 1686. *Documents . . . of New York*, III, 373.

[7] *Documents . . . of New York*, III, 415. Governor Andros had mentioned the Jews in similar fashion in 1678. Ibid., III, 262.

[8] *Ecclesiastical Records of the State of New York*, I, 570 f.

[9] *Documents . . . of New York*, III, 372.

[10] Osgood, *American Colonies in the Eighteenth Century*, II, 14 ff.

[11] Ibid., II, 17 f.

[12] *New York City, Common Council Minutes, 1675–1776*, I, 169.

[13] "Memoir on Acadia, New England, New-York and Virginia 1692," by M. Lamothe-Cadillac. *Documents . . . of New York*, IX, 549.

[14] Joseph J. Mooney, "New York, Archdiocese of," *Catholic Encyclopedia*, XI, 21.

[15] *Documents . . . of New York*, IV, 182 note.

[16] David de Sola Pool, *The Mill Street Synagogue of the Congregation Shearith Israel*, 9. The map is reproduced, 10.

[17] E. T. Corwin, *History of the Reformed Church, Dutch* (*American Church History*, VIII), 108 f.

[18] A. M. Dyer, "Points in the First Chapter of New York Jewish History," *P. A. J. H. S.*, III, 49.

[19] Ibid., III, 47 ff.

[20] Report of the Council of New York, Mar. 24, 1767. *Documents . . . of New York*, III, 304 f.

[21] Pool, 53 ff.

[22] Cantor or Reader.

[23] Brodhead, *History of the State of New York*, II, 426, 427 note.

[24] *New York Common Council Minutes*, I, 168 f.

[25] "The Burghers of New Amsterdam and the Freemen of New York," *Collections of the New-York-Historical Society*, 1885, 104.

[26] "Travels into North America," in Pinkerton, *Voyages and Travels*, XIII, 455.

[27] "The Burghers of New Amsterdam," 95.

[28] Ibid., 164.

[29] Ibid., 169.

[30] Ibid., 174.

[31] Ibid., 183.

[32] "A New York Jewish Silversmith of the Eighteenth Century," *P. A. J. H. S.*, XXVIII, 237.

[33] O'Callaghan, *The Documentary History of the State of New York*, III, 263.

[34] Pious works.

[35] Lyons Collection, *P. A. J. H. S.*, XXI, 26.

[36] Beadle.

[37] Lyons Collection, *P. A. J. H. S.*, XXI, 80.

[38] Ibid., *P. A. J. H. S.*, XXVII, 22.

[39] A *mitzvah*.

[40] Mrs. Schuyler Van Rensselaer, *History of the City of New York in the Seventeenth Century*, I, 427.

[41] "Minute Book of Congregation Shearith Israel," *P. A. J. H. S.*, XXI, 72.

[42] Ibid., 85.

[43] Leon Huhner, "Jews and Colleges of the Original States," *P. A. J. H. S.*, XIX, 118.

[44] My light is God.

[45] Huhner, *P. A. J. H. S.*, XIX, 118 f.

[46] D. de Sola Pool, *The Mill Street Synagogue*, 49.

[47] *Documents . . . of New York*, II, 250.

[48] Attorney General Northey to the Lords of Trade, Jan. 2, 1718. Ibid., V, 496.

[49] Supra, 10 f.

[50] Hollander, "Naturalization of Jews in the American Colonies under the Act of 1740," *P. A. J. H. S.*, V, 116 f.

[51] McKinley, *Suffrage Franchise in the Thirteen English Colonies*, 211 f.

[52] Ibid., 217.

[53] Ibid., 214 note.

[54] Stokes, *The Iconography of Manhattan Island*, IV, 507.

[55] *Journal of the General-Assembly of New York*, I, 710 f.

[56] Ibid.

[57] Osgood, II, 474.

[58] McKinley, 214.

[59] *Journal of the General-Assembly*, I, 712.

[60] Ibid., I, 717.

[61] McKinley, 215.

[62] "Travels into North America," in Pinkerton, *Voyages and Travels*, XIII, 455.

[63] *Jewish Encyclopedia*, "New York," IX, 266.

[64] Poore, *Federal and State Constitutions*, part II, 1338.

NOTES   217

NOTES TO CHAPTER VII.

1 *Jewish Encyclopedia*, "Sweden," XI, 607 f.
2 Amandus Johnson, *Instructions for Johan Printz*, 95 f.
3 Supra, 90 f., 92 f.
4 Oppenheim, "Early History of the Jews in N. Y.," *P. A. J. H. S.*,
XVIII, 27 f.
5 Berthold Fernow, *Records of New Amsterdam*, II, 80 f.
6 *Documents . . . of New York*, XII, 136.
7 Oppenheim, *P. A. J. H. S.*, XVIII, 29.
8 *Documents . . . of New York*, XII, 148.
9 Ibid., XII, 450.
10 Note in *P. A. J. H. S.*, I, 123.
11 Samuel Hazard, *Annals of Pennsylvania*, 237.
12 *Pennsylvania Archives*, 2nd Series, V, 436 f.
13 Christopher Ward, *Dutch and Swedes on the Delaware*, 333.
14 John Brodhead, *History of the State of New York*, I, 698.
15 Ibid., I, 745.
16 *Documents . . . of New York*, XII, 457.
17 Ibid., III, 71.
18 Samuel Smith, *History of Nova-Caesaria*, 513.
19 Ibid., 529.
20 Andrews, *Colonial Period of American History*, III, 152.
21 Edward Beatty, *William Penn as Social Philospher*, 124.
22 Ibid., 125.
23 William Hull, *William Penn*, 206.
24 Beatty, 134.
25 Ibid., 151 ff.
26 *Collected Works*, II, 848.
27 Samuel Hazard, *Annals of Pennsylvania*, 523.
28 Ibid., 569.
29 Ibid., 573.
30 Ibid.
31 *Pennsylvania Colonial Records*, I, 398.
32 *A Quaker Experiment in Government*, 128.
33 Albert McKinley, *Suffrage Franchise in the English Colonies*, 279.
34 Ibid., 290 ff.
35 Patrick M'Robert, *A Tour of America*, 31.
36 Carl and Jessica Bridenbaugh, *Rebels and Gentlemen*, 3 f.
37 Letter to Henry Goldney, Mar. 7, *Pennsylvania Archives*, 2nd
Series, VII, 82.
38 Ibid., IX, 632.
39 "Reise-Diarium," in Samuel Urlsperger, *Ausführliche Nachricht
von der Saltzburgischen Emigranten*, I, 156.

[40] Scharff and Westcott, *History of Philadelphia*, II, 1436.

[41] Ibid., II, 1436 f.

[42] Ibid.

[43] Henry Morais, *Jews of Philadelphia*, 201.

[44] Scharff and Wescott, II, 1436.

[45] Letter from Jacob Henry to Barnard Gratz, Jan. 7, 1761. William Byars, ed., *B. and M. Gratz*, 52. The originals of these letters were in Yiddish. The editor transliterated the word as *shiloh* instead of *shuleh (Schule)*, which does not make sense.

[46] John Watson, *Annals of Philadelphia and Pennsylvania*, I, 283.

[47] Ibid., I, 284. Scharff and Westcott, II, 1437.

[48] Byars, 74.

[49] Ibid., 30.

[50] N. Taylor Phillips, "Levy and Seixas Families," *P. A. J. H. S.*, IV, 199.

[51] Israel Solomons, "Genealogy of the Franks Family," *P. A. J. H. S.*, XVIII, 213 f.

[52] William Riddell, "Pre-Revolutionary Pennsylvania and the Slave Trade," *Pennsylvania Magazine of History*, LII, 16 f.

[53] *Pennsylvania Archives*, 5th Series, I, 50.

[54] Edward Cheyney, *History of the University of Pennsylvania*, 32.

[55] Thomas Montgomery, *History of the University of Pennsylvania to 1770*. List of students in the Academy found in the appendix.

[56] University Catalogue, 1917, 20.

[57] Benjamin Owen, "Letters of Richard Locke," *Pennsylvania Magazine of History*, XXIV, 475.

[58] Gustavus Hart, "Notes on Myer Hart," *P. A. J. H. S.*, VIII, 127 f.

[59] *History of Berks and Lebanon Counties*, 345.

[60] A thoroughly untrustworthy account may be found in Julius Sachse's *German Sectarians in Pennsylvania*, II, 116 ff.

[61] Byars, 14.

[62] David Philipson, *Letters of Rebecca Gratz*, viii f., xix f.

[63] Ibid., 18 f.

[64] Ibid., 18.

[65] Ibid., 16.

[66] Charles Thomas, "Merchants in the Illinois Country," *Illinois Historial Society Journal*, XXX, 430 f.

[67] Ms. Gage Papers, Am. Series, IC, Clements Library, University of Michigan.

[68] McKinley, 270.

[69] *New Jersey Archives*, 1st Series, II, 460.

[70] Leonard Labaree, *Royal Instructions to British Colonial Governors*, II, 494.

[71] *New Jersey Archives*, 1st Series, IV, 342 ff.

NOTES TO CHAPTER VIII.

[1] Godfrey Davies, *The Early Stuarts*, 205 ff.
[2] "Calvert Papers," No. 1, *Maryland Historical Society*, XXVIII, 32.
[3] Hollander, "Some Unpublished Material Relating to Dr. Jacob Lumbrozo," *P. A. J. H. S.*, I, 35.
[4] *Maryland Archives*, III, 488.
[5] Raphael Semmes, *Crime and Punishment in Early Maryland*, 226.
[6] *Maryland Archives*, XLI, 203.
[7] Ibid., III, 526.
[8] Ibid., XLI, 590.
[9] Ibid., III, 210, 214.
[10] James McSherry, *History of Maryland*, 66.
[11] *Maryland Archives*, I, 244 f.
[12] Ibid., 246.
[13] Matthew Andrews, *Founding of Maryland*, 154 n.
[14] Max Farrand, *Laws and Liberties of Massachusetts*, 5.
[15] "For the Colony in Virginea Britannia," Force's *Tracts*, III, no. 2, 10.
[16] *Maryland Archives*, III, 313.
[17] Hall, *Narratives of Early Maryland*, 264, 312.
[18] *Maryland Archives*, III, 313.
[19] Ibid., I, 340.
[20] Ibid., I, 343.
[21] White, "Narrative of a Voyage to Maryland," *Maryland Historical Society Fund Publication*, no. 7, 92 f.
[22] *Maryland Archives*, III, 324.
[23] Ibid., 325.
[24] *Proceedings of General Assembly of Maryland 1637-1664, Archives of Maryland*, 339.
[25] *Maryland Archives*, III, 353.
[26] Rufus Jones, *Quakers in the American Colonies*, 276 n.
[27] *Maryland Archives*, XLI, 203.
[28] *Quakers in the American Colonies*, 73 f.
[29] Ibid., 74.
[30] *Maryland Archives*, XLI, 104.
[31] Ibid., III, 353.
[32] Ibid., XLI, 203.
[33] William Braithwaite, *Beginnings of Quakerism*, 427.
[34] *Maryland Archives*, XLI, 202.
[35] Ibid., 203.
[36] Ibid.
[37] Ibid.
[38] Ibid.
[39] Ibid.

[40] Ibid., 258 f.
[41] Ibid., X, 511.
[42] Ibid., XLIX, 53.
[43] Ibid., III, 488.
[44] Ibid., XLI, 513.
[45] Ibid., LIII, 319 f.
[46] Ibid., 355 ff.
[47] Ibid., 387 ff.
[48] Ibid., 609, 616.
[49] The papers of administration are in the Hall of Records, Annapolis.
[50] J. H. Hollander, "Civil Status of the Jews of Maryland, 1634–1776," *P. A. J. H. S.*, II, 40 n.
[51] Labaree, *Royal Instructions to British Colonial Governors*, II, 494.
[52] *Maryland Archives*, LII, vii, xix.
[53] Ibid., XXXIII, 288.
[54] Ibid., XXVI, 340 f.
[55] Ibid., 341.
[56] Eugene McCormac, *White Servitude in Maryland* (*Johns Hopkins University Studies*, XXII), 31.
[57] Ibid., 98 f.
[58] "Leibzoll," *Jewish Encyclopedia*, VII, 670.
[59] Marvin Lowenthal, *The Jews of Germany*, 210.
[60] *Maryland Archives*, LII, 426.
[61] Ibid., 89.
[62] Ibid., 90.
[63] Ibid., 92.
[64] Ibid., LII, 293.
[65] Ibid., LV, xix.
[66] Ibid., 306.
[67] *William and Mary Quarterly*, 1901–2, X, 95.
[68] Edgar Woods, *Albermarle County in Virginia*, 359.
[69] Samuel Oppenheim, "The Jews and Masonry," *P. A. J. H. S.*, XIX, 58.
[70] Saul Padover, *Jefferson*, 82.

NOTES TO CHAPTER IX.

[1] *Colonial Records of North Carolina*, I, 32 f.
[2] Ibid., I, 113 f.
[3] H. R. F. Bourne, *Locke*, I, 238 f.; Louise Brown, *The First Earl of Shaftesbury*, 156. There seems to be some doubt concerning the authorship of *The Fundamental Constitutions*. See Andrews, *Colonial Period of American History*, III, 212.

[4] Alexander Frazer, *Locke*, 90.
[5] *Letters on Toleration*, 1.
[6] Bourne, I, 236.
[7] Ibid., I, 239.
[8] Article 96, *Colonial Records of North Carolina*, I, 202.
[9] Ibid., I, 202 f.
[10] Article 101, ibid., I, 203.
[11] Article 106, ibid., I, 204.
[12] Andrews, *Colonial Period of American History*, 220 f.
[13] *Colonial Records of North Carolina*, II, 856 f.
[14] R. D. W. Conner, *History of North Carolina*, I, 97.
[15] Leon Huhner's article, "The Jews of North Carolina prior to 1800," mentions but one indisputable Jew in pre-Revolutionary North Carolina, although he lists a number of Jewish-sounding names, signifying nothing. *P. A. J. H. S.*, XXIX, passim.
[16] Stephen Beauregard Weeks, *Church and State in North Carolina* (*Johns Hopkins University Studies*, 11th series), passim.
[17] Huhner, "The Struggle for Religious Liberty in North Carolina," *P. A. J. H. S.*, XVI, 68.
[18] Archdale, "Description of Carolina," in B. R. Carroll, *Historical Collections of South Carolina*, II, 106.
[19] Arthur Hirsch, *Huguenots of Colonial South Carolina*, 10 ff.
[20] Ibid., 113 f.
[21] Ibid., 90 ff., 105.
[22] Ibid., 113.
[23] *South Carolina Commons Assembly Journals*, 1693, 36.
[24] Ibid.
[25] *Commons Assembly Journals*, 1697, 5 f.
[26] Ibid., 6.
[27] Ibid., 18.
[28] *Statutes of South Carolina*, II, 131.
[29] Ibid., II, 133.
[30] Ibid., II, 132.
[31] Ibid.
[32] Huhner, "Asser Levy," *P. A. J. H. S.*, VIII, 22 n.
[33] Barnett Elzas, *The Jews of South Carolina*, 20 f.
[34] Ibid., 21 f.
[35] *Colonial Records of North Carolina*, I, 199.
[36] *Statutes of South Carolina*, II, 73.
[37] William Rivers, *Early History of South Carolina*, 437.
[38] Ibid., 456.
[39] Ibid., 457 f.
[40] Ibid., 458 f.
[41] Ibid., 453 ff.

[42] Ibid., 455.

[43] Ibid., 459.

[44] Ibid., 459 f.

[45] Alexander Salley, *Narratives of Early Carolina*, 275.

[46] Ibid., 268.

[47] Rivers, 222 f.

[48] Frederick Dalcho, *Protestant Episcopal Church in South Carolina*, 64 f.

[49] Salley, 223 f.

[50] Ibid., 245.

[51] *Statutes of South Carolina*, II, 232 f.

[52] Ibid., II, 252 f.

[53] Ibid., II, 252 f.

[54] Ibid., II, 249.

[55] Ibid., III, 140.

[56] Ibid., III, 136.

[57] Ibid., III, 137.

[58] Hirsch, 315 ff.

[59] Elzas, 277.

[60] Ibid.

[61] Nathaniel Levin, "Beth Elohim," *Charleston Year Book, 1883*, 301.

[62] Ibid., 302.

[63] Elzas, 35 f.

[64] Supra, 62 f.

[65] Elzas, 48.

[66] Ibid., 49.

[67] *Charleston Year Book, 1883*, 403.

[68] Elzas, 53 ff.

[69] Supra, 61 ff.

[70] Elzas, 64.

[71] Ibid., 66.

[72] Mrs. St. Julien Ravenel, *Charleston*, 119 f.; Elzas, 28.

[73] Elzas, 36.

[74] Ibid., 42.

[75] Edward McCrady, *South Carolina Under the Royal Government*, 350.

[76] McKinley, 155.

[77] Ibid., 157.

[78] McCrady, 326 ff.

[79] Elzas, 68 ff.

[80] Infra, 172 ff.

[81] Elzas, 76 n. 21.

[82] Elzas, 68.

[83] Ibid., 70.

[84] *Journal of Provincial Congress, 1775*, 29.

[85] Drayton, II, 338 ff.

[86] *Philosophico-Historico-Hydrogeography*, Plowden Weston, ed. (*Documents Connected with History of South Carolina*), 161 f.

[87] Ibid., 195 f.

NOTES TO CHAPTER X.

[1] Amos Ettinger, *James Edward Oglethorpe*, 90 ff.; *Commons Journals*, XXI, 274 ff.

[2] *Commons Journals*, XXI, 578.

[3] *Diary of Viscount Percival*, I, 45 f.

[4] Vernon Crane, *The Southern Frontier*, 304 ff.

[5] *Diary of Viscount Percival*, I, 90, 98, 214, 272 ff., 292.

[6] Ibid., I, 26.

[7] Ibid., I, 12.

[8] *Georgia Colonial Records*, I, 21.

[9] *Diary of Viscount Percival*, I, 299.

[10] Crane, *Southern Frontier*, 320 f.

[11] *Georgia Colonial Records*, I, 12.

[12] Albert McKinley, *The Suffrage Franchise in the English Colonies*, 163 f.

[13] *Georgia Colonial Records*, I, 14.

[14] Lee R. A. Roberts, introduction to *Diary of Viscount Percival*, I, v ff.

[15] *Diary*, I, 298.

[16] Charles Linn, *Georgia Colony of Salzburgers*, ch. II.

[17] *Diary*, I, 287 f.

[18] "The Promotion Literature of Georgia," in *Bibliographical Essays, a Tribute to Wilberforce Eames*, 81.

[19] Ibid., passim.

[20] *Georgia Colonial Records*, I, 70.

[21] Ibid., I, 75 f.

[22] *Diary*, I, 313.

[23] Supra, 165 f.

[24] M. J. Landa, "Kitty Villareal, the Da Costas and Samson Gideon," *Transactions of Jewish Hist. Soc. of England*, XIII.

[25] Ibid., XIII, 272.

[26] Ibid., XIII, 276.

[27] Ibid.

[28] Ettinger, *James Oglethorpe*, 130.
[29] J. Rumney, "Anglo-Jewry as Seen Through Foreign Eyes," *Transactions of Jewish Hist. Soc. of England*, XIII, 328 f.
[30] *Diary*, I, 301.
[31] Ibid., II, 41.
[32] Ibid., I, 309.
[33] Ibid., I, 313.
[34] *Georgia Colonial Records*, I, 98.
[35] Ibid.
[36] Letter from Martyn to Oglethorpe, Feb. 21, 1732–3, Colonial Office Ms., 5: 666, p. 10.
[37] *Diary*, I, 463.
[38] "Progress of Georgia," 11, Force's *Tracts*, I.
[39] *Diary*, I, 463 f.
[40] Ibid.
[41] *Occident*, I, 380 ff., 486 ff.
[42] Ibid., I, 382 f.
[43] Huhner, "The Jews of Georgia in Colonial Times," *P. A. J. H. S.*, X, 78.
[44] *Occident*, I, 381 f.
[45] Ibid., I, 382 f.
[46] George White, *Statistics of the State of Georgia*, 619 f.
[47] *Diary*, I, 440.
[48] Ettinger, 137 n.
[49] Nov. 25, 1733, *Colonial Records of Georgia*, XXIX (Ms.), 40–42.
[50] Infra, 184.
[51] *Diary*, I, 463 f.
[52] Ibid., I, 464.
[53] *Georgia Colonial Records*, I, 149 f.
[54] *Diary*, I, 476.
[55] Ibid., II, 3.
[56] *Georgia Colonial Records*, I, 151 f.
[57] Ibid., I, 153.
[58] Ibid., II, 62.
[59] Ettinger, 144 ff.
[60] "Thomas Coram," *Dictionary of National Biography*, XII, 194 f.
[61] "Letters of Thomas Coram," *Massachusetts Historical Society Proceedings*, LVI, 15 ff.
[62] "Brief Account of Cuases that Retarded Progress of Georgia," *Georgia Historical Society Collections*, II, 96 ff.
[63] *Diary*, II, 199.
[64] Sept. 22, 1738, *Massachusetts Historical Society Collections*, LVI, 47 f.

NOTES TO CHAPTER XI.

[1] *Diary of Viscount Percival*, II, 69.

[2] Supra, pp. 175 f. and 177.

[3] Tailfer, Anderson and Douglas, "Narrative of Georgia," Force, *Tracts*, I, no. 4.

[4] Charles C. Jones, Jr., *History of Georgia*, I, 157 f.

[5] Ibid., I, 158. Only eleven Jewish names are listed there, but a twelfth is found in the Sheftall record. *Occident*, I, 381 f.

[6] Supra, 176.

[7] Sam. Urlsperger (ed.), *Ausführliche Nachricht von den Saltzburgischen Emigranten*, 82.

[8] Ibid., 97.

[9] Ibid., 97.

[10] W. Guenther Plant, "Two Notes on the History of the Jews in America," *Hebrew Union College Annual*, XIV, 581.

[11] *Ausführliche Nachricht*, 91.

[12] Ms. in Georgia State Archives.

[13] Letter to Prof. Francken, Mar. 23, 1734, *Ausführliche Nachricht*, 215.

[14] "Callenberg," in *Allgemeine Deutsche Biographie*, III, 707 f.

[15] *H. U. C. Annual*, XIV, 580.

[16] *Diary of Viscount Percival*, II, 119.

[17] Letter, July 3, 1739, *Ausführliche Nachricht*, 2277.

[18] *Georgia Colonial Records*, IV, 330.

[19] "Establishment of the Colony of Georgia," Force, *Tracts*, I, no. 2, p. 6.

[20] *Georgia Colonial Records*, II, 190 f.

[21] Ibid., IV, 43.

[22] "Historic Narrative of the Colony of Georgia," Force, *Tracts*, I, no. 4, xii.

[23] *H. U. C. Annual*, XIV, 581; letter, July 3, 1739, *Ausführliche Nachricht*, 2277.

[24] *Georgia Colonial Records*, II, 195.

[25] Letter, July 3, 1739, *Ausführliche Nachricht*, 2277.

[26] *H. U. C. Annual*, XIV, 581.

[27] Letter to Henry Newman, Ms. in Georgia State Archives.

[28] Letter of Wm. Stephens to the trustees, May 27, 1738, *Georgia Colonial Records*, XXII, pt. I, 166.

[29] *H. U. C. Annual*, XIV, 582.

[30] Letter of Bartholomew Zouberbuhler to Benj. Martyn, Dec. 20, 1750, *Georgia Colonial Records*, XXVI, 104.

[31] *H. U. C. Annual*, XIV, 581.

[32] Letter to Henry Newman.

[33] *H. U. C. Annual*, XIV, 580.

[34] Letter to Henry Newman.

[35] Edition of 1906, 46.

[36] *H. U. C. Annual*, XIV, 580.

[37] Ibid., 581.

[38] Letter, July 3, 1739, *Ausführliche Nachricht*, 2277.

[39] *H. U. C. Annual*, XIV, 581.

[40] *Occident*, I, 384.

[41] Reba Strickland, *Religion and the State in Georgia in the Eighteenth Century*, 44 ff.

[42] Ibid., 69 f.

[43] Ibid., 71 ff.

[44] Ibid., 70 f.

[45] Ibid., 76 ff.

[46] E. Merton Coulter, *Short History of Georgia*, 61 ff.; Ettinger, *Oglethorpe*, 208 ff.

[47] Force, *Tracts*, I, no. 4, 42 f.

[48] Ibid., I, no. 4, v.

[49] Ibid., I, no. 4, 27.

[50] *Georgia Colonial Records*, XXII, pt. 1, 295.

[51] *Diary*, III, 188.

[52] Coulter, *History of Georgia*, 74.

[53] Leonard Labarée, *Royal Instructions to British Colonial Governors*, II, 494.

[54] *Georgia Colonial Records*, XVIII, 258 ff.

[55] Strickland, 97, 103 f.

[56] *Georgia Colonial Records*, XIII, 758 f.

[57] Strickland, 126; Letter of John J. Zubly to Ezra Stiles, *Massachusetts Historical Society Proceedings*, 1864–5, 217.

[58] *Georgia Colonial Records*, XVII, 559.

[59] Ibid., XVII, 560 ff.

[60] Ibid., XV, 145 f.

[61] Ibid., XV, 172.

[62] Ibid., XVII, 572 f.

[63] Ibid., XVII, 574.

[64] Ibid., XVII, 575.

[65] *Massachusetts Historical Society Transactions*, 1864–5, 217. Zubly charged that discussion on his bill was postponed till the king's birthday, June 4, when there would be no session. The records, however, report the date for further discussion as June 1.

[66] Edmund Abrahams, "Early History of the Sheftalls," *P.A.J.H.S.*, XVII, 172 f.

[67] *Occident*, I, 486.

[68] *Minutes of the Union Society*, 122 f., page in back of book numbered 1, note.

[69] *Georgia Colonial Records*, XVII, 190.

[70] George White, *Historical Collections of Georgia*, 40.

[71] Ibid., 38.

[72] Supra, 111.

[73] White, 39.

[74] Ibid., 41.

[75] Ettinger, 304, 306 ff.

[76] Ibid., 326.

[77] Leon Huhner, "First Jew to Hold the Office of Governor," *P. A. J. H. S.*, XVII, 187 ff.

NOTE TO CHAPTER XII.

[1] Carl Van Doren, *Benjamin Franklin*, 760.

BIBLIOGRAPHY

Primary Sources

ABRAHAMS, EDMUND H., "Some Notes on the Early History of the Sheftalls of Georgia," *P.A.J.H.S.*,* XVII. New York, 1909.

ADAMS, JAMES TRUSLOW, Album of American History, 3 vols. New York, 1944–1946.

ARCHDALE, JOHN, "A New Description of that Fertile and Pleasant Province of Carolina," in B. R. Carroll, *Historical Collections of South Carolina*, 2 vols. New York, 1836.

AUSTIN, JOHN OSBORNE, The Genealogical Dictionary of Rhode Island. Albany, 1887.

BARTLETT, JOHN RUSSELL, ed., Records of the Colony of Rhode Island and Providence Plantations in New England, 10 vols. Providence, 1856–1865.

BLOOM, HERBERT I., "A Study of Brazilian Jewish History 1623–1654, Based Chiefly upon the Findings of the Late Samuel Oppenheim," *P.A.J.H.S.*, XXXIII. New York, 1934.

——, Economic Activities of the Jews of Amsterdam in the Seventeenth and Eighteenth Centuries. Williamsport, 1937.

BRIGHAM, CHARLES SAUNDERS, ed., The Fourth Paper presented by Major Butler with other papers edited and published by Roger Williams in London 1652. Providence, 1903.

Brown University Records (Manuscripts), John Carter Brown Library, Providence.

* Publications of the American Jewish Historical Society.

229

BROWNE, WILLIAM HAND, ed., Judicial and Testamentary Records of the Provincial Court, 1649/50–1657. Archives of Maryland, X. Baltimore, 1891.

————, ed., Proceedings and Acts of the General Assembly of Maryland, January 1637/8–September 1664. Archives of Maryland, I. Baltimore, 1883.

————, ed., Proceedings and Acts of the General Assembly of Maryland, April 1684–June 1692. Archives of Maryland, XIII. Baltimore, 1894.

————, ed., Proceedings and Acts of the General Assembly of Maryland, September 1704–April 1706. Archives of Maryland, XXVI. Baltimore, 1906.

————, ed., Proceedings of the Council of Maryland, 1636–1667. Archives of Maryland, III. Baltimore, 1885.

————, ed., Proceedings of the Council of Maryland, 1667–1687/8. Archives of Maryland, V. Baltimore, 1887.

————, ed., Proceedings of the Council of Maryland, 1687/8–1693. Archives of Maryland, VIII. Baltimore, 1890.

The Burghers of New Amsterdam and the Freemen of New York, 1675–1776. Collections of the New York Historical Society for the Year 1885. New York, 1886.

BYARS, WILLIAM VINCENT, B. and M. Gratz. Jefferson City, 1916.

Calvert Papers, The, no. 1, Maryland Historical Society Publications, no. 28. Baltimore, 1889.

CANDLER, ALLEN D., ed., Journal of the Commons House of Assembly, 1755–1762. The Colonial Records of the State of Georgia, XIII. Atlanta, 1907.

————, ed., Journal of the Commons House of Assembly, 1769–1782. The Colonial Records of the State of Georgia, XV. Atlanta, 1907.

————, ed., Journal of the Trustees for Establishing the Colony of Georgia in America. The Colonial Records of the State of Georgia, I. Atlanta, 1904.

————, ed., Journal of the Upper House of Assembly, 1763–1774. The Colonial Records of the State of Georgia, XVII. Atlanta, 1908.

CANDLER, ALLEN D., ed., The Minutes of the Common
    Council of the Trustees for Establishing the Colony of
    Georgia in America. The Colonial Records of the State
    of Georgia, II. Atlanta, 1904.

——, ed., Original Papers Correspondence, Trustees, General
    Oglethorpe, and Others. The Colonial Records of the
    State of Georgia, XXI, XXII. Atlanta, 1910–1913.

——, ed., Statutes Enacted by the Royal Legislature of
    Georgia 1754 to 1768. The Colonial Records of the State
    of Georgia, XVIII. Atlanta 1910.

Charter of the Province of Massachusetts Bay 1691. Publica-
    tions of the Colonial Society of Massachusetts, II. Boston,
    1913.

The Colonial Laws of Massachusetts Reprinted from the
    Edition of 1660, with the Supplements to 1672. Boston,
    1889.

Commerce of Rhode Island. Collections of the Massachu-
    setts Historical Society, 7th series, IX–X, 2 vols. Boston,
    1915.

CONE, G. HERBERT, "The Jews in Curaçao," *P.A.J.H.S.*, X.
    New York, 1902.

Connecticut Colonial Records. New England Records of the
    Court of Assistants, 1669–1701. Manuscripts in Con-
    necticut State Library, Hartford.

Connecticut Historical Society. Collections of Hartford Town
    Votes, 1635–1716, VI. Hartford, 1897.

——. Collections of the Wyllys Papers, XXI. Hartford,
    1924.

Connecticut, State of, Public Acts, October 1842. Hartford,
    1843.

CRANE, VERNON W., "The Promotion Literature of Georgia,"
    Bibliographical Essays, a Tribute to Wilberforce Eames.
    Cambridge, 1924.

COOPER, THOMAS and DAVID J. McCORD, eds., The Statutes
    at Large of South Carolina, 10 vols. Columbia, 1836–1841.

CUNDALL, FRANK, DAVIS, N. DARNELL and FRIEDENBERG,
    ALBERT M., "Documents Relating to the History of the

Jews in Jamaica and Barbados in the Time of William III,"
   P.A.J.H.S., XXIII. New York, 1915.

DE BRAHM, WILLIAM GERARD, Philosophico-Historico-Hydrogeography of South Carolina, Georgia, and East Florida.
   Plowden Charles Jennett Weston, *Documents Connected
   with the History of South Carolina*. London, 1856.

DEXTER, FRANKLIN BOWDITCH, Biographical Sketches of the
   Graduates of Yale College. vols. I–V, New York, 1885
   seq.; vol. VI. New Haven, 1912.

——, ed., Extracts from the Itineraries and Other Miscel-
   lanies of Ezra Stiles. New Haven, 1916.

——, ed., The Literary Diary of Ezra Stiles, D. D., LL. D.,
   3 vols. New York, 1901.

Documents Relating to the Colonial History of the State of
   New York, 15 vols. Albany, 1853–1887.

DONNAN, ELIZABETH, Documents Illustrative of the History
   of the Slave Trade to America. 4 vols. Washington,
   1930–1935.

DRAYTON, JOHN, Memoirs of the American Revolution. 2 vols.
   Charleston, 1821.

DYER, ALBION MORRIS, "Points in the First Chapter of New
   York Jewish History," *P.A.J.H.S.*, III. New York, 1895.

Extracts from the Journals of the Provincial Congress of South
   Carolina held at Charles-Town June 1st to 22nd, 1775.
   Charleston, 1775.

FERNOW, BERTHOLD, ed., The Records of New Amsterdam
   from 1653 to 1674 Anno Domini, 7 vols. New York, 1897.

——, The Minutes of the Orphanmasters of New Amsterdam,
   1655–1663. 2 vols. New York, 1902–1907.

[FERRAND, MAX, ed.,] The Laws and Liberties of Massachusetts.
   Cambridge, 1929.

First Report of the Record Commissioners of the City of Boston. 2nd Edition, Boston, 1881.

FORCE, PETER, ed., "A Brief Account of the Establishment of
   the Colony of Georgia," *Tracts and Other Papers*, I, no. 2.
   Washington, 1836.

——, ed., "An Extract of the Journals of Mr. Commissary

Von Reck and the Reverend Mr. Bolzius," *Tracts and Other Papers*, IV. Washington, 1846.

FORD, WORTHINGTON CHAUNCEY, "Letters of Thomas Coram," *Massachusetts Historical Society Proceedings*. Boston, 1923.

FORTESCUE, J. W., ed., Calendar of State Papers, Colonial Series, America and West Indies, 1681–1685. London, 1898.

FRIEDENWALD, HERBERT, "Material for the History of the Jews in the British West Indies," *P.A.J.H.S.*, V. New York, 1897.

GROSS, CHARLES, "Documents from the Public Record Office (London)," *P.A.J.H.S.*, II. New York, 1894.

HALL, CLAYTON COLMAN, Narratives of Early Maryland, 1633–1684. Original Narratives of Early American History. New York, 1910.

———, ed., Proceedings and Acts of the General Assembly of Maryland, May 1717–April 1720. Archives of Maryland, XXXIII. Baltimore, 1913.

HARPER, LAWRENCE A., The English Navigation Laws. New York, 1939.

Harvard College Records, *Colonial Society of Massachusetts Publication*, XV, XVI. Boston, 1925.

HASTINGS, HUGH, ed., Ecclesiastical Records, State of New York, 7 vols. Albany, 1901–1916.

HAZARD, SAMUEL, Annals of Pennsylvania. Philadelphia, 1850.

HEADLAM, CECIL, ed., Calendar of State Papers, Colonial Series, America and West Indies, August 1717–December 1718. London, 1930.

Historical Catalogue of Brown University. Providence, 1905.

HOLLANDER, J. H., "Some Unpublished Material relating to Dr. Jacob Lumbrozo, of Maryland," *P.A.J.H.S.*, I. New York, 1893.

HUHNER, LEON, "Asser Levy: A Noted Jewish Burgher of New Amsterdam," *P.A.J.H.S.*, VIII. New York, 1900.

———, "Naturalization of Jews in New York under the Act of 1740," *P.A.J.H.S.*, XIII. New York, 1905.

HUHNER, LEON, "Whence Came the First Jewish Settlers of New York?" *P.A.J.H.S.*, IX. New York, 1900.

The Hutchinson Papers, 2 vols. Albany, 1865.

JAMESON, J. FRANKLIN, Narratives of New Netherland, 1609–1664. New York, 1909.

JASTROW, MORRIS, JR., "Notes on the Jews of Philadelphia from Published Annals," *P.A.J.H.S.*, I. New York, 1893.

JOHNSON, AMANDUS, The Instruction for Johan Printz, Governor of New Sweden. Philadelphia, 1930.

Journals of the House of Commons. London, 1547 —.

Journals of the House of Lords. London, 17 —.

Journal of the Provincial Congress of South Carolina 1776. Charleston, 1776.

Journal of the Votes and Proceedings of the General Assembly of the Colony of New York, I. New York, 1764.

JUDAH, GEORGE FORTUNATUS, "The Jews' Tribute in Jamaica," *P.A.J.H.S.*, XVIII. New York, 1909.

KALM, PETER, Travels into North America (translated by John Reinhold-Forster), in John Pinkerton, A General Collection of the Best and Most Interesting Voyages and Travels in All Parts of the World, XIII. London, 1812.

KNIGHT, LUCIAN LAMAR, ed., Original Papers: Trustees, President and Assistants, and Others, 1750–1752. The Colonial Records of the State of Georgia, XXVI. Atlanta, 1916.

KORN, HAROLD, "Documents Relative to the Estate of Aaron Lopez," *P.A.J.H.S.*, XXXV. New York, 1939.

LABAREE, LEONARD WOODS, Royal Instructions to British Colonial Governors, 1670–1776, 2 vols. New York, 1935.

LANDA, M. J., "Kitty Villareal, the Da Costas and Samson Gideon," *Jewish Historical Society of England Transactions*, XIII. London, 1936.

LINN, CHARLES ADOLPHUS, The Georgia Colony of Salzburgers, Ms. Ph. D. dissertation, Hartford Theological Seminary, 1931.

"A List and Abstract of Documents Relating to South-Carolina now existing in the State Paper Office London," *Collections of the South-Carolina Historical Society*, I. Charleston, 1857.

LOCKE, J. H., Four Letters on Toleration. London, n. d.

The Lyons Collections, *P.A.J.H.S.*, XXI, XXVII. New York, 1913, 1920.

[MARTYN, BENJAMIN,] "An Account Showing the Progress of the Colony of Georgia in America," *Tracts and Other Papers*, no. 5 (Peter Force, ed.). Washington, 1836.

MATHER, COTTON, Magnalia Christi Americana, 2 vols. Hartford, 1855.

McCORMAC, EUGENE IRVING, White Servitude in Maryland (Johns Hopkins University Studies in History and Political Science, Series XXII). Baltimore, 1904.

MILLER, JOHN, New York Considered and Improved, 1695. Cleveland, 1903.

Minutes of the Provincial Council of Pennsylvania, 10 vols. Philadelphia, 1852.

MODE, PETER G., Source Book and Bibliographical Guide for American Church History. Menasha, Wis., 1921.

MOORE, FRANCIS, "A Voyage to Georgia, Begun in the Year 1735," *Collections of the Georgia Historical Society*, I. Savannah, 1840.

M'ROBERT, PATRICK, A Tour through Part of the North Provinces of America. Philadelphia, 1935.

New Hampshire, The Revised Laws of the State of. Concord, 1942.

New Jersey Archives. Newark, Trenton, 1880 —.

Newport Historical Society, *Manuscript Papers*.

New York City, Common Council Minutes, 1675–1776, 8 vols. New York, 1905.

O'CALLAGHAN, E. B., The Documentary History of the State of New York, 4 vols. Albany, 1850–1856.

———, Laws and Ordinances of New Netherland, 1638–1674. Albany, 1868.

OLDMIXON, J., "The History of Carolina," in B. R. Carroll, *Historical Collections of South Carolina*, 2 vols. New York, 1836.

OPPENHEIM, SAMUEL, "More about Jacob Barsimson, the First Jewish Settler in New York," *P.A.J.H.S.*, XXIX. New York, 1925.

——, "The Early History of the Jews in New York, 1654–1664," *P.A.J.H.S.*, XVIII. New York, 1909.

OWEN, BENJAMIN F., "Letters of Rev. Richard Locke and Rev. George Craig," *Pennsylvania Magazine of History*, XXIV. Philadelphia, 1900.

PENN, WILLIAM, "A Visitation to the Jews," *A Collection of the Works of William Penn,* 2 vols. London, 1726.

Pennsylvania Archives. Philadelphia, 1852 —.

PERCIVAL, VISCOUNT, afterwards First Earl of Egmont, Diary of, Historical Manuscripts Commission, 3 vols. London, 1920–1923.

PHILLIPS, N. TAYLOR, "The Levy and Seixas Families of Newport and New York," *P.A.J.H.S.*, IV. New York, 1896.

PHILLIPS, ULRICH B., "New Light upon the Founding of Georgia," *Georgia Historical Quarterly*, VI. Macon, 1922.

PLEASANTS, J. HALL, ed., Proceedings and Acts of the General Assembly of Maryland, 1755–1756. Archives of Maryland, LII. Baltimore, 1935.

——, ed., Proceedings and Acts of the General Assembly of Maryland, 1757–1758. Archives of Maryland, LV. Baltimore, 1938.

——, ed., Proceedings of the County Court of Charles County, 1658–1666, and Manor Court of St. Clement's Manor, 1659–1672. Archives of Maryland, LIII. Baltimore, 1936.

——, ed., Proceedings of the Court of Chancery of Maryland, 1669–1679. Archives of Maryland, LI. Baltimore, 1934.

——, ed., Proceedings of the Provincial Court of Maryland, 1663–1666. Archives of Maryland, XLIX. Baltimore, 1932.

POORE, BENJAMIN PERLEY, The Federal and State Constitutions, Colonial Charters and Other Organic Laws of the United States, 2 parts. Washington, 1878.

PRESTON, HOWARD W., CHAPIN, HOWARD M. and MORIARTY,

G. ANDREWS, JR., The Letter Book of Peleg Sanford. Providence, 1928.

Records and Files of the Quarterly Courts of Essex County, Massachusetts, 5 vols. Salem, 1911–1916.

Records of the Suffolk County Court, 1671–1680. Publications of the Colonial Society of Massachusetts, XXIX, XXX. Boston, 1933.

A Report of the Record Commissioners of the City of Boston Containing the Boston Records from 1700–1728. Boston, 1883.

RIDER, SIDNEY S., "An Inquiry Concerning the Origin of the Clause in the Laws of Rhode Island (1719–1783) Disfranchising Roman Catholics," *Rhode Island Historical Tracts*, Second Series, no. 1. Providence, 1889.

———, ed., The Charter and the Acts and Laws of His Majesties Colony of Rhode-Island, and Providence-Plantations in America, 1719. Providence, 1895.

ROBINSON, CHARLES J., Register of Merchant Taylor's School, 2 vols. London, 1882–1883.

ROSENDALE, SIMON W., "An Act Allowing Naturalization of Jews in the Colonies," *P.A.J.H.S.*, I. New York, 1893.

RUMNEY, J., "Anglo-Jewry as Seen Through Foreign Eyes (1730–1830)," *Jewish Historical Society of England Transactions*, XIII. London, 1936.

SAINSBURY, W. NOEL, Calendar of State Papers, Colonial Series, America and West Indies, 1661–1668. London, 1880.

SALLEY, A. S., JR., ed., Journals of the Commons House of Assembly of South Carolina for the Four Sessions of 1693. Columbia, 1907.

———, ed., Journals of the Commons House of Assembly of South Carolina for the Two Sessions of 1697. Columbia, 1913.

SALLEY, ALEXANDER S., Narratives of Early Carolina. New York, 1911.

SAMUEL, WILFRED S., "A Review of the Jewish Colonists in

Barbados in the Year 1680," *Jewish Historical Society of England Transactions*, XIII. London, 1936.

SAUNDERS, WILLIAM L., ed., The Colonial Records of North Carolina, 10 vols. Raleigh, 1886–1890.

SCHNEIDER, HERBERT and CAROL, Samuel Johnson, His Career and Writings, 4 vols. New York, 1929.

SEMMES, RAPHAEL, Captains and Mariners of Early Maryland. Baltimore, 1937.

———, Crime and Punishment in Early Maryland. Baltimore, 1938.

Shaftesbury Papers. *Collections of the South Carolina Historical Socliety*, V. Charleston, 1897.

SHEFTALL, LEVI, "The Jews of Savannah," *The Occident and American Jewish Advocate*, I. Philadelphia, 1843.

SHURTLEFF, NATHANIEL B., Records of the Governor and Company of the Massachusetts Bay in New England. 5 vols. Boston, 1853–1854.

SMITH, SAMUEL, The History of the Colony of Nova-Caesaria, or New-Jersey. 2nd edition. Trenton, 1877.

SOLOMONS, ISRAEL, "The Genealogy of the Franks Family," *P.A.J.H.S.*, XVIII. New York, 1909.

Southern Jew, A, "Jews in Savannah," *The Occident and American Jewish Advocate*, I. Philadelphia, 1843.

[STEPHENS, THOMAS and EVERHARD, SIR WILLIAM] "A Brief Account of the Causes that Have Retarded the Progress of the Colony of Georgia in America," *Collections of the Georgia Historical Society*, II. Savannah, 1842.

STEPHENS, WILLIAM, A Journal of the Proceedings in Georgia. The Colonial Records of the State of Georgi a, IV. Atlanta, 1906.

STEINER, BERNARD CHRISTIAN, ed., Proceedings of the Provincial Court of Maryland, 1658–1662. Archives of Maryland, XLI. Baltimore, 1922.

[STRACHEY, WILLIAM, ed.] "For the Colony of Virginea, Britannia, Lavves, Diuine, Morall and Martiall, etc." *Tracts and Other Papers*, III, no. 2 (Peter Force, ed.). Washington, 1844.

STRICKLAND, REBA CAROLYN, Religion and the State in Georgia in the Eighteenth Century. New York, 1939.

TAILFER, PAT., ANDERSON, HUGH and DOUGLAS, D. A., A True and Historical Narrative of the Colony of Georgia, *Tracts and Other Papers.* Collections of the Georgia Historical Society. Savannah, 1842.

TOPPAN, ROBERT MAXON and GOODRICK, ALFRED THOMAS SCROPE, eds., Edward Randolph, including his letters and official papers, 7 vols. Boston, 1898–1909.

TRUMBULL, J. HAMMOND and HOADLEY, CHARLES F., eds., The Public Records of the Colony of Connecticut, 15 vols. Hartford, 1850–1890.

Trustees of Georgia, publishers, "An Account, Showing the Progress of the Colony of Georgia in America," *Tracts and Other Papers*, I, (Peter Force, ed.). Washington, 1836.

Union Society, Minutes of the. Savannah, 1860.

University of Pennsylvania, General Alumni Catalogue of the. Philadelphia, 1917.

URLSPERGER, SAMUEL, Ausführliche Nachricht von den Saltzburgischen Emigranten, Die sich in America niedergelassen haben. Halle, 1744.

———, Briefe der Prediger in Ebenezer. Ausführliche Nachricht von den Saltzburgischen Emigranten, Die sich in America niedergelassen haben, Fourth Continuation. Halle, 1744.

VAN LAER, A. J. F., ed. and tr., Minutes of the Court of Fort Orange and Beverwyck, 1652–1660, 2 vols. Albany, 1920–1923.

A Volume of Records Relating to the Early History of Boston Containing Miscellaneous Papers. Boston, 1900.

VON RECK [PHILIPP], "Reise-Diarium," in Urlsperger, Samuel, Ausführliche Nachricht von der Saltzburgischen Emigranten, Die sich in America niedergelassen haben, I. Halle, 1744.

WATERS, HENRY F., "Genealogical Gleanings in England," *New England Historical and Genealogical Register*, XLVIII. Boston, 1894.

WATSON, JOHN F., Annals of Philadelphia and Pennsylvania in Olden Time, 2 vols. Philadelphia, 1870.

WESLEY, REV. JOHN, A. M., The Journal of John Wesley, 4 vols. London, 1906.

WHITE, FATHER ANDREW, Narrative of a Voyage to Maryland (Maryland Historical Society Fund Publications, no. 7). Baltimore, 1874.

WHITNEY, EDSON L., "Bibliography of the Colonial History of South Carolina," *Annual Report of the American Historical Association for the Year 1894*. Washington, 1895.

WILLARD, JOSEPH N., "Naturalization in the American Colonies," *Proceedings of the Massachusetts Historical Society, 1858–1860*. Boston, 1860.

WILLIAMS, ROGER, The Bloudy Tenent of Persecution (Publications of the Narragansett Club, First Series, III). Providence, 1867.

Yale University, Catalogue of. New Haven, 1924.

ZUBLY, JOHN J., "Letters to Ezra Stiles," *Proceedings of the Massachusetts Historical Society, 1864–1865*. Boston, 1866.

SECONDARY SOURCES

ADAMS, BROOKS, The Emancipation of Massachusetts, Boston and New York, 1893.

ADAMS, JAMES TRUSLOW, Provincial Society (A History of American Life, III). New York, 1927.

———, Revolutionary New England, 1691–1776. Boston, 1923.

———, The Founding of New England. Boston, 1927.

ALTFELD, E. MILTON, The Jews Struggle for Religious and Civil Liberty in Maryland. Baltimore, 1924.

ANDRADE, JACOB A. P. M., A Record of the Jews in Jamaica from the English Conquest to the Present Time. Kingston, Jamaica, 1941.

ANDREWS, CHARLES McLEAN, Colonial Self-Government (The American Nation, V). New York, 1904.

ANDREWS, CHARLES MCLEAN, The Colonial Period of American History, 5 vols. New Haven, 1934–1938.

ANDREWS, MATTHEW PAGE, The Founding of Maryland. Baltimore, 1933.

Anonymous, "Coram, Thomas," *Dictionary of National Biography*, XII. London, 1887.

ARNOLD, SAMUEL GREENE, History of the State of Rhode Island and Providence Planatations, 2 vols. Providence, 1894.

BALDWIN, EBENEZER, Annals of Yale College. New Haven, 1838.

BARNOUW, ADRIAN J., "Megapolensis, Johannes," *Dictionary of American Biography*, XII. New York, 1933.

BEATTY, EDWARD CORBYN OBERT, William Penn as Social Philosopher. New York, 1939.

BENTON, JOSIAH HENRY, Warning Out in New England. Boston, 1911.

BIGELOW, BRUCE M., "Aaron Lopez, Merchant of Newport," *The New England Quarterly*, IV, no. 4. Portland, Me., 1931.

BOURNE, H. R. Fox, The Life of John Locke, 2 vols. London, 1876.

BOZEMAN, JOHN LEEDS, The History of Maryland to 1660, 2 vols. Baltimore, 1837.

BRAITHWAITE, WILLIAM C., The Beginnings of Quakerism. London, 1923.

BRIDENBAUGH, CARL and JESSICA, Rebels and Gentlemen; Philadelphia in the Age of Franklin. New York, 1942.

BROCKUNIER, SAMUEL HUGH, The Irrepressible Democrat — Roger Williams. New York, 1940.

BRODHEAD, JOHN ROMEYN, History of the State of New York, 2 vols. New York, 1853–1871.

BRONSON, HENRY, Chapters on the Early Government of Connecticut (Papers of the New Haven Colony Historical Society, III). New Haven, 1882.

BRONSON, WALTER C., The History of Brown University. Providence, 1914.

BROWN, LOUISE FARGO, The First Earl of Shaftesbury. New York, 1933.

CARPENTER, A. M., "Naturalization in England and the American Colonies," *The American Historical Review*, New York, January, 1904.

"Centennial of the Incorporation, The," *Year Book-1883, City of Charleston*. Charleston, 1884.

CHANNING, EDWARD, A History of the United States, 6 vols. New York, 1905–1925.

CHEYNEY, EDWARD POTTS, European Background of American History (The American Nation: A History, I). New York, 1904.

——, History of the University of Pennsylvania. Philadelphia, 1940.

COBB, SANFORD H., The Rise of Religious Liberty in America. New York, 1902.

CONNER, R. D. W., History of North Carolina, 2 vols. Chicago and New York, 1919.

CORWIN, E. T., A History of the Reformed Church, Dutch (American Church History, VIII). New York, 1895.

COULTER, E. MERTON, A Short History of Georgia. Chapel Hill, 1933.

CRANE, VERNON, The Southern Frontier, 1670–1732. Philadelphia, 1929.

DALCHO, FREDERICK, An Historical Account of the Protestant Episcopal Church in South Carolina. Charleston, 1820.

DALY, CHARLES P., The Settlement of the Jews in North America. New York, 1893.

DAVIES, GODFREY, The Early Stuarts, 1603–1660. Oxford, 1937.

DAVIS, DANIEL, "Lancaster," *Universal Jewish Encyclopedia.*, VI. New York, 1942.

DAVIS, GEORGE LYNN-LACHLAN, The Day-Star of American Freedom. New York, 1855.

DAVIS, N. DARNELL, "Notes on the History of the Jews in Barbados," *P.A.J.H.S.*, XVIII. New York, 1909.

DEUTSCH, GOTTHARD and GOTTHEIL, RICHARD, "Leibzoll,"
    Jewish Encyclopedia, VII. New York, 1904.

DEUTSCH, GOTTHARD, "Oath More Judaico," *Jewish Encyclo-
    pedia*, IX. New York, 1905.

DOW, GEORGE FRANCIS and EDMONDS, JOHN HENRY, The
    Pirates of the New England Coast, 1630–1730. Salem, 1923.

DURFEE, THOMAS, "Gleanings from the Judicial History of
    Rhode Island," *Rhode Island Historical Tracts*, no. 18.
    Providence, 1883.

ELTON, OLIVER, A Survey of English Literature, 1730–1780,
    2 vols. New York, 1928.

ELZAS, BARNETT A., The Jews of South Carolina. Philadelphia,
    1905.

ERNST, CARL W., Constitutional History of Boston, Massa-
    chusetts. Boston, 1892.

ERNST, JAMES, Roger Williams. New York, 1932.

ETTINGER, AMOS ASCHBACH, James Edward Oglethorpe, Im-
    perial Idealist. Oxford, 1936.

FELDMAN, ABRAHAM J., "Hartford," *Universal Jewish Encyclo-
    pedia*, V. New York, 1941.

FELT, JOSEPH B., The Ecclesiastical History of New England,
    2 vols. Boston, 1855–1862.

FOWLER, THOMAS, Locke. London, 1909.

FRASER, ALEXANDER CAMPBELL, Locke. Edinburgh, 1890.

FRIEDENBERG, ALBERT M., "The Jews of New Jersey from the
    Earliest Times to 1850," *P.A.J.H.S.*, XVII. New York,
    1909.

FRIEDENWALD, HERBERT, "Barbados," *Jewish Encyclopedia*, II.
    New York, 1902.

FRIEDMAN, Lee M., "Cotton Mather and the Jews,"
    P.A.J.H.S., XXVI. New York, 1918.

——, Early American Jews. Cambridge, 1934.

——, "Early Jewish Residents of Massachusetts," *P.A.J.H.S.*,
    XXIII. New York, 1915.

——, Jewish Pioneers and Patriots. Philadelphia, 1942.

——, "Judah Monis, First Instructor in Hebrew at Harvard
    University," *P.A.J.H.S.*, XXII. New York, 1914.

GOLDBERG, ISAAC, Major Noah: American-Jewish Pioneer. Philadelphia, 1936.

GORDON, ALEXANDER, "Wesley, John," *Dictionary of National Biography*, LX. London, 1899.

———, "Wesley, Samuel," *Dictionary of National Biography*, LX. London, 1899.

GUILD, REUBEN A., History of Brown University. Providence, 1867.

GUTSTEIN, MORRIS A., The Story of the Jews of Newport. New York, 1936.

HART, GUSTAVUS N., "Notes on Myer Hart and Other Jews of Easton, Pennsylvania," *P.A.J.H.S.*, VIII. New York, 1900.

HIRSCH, ARTHUR HENRY, The Huguenots of Colonial South Carolina. Durham, 1928.

HOLLANDER, J. H., "The Civil Status of the Jews in Maryland, 1634–1776," *P.A.J.H.S.*, II. New York, 1894.

HUGHES, THOMAS, History of the Society of Jesus in North America, 4 vols. London, 1908–1910.

HUHNER, LEON, "The First Jew to Hold the Office of Governor of One of the United States," *P.A.J.H.S.*, XVII. New York, 1909.

———, "Francis Salvador, a Prominent Patriot of the Revolutionary War," *P.A.J.H.S.*, IX. New York, 1901.

———, "Jews in Connection with Colleges of the Thirteen Original States prior to 1800," *P.A.J.H.S.*, XIX. New York, 1910.

———, "The Jews of Georgia in Colonial Times," *P.A.J.H.S.*, X. New York, 1902.

———, "The Jews of New England (other than Rhode Island) prior to 1800," *P.A.J.H.S.*, XI. New York, 1903.

———, "The Jews of North Carolina prior to 1800," *P.A.J.H.S.*, XXIX. New York, 1925.

———, "The Jews of South Carolina from the Earliest Settlement to the End of the American Revolution," *P.A.J.H.S.*, XII. New York, 1904.

———, "The Jews of Virginia from the Earliest Times to the

Close of the Eighteenth Century," *P.A.J.H.S.*, XX. New York, 1911.

————, "The Struggle for Religious Liberty in North Carolina, with Special Reference to the Jews," *P.A.J.H.S.*, XVI. New York, 1907.

HULL, WILLIAM I., William Penn, A Topical Biography. New York, 1937.

INNES, J. H., New Amsterdam and Its People. New York, 1902.

IVES, J. Moss, The Ark and the Dove. New York, London, Toronto, 1936.

JACOBS, HENRY EYSTER, A History of the Evangelical Lutheran Church in the United States. (American Church History, IV). New York, 1893.

JOHNSON, AMANDA, Georgia as Colony and State. Atlanta, 1938.

JOHNSON, AMANDUS, The Swedish Settlements on the Delaware, 2 vols. New York, 1911.

JOHNSON, BRADLEY T., "The Foundation of Maryland," Fund-Publication, no. 18, Maryland Historical Society. Baltimore, 1883.

JOHNSON, MELVIN M., The Beginnings of Freemasonry in America. Washington, 1924.

JONES, CHARLES C., JR., The History of Georgia, 2 vols. Boston, 1883.

————, "The Settlement of the Jews in Georgia," *P.A.J.H.S.*, I. New York, 1893.

JONES, RUFUS M., The Quakers in the American Colonies. London, 1911.

KEITH, CHARLES P., Chronicles of Pennsylvania from the English Revolution to the Peace of Aix-la-Chapelle, 2 vols. Philadelphia, 1917.

KELLER, NATHANIEL M., "New Brunswick," *Universal Jewish Encyclopedia*, VIII. New York, 1942.

KEMMERER, DONALD L., Path to Freedom. The Struggle for Self-Government in Colonial New Jersey. Princeton, 1940.

KOHLER, MAX, J., "The Jews in Newport," *P.A.J.H.S.*, VI. New York, 1897.

———, "Civil Status of the Jews in Colonial New York," *P.A.J.H.S.*, VI. New York, 1897.

———, "New York" (in part), *Jewish Encyclopedia*, IX. New York, 1905.

———, Rebecca Franks. New York, 1894.

LEBESON, ANITA LIBMAN, Jewish Pioneers in America. New York, 1931.

LEBOWICH, JOSEPH, "The Jews of Boston till 1875," *P.A.J.H.S.* XII. New York, 1910.

LECKY, WILLIAM EDWARD HARTPOLE, A History of England in the Eighteenth Century, 4 vols. New York, 1883.

LEVIN, NATHANIEL, "The Congregation 'Beth Elohim'," *Year Book-1883, City of Charleston*. Charleston, 1884.

LINDNER, GUSTAVE, "Sweden," *Jewish Encyclopedia*, XI. New York, 1905.

LOWENTHAL, MARVIN, The Jews of Germany. Philadelphia, 1936.

MARCUS, JACOB R., The Jew in the Medieval World. Cincinnati, 1938.

MASON, GEORGE CHAMPLIN, Reminiscences of Newport. Newport, 1884.

MAYNARD, THEODORE, The Story of American Catholicism. New York, 1941.

McCAIN, JAMES ROSS, Georgia as a Proprietary Province. Boston, 1917.

McCRADY, EDWARD, The History of South Carolina under the Proprietary Government. New York, 1897.

———, The History of South Carolina under the Royal Government, 1719–1776. New York, 1899.

McKINLEY, ALBERT EDWARD, The Suffrage Franchise in the Thirteen English Colonies in America (Publications of the University of Pennsylvania, Series in History, II). Philadelphia, 1905.

McSHERRY, JAMES, History of Maryland. Baltimore, 1849.

MENDES, REV. A. P., "The Jewish Cemetery at Newport,

Rhode Island," *The Rhode Island Historical Magazine*, VI, no. 2, Newport, October, 1885.

MERENESS, NEWTON D., Maryland as a Proprietary Province. New York, 1901.

MONTGOMERY, THOMAS HARRISON, A History of the University of Pennsylvania from Its Foundation to A. D. 1770. Philadelphia, 1900.

MOORE, GEORGE FOOT, "Judah Monis," *Proceedings of the Massachusetts Historical Society*, LII. Boston, 1915.

MORAIS, HENRY SAMUEL, The Jews of Philadelphia. Philadelphia, 1894.

MORISON, SAMUEL ELIOT, Builders of the Bay Colony. Boston, New York, 1930.

———, Harvard College in the Seventeenth Century, 2 vols. Cambridge, 1936.

NECARSULMER, HENRY, "The Early Jewish Settlers at Lancaster, Pennsylvania," *P.A.J.H.S.*, IX. New York, 1900.

"A New York Jewish Silversmith of the Eighteenth Century," *P.A.J.H.S.*, XXVIII. New York, 1922.

O'CALLAGHAN, EDMUND B., History of New Netherland. New York, 1848.

ONDERDONK, HENRY, JR., "Persecution of An Early Friend, A Quaker," *American Historical Record*, I. Philadelphia, 1872.

OPPENHEIM, SAMUEL, "The Jews and Masonry in the United States before 1810," *P.A.J.H.S.*, XIX. New York, 1910.

OSGOOD, HERBERT, L., The American Colonies in the 18th Century, 2 vols. New York, 1924.

———, The American Colonies in the 17th Century, 3 vols. New York, 1907.

OSTERWEIS, ROLLIN G., "New Haven," *Universal Jewish Encyclopedia*, VIII. New York, 1942.

PALFREY, JOHN GORHAM, History of New England, 3 vols. Boston, 1892.

PALTSITS, VICTOR H., "Stuyvesant, Petrus," *Dictionary of American Biography*, XVIII. New York, 1936.

PARRINGTON, VERNON LOUIS, The Colonial Mind. New York, 1927.

"Patents Issued During the Regal Government, James City County. *William and Mary Quarterly*, X. Williamsburg, Va., 1907.

PENNINGTON, EDGAR LEGARE, "The Reverend Samuel Quincy, S. P. G. Missionary," *The Georgia Historical Quarterly*, XI. Savannah, 1927.

PETERSON, EDWARD, History of Rhode Island and Newport. New York, 1853.

PHILIPSON, DAVID, Letters of Rebecca Gratz. Philadelphia, 1929.

PICCIOTTO, JAMES, Sketches of Anglo-Jewish History. London, 1875.

PLITT, "CALLENBERG," *Allgemeine Deutsche Biographie*, III. Leipzig, 1876.

POMERANTZ, SIDNEY I., New York, an American City, 1783–1803. New York, 1938.

POOL, REV. DAVID DE SOLA, "Hebrew Learning Among the Puritans of New England prior to 1700," *P.A.J.H.S.*, XX. New York, 1911.

PRESTON, HOWARD W., Rhode Island and the Sea. Rhode Island State Bureau of Information. (Historical Publication no. 4) Providence, 1932.

RAVENEL, MRS. ST. JULIEN, Charleston. New York, 1906.

(RAY) SISTER MARY AUGUSTINE, American Opinion of Roman Catholicism in the Eighteenth Century. New York, 1936.

RICHMAN, IRVING BERDINE, Rhode Island. Boston and New York, 1905.

———, Rhode Island, Its Making and Its Meaning, 2 vols. New York and London, 1902.

RIDDELL, WILLIAM RENWICK, "Pre-Revolutionary Pennsylvania and the Slave Trade," *Pennsylvania Magazine of History*, LII. Philadelphia, 1928.

RILEY, ARTHUR J., Catholicism in New England to 1788. Washington, 1936.

RIVERS, WILLIAM JAMES, A Sketch of the History of South
Carolina. Charleston, 1856.

ROSENBACH, ABRAHAM S. WOLF, "Philadelphia," *Jewish Encyclopedia*, IX. New York, 1905.

———, "Notes on the First Settlement of Jews in Pennsylvania, 1655–1703," *P.A.J.H.S.*, V. New York, 1897.

ROTH, CECIL, A History of the Marranos. Philadelphia, 1932.

RUPP, I. DANIEL, History of the Counties of Berks and Lebanon. Lancaster, 1844.

SCHAFER, WILLIAM A., "Sectionalism and Representation in South Carolina," *Annual Report of the American Historical Association for the Year 1900*, I. Washington, 1901.

SCHARF, J. THOMAS, History of Maryland, 3 vols. Baltimore, 1879.

SCHARF, J. THOMAS and WESCOTT, THOMPSON, History of Philadelphia 1609–1884, 3 vols. Philadelphia, 1884.

SCHOLES, PERCY A., The Puritans and Music in England and New England. London, 1934.

SEELIGMAN, SIGMUND, "Amsterdam," *Jewish Encyclopedia*, I. New York, 1897.

SHARPLESS, ISAAC, A Quaker Experiment in Government. Philadelphia, 1898.

SLIJPERE, E., "Netherlands," *Jewish Encyclopedia*, IX. New York, 1905.

SMITH, C. HENRY, The Story of the Mennonites. Berne, Indiana, 1941.

SMITH, GEORGE GILLMAN, The Story of Georgia and the Georgia People. Macon, 1900.

SMITH, WILLIAM, History of New York. Albany, 1814.

SMITH, W. ROY, South Carolina as a Royal Province, 1719–1776. New York, 1903.

START, CORA, "Naturalization in the English Colonies of America", *Annual Report of the American History Association for the Year 1893*. Washington, 1894.

STEINER, BERNARD C., Maryland During the English Civil Wars (*Johns Hopkins University Studies in History and*

Political Science. Series XXIV, XXV). Baltimore, 1906–1907.

STEINER, BERNARD C., Maryland Under the Commonwealth (*Johns Hopkins University Studies in History and Political Science.* Series XXIX). Baltimore, 1911.

STEVENS, WILLIAM BACON, A History of Georgia, 2 vols. New York, 1847–1859.

STOKES, N. PHELPS, The Iconography of Manhattan Island, 6 vols. New York, 1915–1928.

STOMBERG, ANDREW A., A History of Sweden. New York, 1931.

SUTHERLAND, STELLA H., Population Distribution in Colonial America. New York, 1936.

SWEET, WILLIAM WARREN, Religion in Colonial America. New York, 1942.

THOMAS, CHARLES M., "Successful and Unsuccessful Merchants in the Illinois Country," *Journal of the Illinois State Historical Society*, XXX. Springfield, 1938.

TROTH, SAMUEL, "Richard Preston, Sr., Puritan Quaker of Maryland," *Pennsylvania Magazine of History and Biography*, XVI. Philadelphia, 1892.

TRUMBULL, J. HAMMOND, ed., The Memorial History of Hartford County, Connecticut, 2 vols. Boston, 1886.

VAN RENSSELAER, MRS. JOHN KING, Newport, Our Social Capital. Philadelphia and London, 1905.

VAN RENSSELAER, MRS. SCHUYLER, History of the City of New York in the Seventeenth Century, 2 vols. New York, 1909.

WARD, CHRISTOPHER, The Dutch and Swedes on the Delaware, 1609–1664. Philadelphia, 1930.

WÄTJEN, HERMANN, Das holländische Kolonialreich in Brazilien. The Hague and Gotha, 1921.

WEEDEN, WILLIAM B., Early Rhode Island. New York, 1910.

WEEKS, STEPHEN BEAUREGARD, Church and State in North Carolina (*Johns Hopkins University Studies in Historical and Political Science.* Series XI). Baltimore, 1893.

WHITE, GEORGE, Statistics of the State of Georgia. Savannah, 1849.

WHITNEY, EDSON L., Government of the Colony of South Carolina (*Johns Hopkins University Studies in History and Political Science*, XIII). Baltimore, 1896.

WOLFSON, HARRY A., "Monis, Judah," *Dictionary of American Biography*, XIII. New York, 1934.

WOODS, EDGAR, Albermarle County in Virginia. Charlottesville, 1901.

Work Projects Administration, Maryland. A Guide to the Old Line State. New York, 1940.

ZWIERLEIN, FEDERICK, J., Religion in New Netherland. Rochester, 1910.

INDEX

lina, 150; in Delaware Valley, 119; in
Georgia, 169, 192 f.; in Maryland, 137,
139, 146, 147; in Massachusetts, 18;
in New Jersey, 120, 131; in New
Netherland, 70 ff.; in New York, 97 ff.;
in Pennsylvania, 123; in Rhode Island,
35 f., 45, 58, 60, 63 f.; in South Carolina, 156, 163, 166 f.; in Sweden, 115;
in United States, 201
Freemen: in Connecticut, 24; in Delaware,
131; in London, 17; in Massachusetts
14; in New Netherland, 93 ff., 96,
105; in New York, 106 f., 110; in
Pennsylvania, 122 ff.; in Rhode Island,
36, 43 ff., 53
French, 8, 82, 102, 146, 169; in Canada,
202; in South Carolina, 165, see also
Huguenots; France
French Calvinists; see Huguenots
Frera, David, 92
Frink, Rev. Samuel, 196
Fuller, William, Governor, 140
*Fundamental Constitutions for the Govern-
ment of Carolina, The*, 151, 220; on
franchise, 158; religious provisions,
151 ff.
Fur Trade: in New Netherland, 75 f.,
90 f., 92 f., 96; on Delaware River, 91,
116 ff.

GAGE, GENERAL THOMAS, 130
Gardner, John, Deputy Governor, 57 f.
Gaza, witches of, 13
George II (of England), 169
George III (of England), 24, 165, 199,
226
Georgia, 61, 125, 166, 174; agitation
against authorities, 193 f.; becomes
royal colony, 194 f.; charter on religion,
169; church establishment, 195 ff.;
Coram's protest over conditions, 182 f.;
exodus from, 183, 194; Jewish planters,
185, 187 ff.; Jewish policy, 181 f.;
Jewish-Salzburger relations, 179, 185 ff.,
Jews in office, 199, 200; Jews sail to,
175 ff.; lack of religious spirit, 189;
quarrels between Jewish groups, 190 f.;
religious freedom, 192 f.; vintage of, 187;
see also Savannah and Georgia trustees
Georgia Assembly: anti-Jewish memorial,
197; and Daniel Nunez, 199; Jews'
petition for cemetery enlargement,
195, 196 ff.; Rev. Zubly's petition for
cemetery, 196 ff.
Georgia Trustees, 190, 199; against
Jewish immigrants, 173, 174; aims;

170 f., 173 f.; and Jewish farmers,
187 f., 193 f.; and relations with
Georgia Jews, 187, 188 f.; and resentment of Georgia settlers, 193 ff.;
calibre of men, 169 f.; charter expires,
184 f.; get Oglethorpe's report, 181,
employ Jewish canvassers, 172, 173,
179 ff.; hear Hanson's report, 176, 179;
order canvassers to give up commis-
sions, 174, 179 ff.; publicity campaign,
171; select immigrants, 171; write
Oglethorpe on Jews, 178 f., 181
German Jews; see Ashkenazim
Germans, 129, 130; in Georgia, 166; in
South Carolina, 167; see also Germany;
Salzburgers
Germany, 124, 185, 203; Jews in, 146, 186
Ghettos, 6, 9; in Italy, 141; one sought
for New Amsterdam, 84 f.
Gibbons, Edward, 15
Gideon, Rowland: in court case, 17, 206;
on Boston tax list, 16 f.
Gillam, James, 19
Girlen, Mr., 62 f.
Glover, Elizabeth, 144
Glover, Giles; see Glover, Elizabeth
Gould, John; see Gould, Margery
Gould, Margery, 144
Gould, N. H., 37 f.
Gratz, Barnard: active in western trade,
130 f.; papers of, 130, 218
Gratz, Michael, 127; active in western
trade, 130 f.; papers of, 130, 218
Gratz, Rebecca, 130
Gravesend, 172
Great Britain, 18, 61, 124; Jews unwel-
come in, 33 f.; takes over Delaware,
119; troops in America supplied by
David Franks, 127; see also England;
British Isles
Gustavus Adolphus, 115

HALLE, 186
Hamburg, 38
Hampton, Rev., 101
Handicrafts, Jews in: in Amsterdam,
85 f., 89; in New Netherland, 89, 97;
in New York, 106 f.
Hanson, ship captain, 176, 179, 185, 186
Harper's New Monthly, 50
Hart, Abraham, 59
Hart, Myer, 129
Hartford, Jews in, 24, 25 ff.
Harvard College, 59 f.; and Judah Monis,
21 ff.; founding of, 12; Hebrew at, 12 f.
Hays, Moses M., 58